Dear Brenda,

From one traveling
nomad to another. We've
loved sharing our journey
with you.

love,

Neville & Catherine
xoxoxo

Allow your dreams to take you
to all the places you wish to go

Dream Time

Neville Hockley

Dream Time

Vanguard Press

The characters and events in this publication are drawn
From the author's wide experience

A CIP catalogue record for this title is
available from the British Library
ISBN 1 903489 25 3

All graphics, photographs and drawings
by Neville Hockley

*Vanguard Press is an imprint of
Pegasus Elliot MacKenzie Publishers Ltd.*
www.pegasuspublishers.com

First Published in 2002

**Vanguard Press
Sheraton House Castle Park
Cambridge England**

Printed & Bound in Great Britain

Dedication

Catherine, for her patience,
understanding and love.

Acknowledgement

Many thanks to my friend Lewis Fortuna for sharing his thoughts and memories of the journey, and to Peter Lawton for allowing me to share in his dream.

Contents

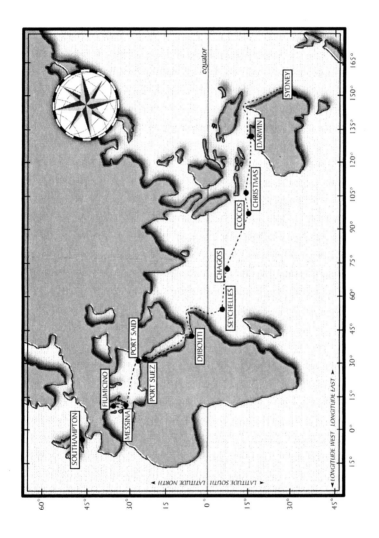

Each entry in this book begins with our exact location and heading. I have included these figures because they symbolize the path I have traveled and the importance of having a direction.

Dreams can only ever be accomplished if they are pursued. Plot the waypoints in your life today and begin the journey that will take you to your land of dreams tomorrow.

Sample co-ordinates:

10° 24.6' S
104° 31.6' E
272°

10° 24.6' S Latitude - Locating a position north or south of the Equator measured from pole to pole

104° 31.6' E Longitude - Measurement of location east to west of the prime meridian

272° - Compass heading

Measurements: 60 minutes (') equals 1 degree (°)
1 knot equals 1.15 miles an hour

INTRODUCTION

On May 6th, 1993, I left the life I knew behind, and began searching for my dream. It was a gray, damp English morning as my girlfriend drove me silently to Heathrow airport. The fine rain hung in the cool country air making everything around us dreary and overcast. The wet M3 reflected the endless stream of headlights as the morning commuters drifted along the motorway, starting the day the same way as they started all their others.

Watching the line of dazzling lights crawling behind one another, it all seemed so predictable as we sped past in the other direction. Just a few weeks earlier I would have been one of those lights heading off to work, consumed by the monotony of my life, unaware of the fact that I wasn't going anywhere. However that day I was heading in the other direction, away from the predictable lights and into the unknown.

Meandering through the towns and woods of southern England, the motorway was like a gray river carrying me in a new direction. The only currents I had to face were my own doubts and fears. The four lane motorway wound its way north towards London, cutting through the green hills of Twyford Down, leaving a huge chalky scar in the once unspoiled countryside of Hampshire.

Looking out across the green-checkered fields, waves of sadness flooded my mind as the reality of leaving family, friends and my home behind, was beginning to register. Watching the wipers push the rain off the windscreen, I stared blankly out of the window, trying to keep my emotions together. I did not want to have the same tear filled goodbye with Catherine as I had endured with my parents the night before. Knowing that I would return to America after Australia, I didn't know when I would see England or my family again.

I was only seven when my family first moved to America but I can still remember the excitement I felt knowing that I was moving to the same country where The Incredible Hulk, The Six Million-Dollar Man, Spiderman and Superman all lived. It was the country of heroes. The country where I fell in love with everything I saw. The final two years of our stay in America, we had spent in New York, where I went to Art College. I knew that one day I would return and live my life there.

The thought of flying back to America after four years of living in England however, felt like too much of a change. When Andy Balcombe, a close friend, told me he was visiting Australia for a year, it seemed like the perfect opportunity to spread my wings and begin the journey back to New York City. With a years worth of traveling under my belt, flying to America to start a new life would seem more manageable.

My flight was due to depart at 11:30. We checked in my backpack and then decided to get a drink before we went through to the departure lounge. I have always preferred quick goodbyes but Catherine insisted on staying at the airport until I had gone, before she would leave. She had always known of my dream to live in America from the first day we met, but the reality of me leaving was something that we were both unprepared for. After spending three years of our lives together we had become a part of each other.

Finally, after almost an hour of hushed conversation, it was time for me to go. I took Catherine's hand in mine and we walked towards the gate. Holding each other we both began to cry. I told Catherine that I would be taking her with me, I placed her hand on my heart and said that we would always be together and that I loved her. I gave her one last kiss and walked to the plane. When I turned to wave goodbye for the last time, I saw her standing alone crying, I couldn't bear to see her upset so I continued through to the gate, not looking back again.

The year I spent in Australia was one of the happiest in my life. A simple existence with nothing to worry about but the pack on my back, travelers are able to experience a freedom few others can. With few responsibilities you are able to enjoy the simplicity of life and at the same time experience different countries and cultures. I have always believed the more you experience the richer and more fulfilling your life will become. To experience nothing at all is death. To experience all life has to offer, good and bad is why I believe we are here. The more you experience, the more you understand life. The more you understand life, the more you want to experience.

A month after Andy and I landed in Brisbane Australia, I was sketching at a marina in Townsville, Queensland, when I met a New Zealander who was taking his Irwin fifty-two foot Ketch, *A True Story*, out of the water to clean and repair. I worked with Neville John Grey, the owner of the boat, for two weeks helping him strip down the masts to respray, anti-foul the hull and re-varnish the woodwork. We built up a good relationship in those short weeks and discovered we had much more in common than just our names. When I explained to Neville I would be flying to America after a year of traveling, he said simply, "Why don't you sail there?" To this day Neville has no idea how that one simple remark changed my life. For the remaining thirteen months in Australia, I spent as much time as possible hanging around marinas, picking up work as a deck hand or helping scrub down a boat; anything to give me more experience to sail such a journey.

Andy and I traveled around Australia for nine months. Working along the way we developed a knack for finding work other than picking fruit, (a favorite for most backpackers). We became skilled in the art of verbal bullshit and talked our way into working on the Great Barrier Reef, the outback as mining researchers for a month, lead roles in television commercials, catwalk modeling for Emporio Armani, promotional work for Pepsi Max, Danon Yoghurt and Gatorade. We built a traffic circle at Brisbane airport with a road gang and worked as an assistant chef in Randwick's Dukes Bistro restaurant outside Sydney. At the end of the year I was confident in my abilities to talk my way into any job. I was also sure I could sail to New York and become the next Art Director at Saachi and Saachi in just a couple of weeks. Time however was not on my side.

After nine months of working and traveling together, Andy flew home to England on April 5th 1994. This was one month before my visa was due to expire and I would also have to leave the country. Andy had become my best friend over the past year, and it was tough saying goodbye to him. Not being as sentimental as I, Andy said, "See ya later mate, probably in New York." With a final wave, he was gone.

With only four weeks left to find a yacht that could take me to America, I quickly put my design and advertising degrees to good use and created a poster to find myself a passage east.

Two weeks later my visa expired and I became an illegal immigrant in Australia, subject to fines and imprisonment, but I was not going to give up. I would have retired in Australia if that was what it was going to take to find that bloody boat! I knew somewhere there was a boat that could take me to America, so I tried another tactic.

CrewFind International is a company that matches crew with boats all over the world. Investing one hundred and fifty dollars I became a member, putting my future in the hands of this organization who assured me they would find me a yacht. Weeks went by and nothing happened. I still made weekly trips down to the marina to check my signs. Other travelers were also looking to crew on boats and were tearing down my signs to eliminate the competition. I kept putting new ones up!

During this time I had stayed in touch with Catherine who was now living in America. She was working as a nanny for the owner of the suntan lotion company Hawaiian Tropic. Looking after his three-year-old child, Catherine would spend a month in Florida with the father, Ron Rice and then a month in California with the mother, Darcy and her new kick boxing husband, Jean Claude Van Damme. She was flying over from America for a week to see me. I was looking forward to seeing her after a year of being separated. She was due to arrive in two weeks so I desperately wanted to find a yacht and surprise her when she landed in Sydney.

I made calls to CrewFind International every day. I am sure they were beginning to feel the membership fee was not nearly enough to cover the aggravation of my constant calling. One day however, I did not get the usual, "Nothing yet Neville, we'll let you know as soon as something comes up." I was told to hold on while he got the paper work.

"It's not what you want, but there is a guy sailing his yacht to Italy and looking for crew, are you interested?" Italy I mused, that does not sound like a bad idea. It was not America but I could see my folks first, and then fly over. I had overstayed my visa now by eight weeks and was getting seriously concerned. "What the heck, when do

I meet this guy?"

Peter Lawton, the owner of *Aphrodite*, lives in Canberra where he owns a successful auto body repair shop. His wife was going to Italy for a year to teach English. She was flying over with their two children while Peter sailed his forty-two foot New Zealand built sloop, *Aphrodite* to Fiumicino, a coastal town about twenty minutes from Rome. Pursuing a lifelong dream to sail around the world, Peter was going to spend a year in Italy with his family then continue the journey west, back to Australia. Peter was making a trip up to Sydney in eighteen days time to check on his boat and interview crew for the journey. If all that stood in the way of this opportunity was a mere interview, it was in the bag, I would just have to put my new found bullshitting skills to work!

Catherine landed at Sydney airport right on time. Waiting at the gate, I felt as nervous as I did over four years ago on our first date. Seeing her for the first time all over again almost made my heart stop. She came over to me smiling and looking incredible. It did not take us long to make up for the year we had been away from each other. Later that day, curled up in bed and holding her in my arms, I told Catherine about the interview I was having with Peter.

He already had a crew of five men and only needed one more. I thought that six guys seemed like a lot for a forty-two footer but I was not going to turn down the opportunity. I spoke to Peter on the phone the day before we were due to meet in Sydney. He sounded like an easygoing sort of chap. I was looking forward to meeting him.

Catherine came with me to Circular Quay where we were to meet. I decided it would be best if I spoke alone with Peter, as I was not sure how it would go. We met outside a deli, shook hands and ordered coffee. Peter was obviously excited by finally fulfilling his dream. I told him that I was in the process of doing the same thing and this trip would be a big part for me to achieve mine. We hit it off.

Wanting to know what sort of person I was, Peter seemed more concerned about my lifesaving abilities rather than my sailing experience. It made sense I guess. If you are going to rely on someone, it's important to know if they are going to come through for you or not. Anyone can learn how to become a competent sailor but trust and dependability are something that you either have or you don't. It's not easily learned. Peter wanted a crew he could rely on no matter what. I told him I was his man. There was only one spot left and he still had a couple of people to interview. I thanked him for meeting with me and went to find Catherine.

Waiting for her on the boardwalk, I saw an old man with a banjo sitting on one of the benches, seemingly waiting for someone. I walked up and asked him what he played. He replied simply, "*Jazz*."

I told him my father was a jazzman and a fan of Ken Colyer, an English jazz musician who traveled to New Orleans and was finally put in jail because he did not have a visa. One of the songs Colyer wrote in jail before he was released to go back to England was *Going Home*.

I asked the old man if he knew it. He looked at me, smiled and started to play the tune my father had played to me so many times before.

Well if home is where the heart is,
Then my home's in New Orleans,
Won't you take me, to that land of dreams,
And if I don't leave now, I won't be going nowhere.

Listening to the old man playing his banjo, it felt right that I should sail to Italy and go home before I went to

America - my land of dreams.

Catherine came up behind me and slipped her arm through mine. Together we listened to the old man play his jazz on the boardwalk.

I got picked for the trip.

1

Sydney to Darwin

(2,485 nautical miles)

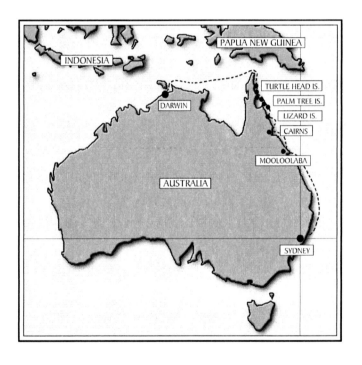

1

Sydney to Darwin

Day 1 - Sydney Harbor

It's July 6th 1994. Today we set sail! It's a good day to raise the canvas. The wind is blowing lightly from the northwest and the sun is shining in a clear blue Australian sky. I have waited for this journey for over a year. It's hard to believe that today, I finally begin to live out my dream.

I was dropped off at Middle Harbor Yacht Club with my entire life in a couple of old bags. Everything that was dear to me I was carrying in my arms or my heart. I called my family, friends and Catherine a couple of days ago to give them the estimated dates we would be sailing to each country and the post office addresses. Once we leave the security of Australian waters it will become harder and harder to contact everyone, I told them that they may not hear from me for a few weeks at a time, but not to worry. Catherine refused to listen to my reasoning and started to worry before she had even got off the phone.

I stowed my gear in the bow cabin and joined the masses of people gathering at the marina to see us off. I met the crew of *Aphrodite* for the first time and their fathers, mothers, brothers, sisters, grandparents, friends, neighbors and pets. I am thankful my family is not here as I am sure there would not be enough tissues to go around. At the same time I feel alone, thinking about the ones I love and when I would see them again.

We seem like the most unlikely group of men ever to be assembled for a voyage that will take us halfway around the world. Watching the crew saying goodbye to loved ones, I am beginning to understand the men I will spend the next five months of my life with.

Peter Lawton is in his late thirties and busy talking to his wife and two children. Overweight and "nervy" he seems as though he cannot wait another second to follow his life's dream to sail around the world, He is obviously excited by the prospect of finally casting off. With thick, oversized square glasses and a scruffy appearance, Peter is a short man and does not give the impression of an adventurous circumnavigator. It must be hard leaving a family behind to follow your dream. I admire him.

Rob is an electrician in his mid thirties, and a friend of Peter's. He is a solid looking bloke with handsome features and a relaxed demeanor. Rob will only be with us for the first month or however long it takes us to reach Darwin, our last port of call in Australia. He must have a real life and is unable to take a mere five months off to travel! I couldn't imagine such a restricted lifestyle, after spending fourteen months backpacking around Australia, I was used to it and loved it. He seems like a nice guy, and like myself, spent his time watching the others saying goodbye from the bench at the stern of the boat that Peter had specially installed for the journey. His girlfriend is back in Canberra. He is only going to be gone for a month no one came to see him off.

Don is the third member of crew and one of two navigators on this trip. He is a big man in his early forties with a strong Italian accent. Already giving orders to the rest of us to organize the equipment he seems to know what he's doing, I get the impression we will be turning to his experience if we run into trouble. The second navigator Tim, is from Canada and will be joining us in a few weeks on the Great Barrier Reef.

Because of the treacherous waters we will be sailing on, Peter has made sure we have two navigators on board. If one of them does not work out we have "a spare" to guide us safely to Italy over eleven thousand miles away.

The fourth member of crew is a fireman from Sydney. Lewis Fortuna is a local guy in his early thirties and a tough looking bastard! He has relatives living in Italy and has taken a leave of absence for a year to do what most Australian men have a reputation of doing, go "walkabout." While everyone was shaking hands with family and friends Lewis was saying goodbye to his dog. Well they do say they're a man's best friend.

Then there's me. I am the youngest in the crew at twenty-four and probably the least qualified to sail on this trip. I have not told anyone about my lack of ocean crossing experience, but looking at this crew I don't think anyone will notice. Looks like I'll fit in just fine.

Born and raised in Southampton, a city on the southern coast of England. I am told the sea is in my blood and I am a natural sailor. If this is true I do not have the confidence in myself I would like to have. The biggest fear I have ever had sailing, was racing in Sydney harbor and not getting back to the yacht club in time to claim my prize of 'greasy chips' and a few beers.

When the skipper told me over a beer after my last race in the harbor to be careful of the pirates, I laughed at him and started to tell Black Beard jokes. When I finally stopped chuckling at my own whimsical sense of humor, he explained to me that every year sailors are lost or killed at sea because they were not prepared. Taking his advice I went to the coast guard office a week before we were due to leave and was surprised to find a number of leaflets on the subject. We were going to sail through some of the worst pirate infested waters on the face of the earth. Indonesia and Africa are two of the most infamous areas. Reading up on what to be prepared for I was surprised to find out just how real this threat really was.

Pirates have a number of ways that they capture a vessel. One of them is to hide over the horizon in a powerful motorboat while a couple of members of crew are left drifting alone in a life raft. By the law of the sea assistance must be offered to people in distress. The unsuspecting yacht would help the men aboard who would then radio their buddies and storm the boat a few minutes later. If you were lucky the pirates would lock you in a room while they ransacked the boat. If you were not so lucky they take the boat and leave you for dead in a life raft with no supplies or radio. If you were really unlucky they would put a bullet in the back of your head and feed you to the sharks. We were sailing only a hundred miles off the coast of Indonesia and up the East Coast of Africa. I took a handful of leaflets and decided that the other members of crew should be made aware of the dangers that we may encounter along the way.

We're finally ready to go! The family and friends fought over who was going to untie the lines from the marina to cast us off. After much tugging and jostling the bow and stern lines were thrown over onto the deck, the journey had begun. Through tears of sadness they waved goodbye from the pontoon in a huddled group as we sailed away.

Sydney harbor was alive with daily traffic. Ferries and JetCats loaded with people raced across the water heading for Manly Beach, Darling Harbor, or Taronga Zoo. Water taxies, motor boats and sailing boats cut up the surface as we quietly sailed for North Head and out to sea. Looking at us no one would have guessed we were destined for

Italy. We looked like a bunch of old friends going out for an afternoon sail. Who would have thought we were five complete strangers embarking on a journey with no ocean crossing experience between us.

I would never dream of turning back. I'm not one for taking the easy path in life. Buddha teaches, the first of the "Four Noble Truths" is "Life is suffering," I had a feeling during the next five month we would all experience this theory.

32° 54.9' S
152° 09.6' E
043° - Day 2

My second shift aboard *Aphrodite*. It's 0230, my first night at sea. We're ten miles from Port Stephens with the wind blowing steady on our beam we're averaging six knots. Swell is up to five feet, water temp is sixty-eight degrees Fahrenheit.

The fact that I have started an adventure that will take me to eight countries over the next five months has not really sunk in. Sitting on the deck, looking into the night I am trying to absorb the enormity of this journey. Having a tendency to forget the moment, I want to truly appreciate what I am doing and not just in reflection. The world around me seems at peace with it itself. We are only twenty miles from land and I can still see the lights of towns as we sail silently past in the night, but I already feel removed from it all. I have a strong feeling from this day on my life will never be quite the same again.

We all managed after a great deal of effort to force down the mammoth meal Don prepared last night. I had to remind him after we washed up all the dishes that we had to ration our food and it would probably be a good idea not to consume it all in the first week! Now I know how the man got so big, I can see I will have to hide my rations from this monster!

Sitting in the cockpit hunched over our plastic bowls the conversation was easy as it usually is in the company of men. Drifting casually from one conversation to the next, I felt as though we were sizing one another up. Lewis, I have discovered, has a quick wit and a sense of humor that parallels my own. In a way he reminds me of Andy. With determined features and a strong personality he seems like a guy you do not want to get on the wrong side of. If you are friends with him however, I get the impression there isn't anything that he wouldn't do for you.

Rob came in very handy today as we were having a few electrical difficulties, nothing major, just everything kept cutting out! Checking the wiring and fuse box, Rob soon discovered that the main battery that runs all the electrical equipment, GPS (global positioning system), radios, autopilot, weather fax, depth gauge, freezer, fridge, nav lights, was not being charged. I can't help but wonder if we are having these problems now what's it going to be like in the middle of the Indian Ocean?

I have drawn up a rotation of four-hour watches with an overlapping change of an hour for each member of crew. Rob will be joining me in thirty minutes, I am looking forward to getting some shut eye.

I had managed to commandeer the bow cabin back in Sydney. The bed is four feet off the ground and shaped like a "V". The base of the "V" is at the front of the yacht with both beds running down the starboard and port sides. I have not had a room to myself in over a year.

Sleeping in hostels around Australia you would often share with three to ten other people. The only consolation in such confined quarters is that you share rooms with both men and women. Women from certain parts of the world are less conscious about their bodies than others. With this thought in my mind I began thinking of Catherine, where she was and what she was doing. I was already looking forward to seeing her but still had a long way to go. The noise of the bow cutting through the waves and the rhythmic motion of the ocean sent me immediately to sleep.

The sea that night was angry. Bucking and reeling trying to shake anything that was on her back, *Aphrodite* was beaten. Her mast that once stood tall and proud was now trailing behind us in the water attached only by a few stays. Like a limb torn from a body she seemed mortally wounded with little hope of survival. The stays that were ripped from the deck now lashed out in the screaming wind, threatening to cut anything in their path.

I was alone on the boat desperately trying to stay alive. The rain beat into my face with the force of a shotgun blast. Giant waves came out of the night relentlessly pounding *Aphrodite*, slowly tearing her to pieces. The thunder from the surf was becoming deafening, I knew I had to abandon ship or I would be pounded against the cliffs with no hope of survival. We did not have a life raft, the inflatable that was strapped to the deck had long since been blown into the black night. All the electrics were dead, I could not radio for help. The tall cliffs towering above me seemed to be waiting patiently for us. Like a predator waiting for its prey, *Aphrodite* was being pushed closer to the inevitable. I had to force myself to move. My hands were wrapped around the railing like the jaws of a vice. Slowly I inched my way to the bow, I did not want to get swept into the mast and entangled in the ropes and wires. *Aphrodite* was taking on water fast. She was going down. With one last look at her,

I hurled myself over the railing and into the blackness.

Landing in a heap on the floor my head struck first. Crumpled upside down and wedged between the two beds I suddenly realized what had happened. Lewis had changed heading and in doing so flipped me right out of bed. Shaken from the fall and the reality of the dream I staggered out of my cabin and made my way up the five steps to the cockpit. The sun was just about to break the horizon. A glow spread across the sky warming everything in its path. When the clouds floating high above us captured the light just a few seconds before the sun appeared, I thought I caught a glimpse of heaven.

Watching the sunrise for the first time I can remember, I was at last lost in the moment. Completely absorbed in this phenomenon I felt a strange peace and lightness. Maybe it was the bump on my head, or maybe it was the magic of the moment, I do not know but I gave myself to it. Lewis broke me from the spell with, "How'd ya sleep Nev?"

31° 47.6' S
153° 05.4' E
025° - Day 3

What a day! Caught my first fish of the trip - a Southern Tuna and saw a whale just after lunch rolling quietly through the calm waters about a mile off our starboard side. We passed Coffs Harbor early this morning and are making good time (good time being about five miles an hour).

Aphrodite is sailing herself, Don is constantly keeping an eye on the autopilot and GPS to monitor our position, but little work is required if the wind remains consistent.

The wind is coming from the east at a steady ten knots and both sails are holding well, what a life!

28° 50.1' S
153° 50.7' E
0° - Day 4

Today is the sort of day you find out if you suffer from sea-sickness. Rob does! We have both the main and the genoa flying high with a strong easterly breeze, swell is up to six feet and hitting us right on the beam causing *Aphrodite* to rock and roll. I have never suffered from sea-sickness before and am determined not to tarnish my record and start hurling now.

We all made our own lunch today because of the conditions. The dish of the day was one-minute noodles, they come in plastic bags and have the consistency of a brick. When you drop them into boiling water the noodles quickly expand to a delicious ready-to-eat feast with very little cleaning up, a prerequisite to any meal on a rough day at sea. To add something special to your banquet each bag of noodles comes with a little sachet of flavoring, chicken or beef seems to be the best. Rob could only manage to force down a slice of bread and spent the remainder of the day hanging onto the railing. We all gave him the support he needed by making fun of his unsettled stomach and telling greasy burger jokes. Oddly, he didn't appreciate our jesting.

Last night was our first of many tests. At 2200 we were hit with a squall which marked the beginning of the eventful evening. We had just finished washing up the dishes when it struck.

Over the last four days we had settled into a comfortable routine. That was our first mistake. The second mistake was after spending a day with winds blowing steadily harder and gusting up to thirty knots we continued to sail into the night with all our canvas up. We had not been in a situation where we had to work quickly together as a crew before. When the squall hit us we had little time to react. We had to reduce sail, and fast.

I turned off the autopilot and steered *Aphrodite* into the squall to take some wind out of the sails, Lewis was busy furling the genoa. With our nose pointing directly in the wind we lost all our momentum and started to get thrown around by the heavy swell. While I tried to hold the boat steady the rest of the crew struggled to bring down the main sail.

Fifteen minutes before the squall hit us there was a small island off our port side about a mile away. Not able to even see the bow spreader through the torrential sheets of rain we were in a bad situation. The strong gusts of wind were forcing us west towards the island, Don started to panic and began yelling at everyone while Peter, Lewis and Rob hung desperately to the swinging boom trying to reef the main. The giant sail, when it was released, crashed back and forth almost throwing Peter into the water. No one had time to put on their harness. The sail dropped down from the top of the mast and fell over the boom. The lazy jacks managed to keep it from spilling onto the deck and getting entangled in the sheets that were being washed around by the waves breaking over the railing.

Five minutes of thrashing around and we finally had the main reefed and part of the genoa out to help stabilize the boat. No sooner had we reduced sail and had *Aphrodite* under control had the squall passed.

The island was now only six hundred feet away. We were all wet and shaken from the experience but learned our first lesson of the trip. If the squall had lasted another three minutes *Aphrodite* would have ended up on the rocks and we would have had a very short trip indeed. We all have a great deal to learn if we expect to make it to Italy.

Later in the night we had the second incident. I woke suddenly in the bow cabin feeling disoriented and groggy. Yelling was coming from the deck so I quickly made my way up to find Lewis and Don in a heated argument. Standing only inches apart and both shouting obscenities at each other I thought we had a mutiny on our hands. Rob was sitting at the back of the boat out of harms way while Peter watched the two fight in amazement puffing on his cigarette.

"What the hell is going on?" I yelled, pissed off that it was my watch next and I wanted some sleep.

Lewis, pointing at Don said, "Ask him!"

It turned out the disorientation I felt in bed was not from a dream but rather from Don's frantic steering whilst trying to avoid some fishing trawlers ahead. Convinced we would have to "go to fucking New Zealand" to avoid collision it took many minutes to reassure him that we need only to change our heading by a few degrees in order to avoid hitting the local fishermen.

This was the second time in a single day Don had lost it. When the squall hit us he shouted and yelled at everyone but did not help. Now he was panicking over a few fishing boats? If the man I thought would lead us safely through the many obstacles yet to come panicked at the mere sight of a few fishing trawlers or a squall, what was going to happen if we were in any real danger?

Later that night I spoke to Lewis alone and asked him what had happened. Don and Lewis share an hour on their watch together and do not seem to be getting on very well. Don, Lewis said has a short temper and is not prepared to listen to him. He said that no amount of reasoning worked with the man. Only when I had carefully explained our options to Don was he prepared to change his mind. Lewis is concerned that although, in theory Don seems to know a lot about sailing and navigation, it appears he has very little practical experience and panics easily. Lewis said that he was impressed with the way I handled the situation. He does not have my patience and said that he was close to smacking him. I was surprised that Peter did not step in and take control of the situation. Maybe he was evaluating his crew to see what we are all made of, or maybe he just did not know what to do?

We are both concerned about Don's attitude and have a bad feeling about what could potentially happen if he is allowed to continue the trip with us to Italy. We will both feel more at ease when we pick up Tim, our second navigator, in Mooloolaba.

27° 31.9' S
153° 36.1' E
0° - Day 5

It's seventy-seven degrees Fahrenheit. We have got fifteen knots of wind in our sails and it seems we are finally settling into a routine. The relationship between Lewis, Don and Peter is becoming increasingly uncomfortable; I fear it will only be a matter of time before it gets physical, (I've got my money on Lewis!) When we pick up Tim in Mooloolaba, Peter is going to break the news to Don that he is welcome to continue the journey to Darwin but no further.

Don's attitude has not changed. In fact it's worse. He is rarely willing to listen to the reason of others and feels that because he is the navigator his decision is the only one that matters. Peter has yet to stand up to him. I do not quite know if it is through tolerance or fear but either way it is not a good sign. Although it is imperative that we all work together as a crew it is equally important to have a captain, someone who can make a final decision. I do not quite know who that is yet.

Peter had planned a sailing trip to Lord Howe, a small island about four hundred nautical miles off the coast of Australia to test the crew and evaluate their abilities. Unfortunately because the repairs and additional changes to *Aphrodite* were not finished in time the trip was cancelled. Consequently meeting each member of crew only for an hour over coffee was in no way a sufficient amount of time to determine their characters. We have spent almost a week together in close quarters, I am discovering the strengths and weaknesses of the other members of crew.

Peter spends most of his time with Rob as they are old buddies and have much in common. He has yet to assert his authority and seems content in letting everyone else make all the decisions. Although it is his boat, he does not have the strength of character I feel is necessary to be a captain. Rob is just enjoying the month away from work and I am sure does not share my concerns. He is a likeable guy and we all wish he could continue the trip to Italy. Although Rob is probably aware of the complications and has spoken to Peter about them, the decisions that have to be made before we leave Australia do not really concern him as he will not be with us.

Lewis and I have talked about the trip ahead and what to expect. We both agree that it will not really begin until we leave Darwin for our first leg across the Indian Ocean. Having a month's sailing under our belts is the perfect way to iron out any kinks in the boat and to test the crew and equipment before we head into the expanse of ocean. As a fire fighter, Lewis is used to dealing with men he can trust and depend on. He is uncomfortable with Don and the potential disasters that could occur if he is allowed to continue with us.

Reading below, Don spends his time mostly to himself and comes up only to check our position and heading. I have tried not to alienate him and have asked him to teach me the basics on navigation. Spending a couple of hours each day, Don seems to enjoy sharing his knowledge with me. I have had a few crash courses in navigation over the past year, taking the sixty-five foot cruiser, *Bird of Dawning* from Sydney to Surfers Paradise and crewing on *The Reef Explorer* for a week, a diving vessel that takes clients from around the world to exclusive parts of the Great Barrier Reef.

With this experience I have caught on quickly and am helping Don plot each leg of our journey through the Great Barrier Reef. Don is excited about the trip ahead but has told me he would much rather sail around the Cape of Good Hope and possibly over to Brazil before heading to Italy. I did not mention to him that unless he changes his attitude, he would not be going anywhere with us when we leave Darwin.

We are now well into Queensland territory and only five miles from Brisbane, the capital of Queensland. Looking at the constellations in the clear night and feeling the wind blowing across the ocean, it's difficult to imagine all the millions of people in the world at this very moment, stuck in traffic leaning on their horns, riding on a subway, or watching TV mesmerized by a sitcom. I can think of no other place I would rather be than here.

Our first port of call is Mooloolaba, about ten hours away. Here we will meet our new navigator for the first time and fix the bits and pieces on the boat for the next leg of our journey up the coast to Cairns, the last major town on the East Coast of Australia. I spent a few weeks in Cairns about ten months ago and loved it there.

Cairns is known for one of the best bungy jump

locations in the world. I decided to confront my fear of heights when I was there and throw myself off a tower with a giant rubber band attached to my ankles in the hope that it would cure me.

Standing on a platform only twenty inches wide and six feet long I felt like I was walking the plank. My legs were bound together making it hard for me to balance. One hundred and forty-seven feet above the rain forest canopy of Northern Australia the air was heavy and humid. I could see the ocean from where I stood and tried to focus on it and not to look down. AJ Hackett has a very good safety record, but before you throw yourself off the platform you have to sign a waiver accepting full responsibility knowing the risks involved. The shallow pool below would offer little consolation if the rubber band attached to my ankles broke.

Wanting to take the bull by the horns I told them while they were tying me up to dunk me. Such is the art of bungy jumping that they can calculate the weight of the jumper to the elasticity of the band and the speed you will reach with the precision of two to three feet. They were going to give me a little extra cord to insure that my upper body would be fully submerged in water before I was wrenched back up into the heavens.

When asked if I was ready, the one thought that came to mind was why I had requested something that would only reduce my chances of survival if they had miscalculated. Putting my life in the hands of a few complete strangers and an old calculator I could only summon a nod as confirmation. The guy to my left in a thick Australian drawl shouted, "No worries mate, wave to the camera!"

With a nervous smile I tried my best to appear calm, confident and in control. Inside I was a mess, a thousand different thoughts were racing through my mind. I decided that mentally counting down from three, was the only way

I was going to do it.

Andy who had jumped before me made it look as though he was merely diving into a swimming pool. Working on scaffolding most of his life I guess you become immune to heights. Stepping up to the edge and throwing himself off without as much as a "yee haaa," he made it seem as though it was an everyday event. I however have no problem admitting my one and only fear.

Bent slightly at the knees I started the countdown. Three, my heart started to pound harder inside my chest. Two, I said a short prayer. One, I stopped breathing. Hurling myself from the platform with as much force as my legs could summon and arms stretched out to my side, I was airborne. Like so many of the dreams I have had over the years I felt like Superman soaring high above the world. This illusion however, did not last for very long before I started to fall. Filling my lungs with the warm tropical afternoon air I let out an almighty "oooohhhh shiiiiiiit," as I plummeted down to earth.

The acceleration was tremendous, I reached seventy miles an hour in the space of a few seconds. The crystal clear pool was rapidly approaching, surely the bungy should have kicked in by now? With nothing to do except hope I waited for the bungy to take up the strain and start slowing me down. If they had miscalculated my weight or speed by just one per cent my head would get driven into the bottom of the pool. Slowly I felt the band tighten, relief and adrenaline flooded my body as the acceleration slowed down and the bungy did its job. So relieved that I was going to live I forgot about the dunk, hitting the surface of the water I was unprepared. Going in was not too bad, being wrenched out again upside down however, water shot up my nose and into every other opening in my head. Punching the air and screaming out "Yeah, yeah" the buzz was out of this world. Blinking to see if I still had my contacts in I enjoyed the rest of the ride bouncing upside down and screaming in triumph.

I still have a fear of heights and will probably always have, but confronting my fear made me realize that although it is something I will always live with, it is something that I am able to face.

Day 6 - Mooloolaba

Tonight is the first night I will not have to brace myself while I sleep. We are anchored safely in a berth at Mooloolaba marina and the only noise vibrating through the yacht is Lewis' snoring, I think I will invest in some earplugs for the journey ahead. We leave tomorrow afternoon for the next leg. Although we have only been anchored for twelve hours I am already looking forward to getting back out to sea.

I called Catherine today. It was a bad line. We spoke for a few minutes and I could barely make out what she was saying, but the worry and concern in her voice came clear through the static. I tried my best to comfort her, telling her we were a good crew with a sturdy boat under our feet. She started to cry and said, "I know it sounds strange, but you feel like you are further away from me than you have ever been before. I have no idea how you are, where you are or when I will hear from you again."

I could only tell her that I loved her and that I would be writing to her everyday. Saying goodbye I imagined her curling up in bed crying herself to sleep. It made me feel sad.

I tried to shake this feeling when I walked out of the harbormaster's office down to the marina. Lewis was busy preparing the gear, when he saw me walking towards him, I could see the concern in his face, "You alright there mate?" He asked.

I told him that Catherine was not taking it too well and that she was concerned for my safety.

"She's got every reason to be concerned mate." Lewis said. "One of our navigators has buggered off to Indonesia and the other one's a wanker!"

I didn't mention to Catherine that the Canadian navigator was not coming with us. Deciding to take another yacht, he had left over a week ago for the Philippines leaving us with only a poorly written note as an apology.

"Have decided to take another boat to the Philippines, good luck with your trip," Tim.

In light of this new situation, Peter has to now rely heavily on Don to navigate the rest of the journey. Not looking forward to spending four months with him, things are not going as planned, and we have not even been gone for a week yet!

24° 16.3' S
153° 07.0' E
260° - Day 7

I am writing today's entry by torch to conserve power. Now the electrical problems have been rectified we have made a rule that no excessive amount of power should be used at night other than for the navigational lights. It's 2230 and a bit of a rough ride. We left Mooloolaba yesterday with renewed vigor, looking forward to whatever lay ahead. I bought a packet of yellow foam earplugs from the local hardware store. I am looking forward to a relatively noise-free sleep.

We are making good time and have decided not to

anchor at Musgrave Reef but to continue north with the wind. Don is upset that we are not stopping off. He would like to take a more scenic route and visit all the islands and reefs along the way. He is not a popular man at the moment but unfortunately we are stuck with him unless we can find another navigator along the way.

The best passage across the Indian Ocean is September to mid-October. Tropical Storms and strong currents in October to November can prove fatal to a small yacht. We are already in the middle of July and have over six thousand nautical miles before we reach the Seychelles to make the leg up the African coast and around the horn. It is important we take advantage of the wind while we have it.

23° 36.5' S
157° 33.4' E
315° - Day 9

Today I went for a swim. After lunch I attached one of the fenders to a twenty-foot piece of line and secured it to the deck. Wearing nothing but a smile I jumped over the railing into the beautiful clear blue water below. It seemed like the right thing to do. Clutching onto the fender being dragged behind *Aphrodite*, I suddenly had a new perspective on the trip. Whatever happens I am going to make the most of every day.

Rob was the first to hear my howls of laughter and quickly joined in the festivities. Peter heard all the commotion and didn't know what to make of two naked men hanging off the back of his beloved boat laughing like a couple of school children. He disappeared into the cabin and returned a few seconds later with another cigarette and his camcorder to capture this momentous occasion on tape.

Lewis and Don forgot their differences and both jumped overboard to join in. After just over a week, we were finally becoming a crew. Nothing has been said about the Canadian navigator. Peter is trying to give Don a little extra room, Don is also making an effort.

Only after Peter had finished his cigarette did he carefully make his way to the railing to jump over. We carried on for about half an hour diving off the railing and swimming along side *Aphrodite* that was sailing at a steady two knots. One by one we all clambered back on deck rejuvenated by the swim. Peter was left enjoying the ride behind his boat. With the camcorder still running we did what men do best in front of a camera and showed off. We were kings of the ocean. We felt alive.

We had all forgotten about our skipper Peter, until we heard his cries for help. The camcorder was dropped as we ran to see what the trouble was. Like I said previously, I have never claimed to be a sailor and I have certainly never claimed I can tie a good knot. It seems that the knot I had used to secure the line was not substantial enough for the weight of our skipper hanging on the end of it. Peter was left bobbing up and down in the sea watching *Aphrodite* sailing away clutching the fender like a security blanket.

Don quickly took the helm as we had all come to expect. Shouting panicked orders to "his crew" trying to bring the situation under control, we all thought it was hysterical which only added to his fury. We brought the boat about to pick up our captain. Dragging him out of the water it made me think of the fishing trawlers we had encountered a few days ago hauling in a heavy catch. Peter spilled out onto the deck looking wet and shaken. He later told us that he had already been lost at sea once before and did not want to relive the experience.

Sailing about ten years ago on a hot summer's day, Peter and his son decided to cool themselves by going for an afternoon dip. Enjoying the swim so much they were unaware that their boat had dragged it's anchor and had drifted away. By the time they realized, it was too late. They found themselves alone in the Tasman Sea with no equipment or food. Peter's wife became concerned when they had not returned from their day's sailing by the early evening. She immediately called the coast guard and told them her husband and son had not returned and a search should begin before it got dark. After four hours Peter heard the chopper coming before he was able to see it. They were rescued and taken back to Canberra. Their boat was never recovered.

After an experience that would send many away from the ocean for life, Peter's dream to circumnavigate the globe was not dampened. It only brought him closer to it.

Later that evening we radioed back to Peter's family to let them know of our position. It turns out our departure was captured on television. A local station was filming whales outside Sydney harbor when *Aphrodite* sailed past.

21° 19.6' S
150° 15.0' E
312° - Day 11

Rob joined me on deck at 0430 to begin his shift. A chilly night breeze was blowing from the east as we sat huddled in the cockpit cupping our hands around mugs of steaming coffee. Talking quietly about all the events over the last two weeks we were unprepared for what was about to happen.

Out of the still night came a sound so powerful, so close that it seemed to vibrate straight through me. Like the air being released from a steam locomotive, warm spray covered us and the deck of *Aphrodite*. Rob and I sat stunned and shocked unable to comprehend what had just happened. The water all around us was unsettled and stirred as though it was alive. Grabbing the spotlight I shone it into the blackness. On our starboard side, as long as *Aphrodite*, close enough to reach out and touch was a whale. As the light reflected off its rubbery skin it dived back into the depths leaving only a ripple of water behind. Following its huge mass we stared in disbelief into the ocean watching it disappear.

Taking gulps of coffee to calm ourselves we started to laugh uncontrollably. Rolling around on the deck at 0445 we soon woke the others. Through fits of laughter we tried to explain what had happened. Lewis took my mug of coffee away and gave it a good sniff, Peter lit up a cigarette, Don started to panic.

Peter has the video *Survive the Savage Sea* aboard *Aphrodite*. Based on a true story, *Survive the Savage Sea*, is about an American family that set sail from Australia to America in their schooner, *Lucette*. Only weeks into their journey they were hit by killer whales forcing them to abandon ship. *Lucette* sunk in seconds and the Robertson family spent thirty-seven days in a life raft with no charts, no compass and rations for just three days. Only hours from death they were sighted by a Japanese fishing boat in the Pacific Ocean far away from the shipping lanes and hundreds of miles from land.

I had prepared myself for the slim possibility of pirates, running aground, storms or getting lost but I had certainly never thought we could be sunk by whales. What else is there that I have to worry about?

Day 14 - Cairns

After Don's yelling and panicking as we approached

the marina in Cairns, he announced that he would not be continuing the trip with us from Darwin. Realizing that he could not change Peter's mind about sailing around the Cape of Good Hope he is abandoning us. That will leave just Lewis, Peter and myself to reach Italy. Peter has said that if he is unable to find another navigator the trip will be cancelled.

Lewis and I made our way through town to pick up any mail that may have been sent to the poste restante and to get away from the tension on the boat. Our spirits were low as we trudged through the streets of Cairns in dirty salty cloths and rough unshaven faces. We hadn't quite got our land legs back so we staggered up Main Street like a couple of drunken vagabonds.

Cairns is the gateway to the Great Barrier Reef and is the last major town on the east coast. North of Cairns lies the wilderness of Cape York Peninsula. The lush rainforests, golden beaches and reefs surrounding Cairns make it a popular destination point for tourists. It is an isolated town and would not be more than a pub and a few shacks next to the muddy estuary if it was not for the tourist dollars that pour in each year. The estuary comes right up to the promenade, when the tide is out there is a huge muddy area the size of a couple of football fields with Mangrove trees to hide the crocodiles. The town council is proposing to fill this huge area with sand to make the city more attractive.

The shops that run parallel to the promenade are either selling t-shirts, opals, didgeridoos, boomerangs or offering reef cruises, diving specials, walkabout tours, rain forest excursions and of course AJ Hackett bungy jumping. There are more backpacking hostels and Castlemain Four X signs than you can shake a stick at!

Relaxing in the grassy park area between the mud and the tourists are the Aborigines. Sitting in the shade of the trees they seem to spend most of their time drinking in small scattered groups. My introduction to Aborigines was not entirely a pleasurable one. I was on my way to work in Townsville, I had to walk through the local park to get to the marina where I was working with Neville Grey on *True Story*, when I saw a group sitting in the morning shade drinking, I nodded a good morning as I passed and thought nothing of it. A few seconds later I was struck on the back with a Duracell D battery, one of the big ones! One of the ladies had got up and hurled it at me. At twenty paces it was a damn good shot too! When I turned around to look at the lady, puzzled as to why she had done it, one of the men stood up on unsteady feet and rushed to her defense. "Don't 'it 'er mate" he said clutching a bottle of meth.

I smiled and like a true Englishman politely said, "No problem," as if it were partly my fault.

The next day I took a wider berth around the group, just to be cautious, and noticed that the same man that had rushed to her defense and asked me not to hit her was now punching her in the face, while the others sat around watching casually as if it were a daily event. Not wanting to get involved I hurried past but mentioned it to the marine officer when I got to the boatyard.

"Oh, don't let that worry you mate, they're always beating each other up, at least it saves us from doing it eh!" he said, nudging me with his elbow.

Lewis and I continued walking up the main street and into the post office where we showed our passports to the lady waiting behind the counter. While she was looking for our letters Lewis noticed the dates on my Australian visa and announced to the world, "Bloody hell Nev, you should have left the country months ago!"

I thanked Lewis for his discretion and asked him if he could speak up a little, as I was sure immigration didn't quite hear him in Darwin. Walking around the supermarket later, I explained to Lewis that my visa expired over two months ago and that I was now staying in Australia illegally, Lewis was genuinely concerned.

"What do you think they'll do to you in Darwin, it'll be another two weeks before we anchor there?" He said stuffing more bags of one-minute noodles into the trolley. "I knew a guy that was fined two thousand dollars because he overstayed his visa!"

Thanking him for putting my mind at ease we continued to fill the trolley up with more noodles, pasta and rice. I asked Lewis not to tell Peter. He had enough on his plate with Don and I did not want to add to his troubles. "We'll cross that bridge when we get to it." I told him.

Day 16 - Lizard Island

Today we are anchored off Lizard Island, a tropical paradise on the Great Barrier Reef with an exclusive resort that hosts celebrities and royalty. Rob, Lewis and myself decided to scale the highest point of Lizard Island to Cook's Lookout 1,074 feet above the turquoise ocean. We left Peter and Don on the boat alone which may not have been a great idea.

The climb took just over an hour but it was worth the effort. It's hard to believe that Captain Cook stood at this very point over two hundred years ago, looking for a way out of the razor sharp reef that circles the island below, with *Endeavour* anchored in the cove where *Aphrodite* now sits. As far as the eye can see the reef seems to stretch to the horizon in every direction. Scattered patches of light blue indicate the shallow waters, the blue sky is broken by light patches of clouds, I have never before seen so many shades of blue.

A sad story hangs over these islands like the cotton wool clouds floating in the warm tropical air. Two hundred years ago Mary Watson was left alone with her baby and two Chinese servants when her husband sailed north to fish. Each night Mary stood at this point looking out to sea hoping for the safe return of her husband. Months after he had left one of her servants went missing and was never seen again. The second servant, while searching for the body was speared by Aborigines but managed to escape to warn Mrs. Watson. The three fled the island in a boiling tub and were left to the mercy of the winds and currents. After weeks at sea they were washed up on an Island now known as Watson Island where they died of thirst.

Only eighty years ago Aborigines would have killed white people if they came to their islands. Those very islands are now the vacation spots for families from all over the world. Colorful umbrellas and deck chairs litter the beaches. The Aborigines have moved back to the bush in the heart of Australia or are drinking in the city parks along the coast.

Hiking back to the beach, we discovered how the island got its name. A giant Iguana six feet from head to tail sat in the center of the path and seemed to resent us for interrupting his sunbathing session. He raised his pointy head and held our gaze in defiance as if to say, "This is my bloody island and I ain't moving!" Not wanting to upset him any further we carefully stepped aside and left him sunning himself.

I spent the rest of the day exploring the island alone. The beach was littered with shells, broken pieces of coral, funny shaped stones and driftwood, by the end of the day I had found a nice piece of native hard wood for my next carving and had a handful of shells and stones to add to my collection. Before returning to the boat I went for a run on the beach and had a power nap for twenty minutes in the shade of a palm tree. When I got back Don was still pissing and moaning about our schedule. Because he had made the decision to leave in Darwin he wants to stop off more along the way and explore the many islands and reefs that we were sailing past. I don't quite understand him. The islands that we have seen so far he never spends any great amount of time on. He just seems to lie there in his cot staring at the ceiling or reading sailing books.

He has managed to upset Peter even more today by underlining all the information in Peter's precious sailing manuals. Every word, sentence or paragraph that Don feels may be pertinent to the journey ahead he has boldly underlined with his HB pencil. When Peter told Don not to write in his books as they cost fifty dollars each, Don's defense was that it was in pencil and if he didn't like it he could rub it out! He couldn't understand why Peter was so angry.

I don't think Don is intentionally being difficult, he's just not sensitive to other people's wishes. He is very thick skinned, which is why the remarks that Peter has made about him never really seem to bother him, which end up upsetting Peter even more. Collectively we told him that the schedule and route was made clear from the very beginning and that we would not be stopping off any more than we had originally planned. Don ended the conversation by saying we were all crazy.

13° 01.9' S
143° 10.5' E
160° - Day 18

It's been pissing down all day. The giant drops of rain beating down hard onto the cabin roof sound like a herd of stampeding buffalo charging over our heads.

I am not on watch right now and am sharing the cabin with Don and Lewis, Peter and Rob have been stuck outside for the last two hours. It's my turn to get wet next. To prevent water from coming into the cabin we have closed the sliding hatch and put up the two pieces of plywood that completely seals the entrance to the cabin area, isolating whoever is outside on watch. The top section of plywood has a small plexiglass window linking the sheltered haven of the cabin to the unfortunate souls outside braving the harsh elements. To pass the time I have been providing a sort of two dimensional puppet show for Peter and Rob by drawing pictures of fish swimming back and forth and sticking them to the inside of the little window. I can see Rob's shoulders shake up and down as he laughs inside the hood of his waterproof jacket. Peter is busy trying to keep his cigarette alight and does not seem to appreciate all my hard work. Don ended the show by drawing a giant penis on a piece of paper and walking it across the window. I don't know if it was a subtle message directed at Peter or just his unique sense of humor that we have all come to love so much. I don't think Peter saw it anyway because his head was in his cupped hands trying to light another cigarette.

13° 29.2' S
143° 40.2' E
143° - Day 21

I no longer know what day it is, although it doesn't really matter. When people dream of being shipwrecked alone on a deserted tropical island, maybe they are dreaming of Palm Tree Island. Framed by golden sand, coral and shells the one palm tree remaining on this small oval island hangs lazily over the sisal trees in the afternoon sun.

A hundred years ago palm trees and sisal trees were planted on such islands. Goats were also left behind for unfortunate pearl divers or shipwrecked sailors. The sisal trees provided long limbs suitable for fires and knocking down coconuts for flesh and milk, the goats I guess provided the company.

An unmarked grave of a long forgotten pearl diver guards the island shaded by the last remaining palm tree. Hungry for something other than one-minute noodles I attempted to climb the palm tree but got a cramp half way up in my right foot trying to grip onto the trunk. My big toe bent painfully over causing me to fall to the ground in a heap, Don found this hysterical. More accustomed to climbing than I, Lewis scaled the palm tree in under a minute and threw down three huge nuts that we split open. We shared the spoils and each walked off in our own direction with our fresh bounty. Munching on fresh coconut meat and picking through the shells on the leeward side of the island I enjoyed a rare moment of solitude. Rob was busy tearing around the island on his windsurfer, Lewis was exploring the windward side of the island, Don was a hundred yards up the beach and Peter was on board drinking another beer and smoking a cigarette.

Lewis and Don returned to the boat leaving me alone on the island with the lost pearl diver. Standing over his grave I began to wonder how he died, what sort of man he was and who he left behind. A variety of exotic reef shells and gifts have been placed carefully around his grave from other sailors that have visited him. For my gift I left a wooden bow divider behind. I had carved the two arms out of wood and joined them together with a peg that enabled the arms to swing back and forth. The bow divider is shaped a little like a compass, both arms have points so it can be used to measure long distances on charts by swinging each arm in front of the other. It is an essential navigational instrument, used for measuring and plotting coordinates. Hoping that my gift would help the soul of the pearl diver find his way off the deserted island and home to his loved ones I made my way to the shore.

Waiting for Lewis to pick me up, I am comfortable knowing that whatever is meant to happen on this trip will happen, and to enjoy each moment while it lasts.

Watching the sun fade to the west the lyrics of *What's new pussy cat* are drifting across the water to where I stand. Tom Jones has never done it for me but I have come to know the lyrics to many of his songs over the past few weeks. Wearing bright red sweat pants and a faded blue shirt Lewis is motoring over in the inflatable to get me. I know I can count on him in the months ahead.

"I'm worried Lewis," I told him as he cut the engine and drifted onto the beach.

Holding the boat steady so I could climb aboard he said, "Yeah mate, we've still got another week with Mr. Panic."

"No, I'm worried that we have to spend another four months listening to that crap!"

Laughing back to the boat we began to sing:

Love is like candy on a shelf,
If you would like a taste then help yourself,
The sweetest things are there for you,
Help yourself, take a few,
That's what I want you to do...

Climbing back on board Peter, Rob and Don joined in the rest of the song. Off key and out of tune we sang Tom Jones, drank Peter's beer and forgot about our differences for the night.

12° 18.3' S
142° 30.8' E
250° - Day 22

We left the pearl diver alone once again on his island. Setting the autopilot and trimming the sails we are now heading for Margaret Bay, a days sailing up the coast. The winds have been blowing from the southeast at fifteen knots. The sea is calm and the days have been clear and warm.

For almost a week I have been navigating under the watchful eye of Don. I have learned much of the art of celestial navigation and the winds, currents and conditions of the journey ahead. Understanding the ocean on which we will be sailing has made me feel more at ease. Nothing has been said about the journey from Darwin or if we will even continue.

The most challenging leg will be the Red Sea. This thin body of water with Ethiopia, Sudan and Egypt on the western side and Yemen and Saudi Arabia on the eastern side is an unforgiving passage for yachts. Saudi Arabia is not known for it's hospitality and forbids any yachts to anchor on the Eastern Shore. If luck is on your side you may have winds blowing from the Gulf of Aden helping you up the first third but you will soon find the wind hitting you on the nose as you battle to make a northerly passage. One of the most dangerous sailing routes in the world, the Red Sea has heavy shipping lanes, uncharted reefs, strong winds and currents.

I have plotted our course around the most northern tip of Australia. Squeezing through Papua New Guinea and Cape York, the Torres Straits are renowned for strong winds and currents. Once we pass through the Straits, we'll head west across the Bay of Carpentaria for Darwin.

Lewis is also taking an interest in navigation and has mastered the noon reading to estimate our latitude with the sextant, Peter has yet to show any interest.

Day 24 - Turtle Head Island

This is our last stop before we reach Darwin. Turtle Head Island is a secure and close anchorage to Cape York. With strong currents through the Torres Straits between Australia and Papua New Guinea, the sea can get nasty so we want to make sure we clear the Cape before nightfall. Once we round it we'll have another ten or eleven days to Darwin.

Our neighbors tonight are three fishing trawlers. As we begin to settle in for a comfortable night at anchor, the men on deck are preparing the nets for another night of trawling. Lewis and Rob took the inflatable over in search for food. It brings a whole new meaning to getting takeout. Returning with a great big bag filled with fresh prawns we lit up the stove and set about cooking them.

While the shrimp were boiling I decided to try my luck and threw a line over the back of the boat. In the space of only a few minutes I pulled two mackerel out of the harbor. Lewis was astonished at the rate I was pulling them in and wanted to know what bait I was using.

"Cheddar Cheese." I told him.

As much as we all like fresh fish we decided to stop fishing. The rations of cheese we have stored in the freezer are far more valuable than the mackerel we were catching.

Supper was superb and to complement the meal we each poured ourselves a mug of whisky and settled down under the stars. I had bought some Indian Beedies back in Cairns. The skipper of the *Reef Explorer* introduced me to them when I worked for him as a deck hand nine months ago. Made of apple leaf, these miniature cigars leave you feeling light headed and happy. Passing them around we all got high and began to sing. Peter had put on his other favorite tape, Neil Diamond. Singing *Cracklin' Rose* we partied late into the night scaring away any remaining fish in the harbor.

10° 50.6' S
136° 53.6' E
259° - Day 26

We have cleared the Gulf of Carpentaria and are heading west across the northern coast of Australia. There is twenty-five knots of good wind gusting over the deck and we are averaging eight knots over ground.

Yesterday afternoon we were buzzed by an Australian coast guard patrolling the coastline in a little two-seater, amphibious airplane. Lewis, Rob and myself were standing naked on the deck showering when it passed. We looked up into the clear sky, shielded our eyes from the sun with one hand and waved with the other as it flew only fifty feet above the mast. We didn't think anything of it until we were radioed by the pilot. The female voice on the end of the line said that she had seen our sails and came over to check on the boat. She said that she had not quite expected the welcome and noted that we all looked to be in good shape. When she came around for a second pass we were ready for her and each struck a pose as the tiny plane dipped its wings as a farewell salute, (either that or she was so impressed with the show she temporarily lost control of the craft. We like to think it's the latter).

I have studied the charts for the Indian Ocean and feel familiar enough with the passage to take on the challenge myself. As my father once told me, "Whether you believe you can, or whether you believe you can't, you're probably right." Great thoughts, potential and dreams are lost around the world each day to people that never attempt to realize them or are too afraid to try. I resent Don for what he has done. Allowing others to influence your decision or change the course of your life can lead to regret. To give up now Peter may never have the opportunity to fulfill his dream again, it would be lost forever. I know the three of us can manage the journey alone, Lewis feels the same way. All we have to do is convince Peter.

Day 31 - Darwin

We have only been in Darwin for three hours and already people are talking about the crew of *Aphrodite*. In our haste to get ashore and have a hot shower we neglected to take note of the high tide that Fannie Bay experiences. We thought we had fed out enough anchor chain to allow for the incoming tide, but when we heard the name of *Aphrodite* mentioned over the loud speaker and the owner to report immediately to the harbormaster, we had a hunch something was wrong.

We quickly raced down to the shore to see *Aphrodite* adrift amongst fifty other yachts. She had already collided with two boats and had now tangled her anchor chain with a third. Peter and Rob raced out in the duck to stop this embarrassing moment. As they approached *Aphrodite*, Peter slowed down allowing Rob to climb aboard. Standing up to steady the boat for Rob, who was now aboard *Aphrodite*, Peter lost his balance and fell back. In doing so he increased the throttle and tumbled over into the water. The inflatable raced off leaving Peter in "the drink" for the second time on this trip.

By now every sailor was looking in amazement at this spectacle in the harbor. With Peter paddling after the inflatable and Rob stuck on *Aphrodite* we did not project the image of an experienced crew. It was later rumored when all vessels had been recovered and egos restored, that the other sailors had little confidence in our ability to successfully reach Italy without a navigator or qualified crew.

That night we ate at the all-you-can-eat-buffet at the Darwin Yacht Club. Piling our plates high, Lewis and I set out to break the record and eat as much bread and meat we could cram into our stomachs. With steak juice dripping down our chins we washed it down with cans of Castlemain's Four X. We felt infinitely better.

Peter is what I would call a "noisy drunk," He does not hold his alcohol very well and started to lecture Don on his attitude problems.

"Your not a bad bloke really," Peter slurred, "It's just that you do not get on well with other people do you!"

Don did not appreciate being psychoanalyzed by Peter, a man that he thought was far from perfect himself. With his pride on the line Don retorted and gave back in full force. Yelling at Peter, saying that he was the worst captain of any boat ever to sail at sea and that we would never make it to Italy because we were a shit crew with no navigator. Not wanting to escalate the situation and knowing Peter was close to throwing a punch I stood up and calmly asked Don for his address.

"What do you want my damn address for Neville?" he yelled with a red face.

"I want to send you a postcard when we reach Italy."

Said in such a matter-of-fact way Don had lost the trip of a lifetime and had now lost the argument. As he stormed off alone we made a toast. Raising our glasses high we shouted out for all to hear, "To Fiumicino!" The decision was made, we were going for it!

Day 37 - Darwin

Peter spoke to me alone today to make sure I really felt comfortable navigating the rest of the journey, I told him I was ready for the challenge, and the three of us was all we needed. I did not tell him that I was full of doubt and apprehension. Knowing that his dream was still on schedule and Don would no longer be with us Peter lit up a cigarette and relaxed in his chair with a smile of contentment stretched across his face.

With the new responsibility of being navigator, I have been carefully studying the charts for the trip ahead and have come to realize that Don never had any intention of sailing through the Suez Canal. He has left me with no charts for the Red Sea, the most hazardous stretch of water on the entire journey! I have managed to get a few I need to help us along the way, but the remaining charts, we will have to pick up on route. The reality of the 8,878 nautical miles ahead that I will have to navigate is only now really beginning to register.

We have been in Darwin for a week preparing for the voyage ahead. The decision that we made the first night to continue the journey to Italy has formed a bond between the three of us that I feel will only strengthen in the months to come. Rob has left to go back home. He will be missed. He wished us luck making us promise to send him a postcard as well.

Don has remained in Darwin staying in a hostel looking for another boat to take him to Brazil. We often see him hanging around the club talking to people. Peter has already spoken to one couple who asked for a reference. He truthfully told them that Don was potentially a good sailor, but had a tendency to panic, which was why he did not get on with the rest of the crew. Don has yet to find another boat.

We are all eager to get back out at sea but it's our last opportunity to buy equipment and supplies for the 4,547 nautical miles across to the Seychelles. We have spent a lot of money in the past week, a new life raft, an EPIRB (emergency position indicating radio beacon), outboard motor, hand held GPS, and a spare RAM for the auto pilot has depleted all of our funds. Peter has paid for most of the equipment as it is his boat and he will use it in the years ahead.

The EPIRB cost $2,800 and we all chipped in for it. This lightweight transmitter when activated sends a signal to the coast guard positioning your exact location. Something that we will all benefit from if we ever have the misfortune of using it, the cost was shared. I exchanged my last pound sterling to US dollars. I now have only $600 for the remaining three months.

Something that did not cost us a cent but could be equally as valuable are the two old car tires we salvaged from the back of the yacht club. We have secured them to the cabin roof on the port side and have prayed that we never need to untie them. The tires will serve as a sea anchor and can help stabilize a boat in severe conditions. If the wind and seas are too great to sail in and there is a danger of being swept to land, a sea anchor will help to hold the boat steady. Some sailors use an old sail, like an underwater parachute, others just throw anything heavy over the back of the boat to slow it down. I can't imagine ever being in such a desperate situation. It's a sailor's final stand against Mother Nature; a last resort.

With everything shipshape, it's time to officially leave Australia. We caught a bus to the immigration office to have our passports stamped. On the way in I told Peter that I may have a few difficulties, as I had overstayed my visa.

"I am sure a few days doesn't really matter Nev." Peter reassured me.

"Well, it's a little more than a few days Peter." I told him.

Lewis and Peter were ready to go within half an hour. Waiting for me by the front desk I told them that they might as well leave as I was being detained for questioning. I had overstayed my visa by ninety-seven days!

Preparing my speech and exercising my bullshitting chords, I began to rehearse as I waited in a small windowless office. To pass the time I studied the world map on the wall. Tracing the route we would make with the tip of my finger it is hard to imagine myself in these places.

In the next four months I will be sailing to uninhabited tropical atolls in the Indian Ocean, visiting the reputed site of the Garden of Eden. I will be shopping at the local bazaars of Africa, haggling over fruit and vegetables in the markets of Sudan, visiting Keops pyramid and the Great Sphinx of Egypt, sailing through the Suez Canal and marveling at the architecture in Rome. The door slammed hard behind me bringing me out of my daydream. I had to remind myself as I turned to greet the officer that I had not made it yet! Without as much as a smile or a handshake I was told to take a seat.

As the officer went over my passport I felt my odds were pretty good. He was a young guy, probably only a few years older than me, I was sure he would sympathize with my situation.

My father has always accused me of being a "lucky bastard." However I have always attributed my good fortune to my charismatic charm and irrepressible sense of humor. Pat asked me a series of routine questions. Were you aware that you overstayed your visa? Have you worked in the past three months? Where have you been in the past three months? Have you been arrested before? I answered his questions honestly and directly. At the end of the interview Pat looked up and asked me where I was heading. I told him Italy.

"Yea? How long will that take you?" He asked with genuine interest.

I told him the whole story and that I had estimated our arrival in Fiumicino to be on November 25th. Pat sat back in his chair and when I had finished said, "Mate, you are a lucky bastard, I would love to go on a journey like that."

"If you can get your kit together by tomorrow morning you are welcome to come along." I said jokingly.

He actually paused to consider it then shook his head as if to wake himself back to reality.

"Naa, my sheila would kill me if I buggered off for four months."

"What can you do about my visa problem?" I finally asked.

Pat explained to me that I would be banned from Australia for six months as my punishment. "Oh, is that all, that's alright" I told him, "I will be sailing for four of those months anyway!"

Getting up from his chair he made his way over to the world map on the wall. "Where will you be sailing again Neville?" He asked.

"Christmas Island and Cocos Keeling are the first two stops."

"Then it won't be alright. Those islands are owned by Australia, if you are banned from Australia you won't be allowed to set foot on them."

I could not believe it! That meant that I would be stuck on the boat for over a month without feeling dry land under my feet. Tropical islands, that most people don't even realize exist would be less than one hundred feet away and still out of reach!

Pat explained that Peter, as the captain of the boat, would be responsible for my actions and fined $2,000 if I attempted to go ashore, I would be thrown in jail for the remainder of our stay. I asked him if there was anything he could do.

Pat said he would fax a letter to the immigration officers at both islands explaining that I was a nice bloke and to turn the other way when *Aphrodite* sailed into their harbors. I thought to myself as he filed away the paperwork that this would not be a very clever idea if other boats were anchored in the area, as I was certain our reputation would precede us.

Wanting to know more about the sailing trip I gave Pat the number of CrewFind International and told him he should give them a call. Although Pat told me to have "No worries mate" and assured me the immigration officers at these islands were pretty easy going and I should not have any problems, I left the interview feeling like a criminal.

A few hundred years ago English convicts were dumped in Australia for their crimes in Europe, I guess this was Australia's way of getting back at us.

When I walked out of the office I was surprised to find that Lewis and Peter had waited for me all that time. We were a crew now, looking out for one another. I told them the news. Lewis said that he would bribe the officers to get me ashore if he had to and not to worry. Peter on the other hand, at the risk of being fined $2,000 was not so carefree.

"You've gotta promise me Nev," looking at me straight in the eyes, "that you do not go ashore unless you have written permission from the authorities."

I told Peter that he had trusted me enough to sail with him half way around the world and that I would not let him down.

Lewis walked away muttering "Don't you worry Nev, I'll sneak you ashore if I have to."

2

Darwin to Christmas Island

(1,487.5 nautical miles)

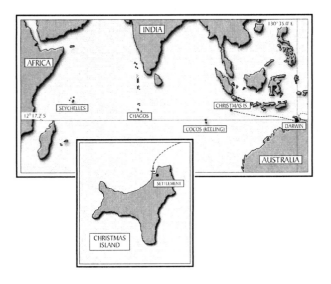

2

Darwin to
Christmas Island

12° 17.2' S
130° 35.0' E
304° - Day 38

After all the preparations and anxiety, we finally left the giant continent of Australia behind us today. Watching the coastline disappear into the horizon we said our silent farewells to loved ones and memories. We are running with the wind. Catching every breath in our canvas, the sails are flared out like the wings of a giant swan. We have only the sea in front of us now, a feeling that none of us have experienced before.

Every direction I look the sea is alive and moving, there is no land in sight and as the days go by we will sail further away from civilization. It feels like we are sailing into the wild, the deeper we go the more alone and vulnerable we will be. The surface of the sea is a continuous movement of waves that have traveled for thousands of miles to greet us. The sunlight reflects off each crest making the world around us twinkle like a giant crumpled sheet of tin foil. The wind is blowing from the southeast, the waves are chasing us from behind as we sail to the west. Australia will shield and protect us for another few days then the waves will have time to build in size and strength, none of us knows what to expect. We each have a thousand different questions but are unable to answer a single one, only time will give us the answers.

The trade winds are blowing a steady fifteen knots from the southeast, we are averaging eight knots over the ground. I have set all the waypoints into the autopilot and plotted our course west across the Indian Ocean. Christmas Island is our first stop, followed by Cocos Keeling, Chagos then the Seychelles before we head north to round the Horn of Africa. If the trade winds are kind we will see the extinct volcano of Christmas Island rise out of the ocean in ten days.

Our passports were stamped for our departure from Australia by the immigration officer who came aboard with the outgoing tide at 1200. Filling out the last of the forms Peter presented the officer with a pump-action shotgun, a .308 rifle and a bottle of morphine for inspection. He was certainly prepared for the worst! Each weapon was accompanied with a license and registration. The bottle of morphine came with a note from Peter's doctor. I could tell by the expression on Lewis's face that he was not comfortable with the guns on board. The weapons were cleared but we were warned to expect trouble with immigration at other countries, especially in Africa.

We have not spoken much about the journey ahead. Peter has not requested to see the waypoints I have programmed into the autopilot nor the charts I am using to navigate to each island. I have suggested that whoever is on watch should take our position every hour, day or night. Although in the expanse of ocean this may seem excessive, we will be better able to determine our average speed and keep on course. In the early hours of the morning when the human body is at its lowest ebb, it is easy to forget about the dangers at sea. Anything to keep the person on watch focused is a good thing. We will not reef the main down tonight, the trade winds have been steady all day and the late afternoon sky is clear.

With just three of us now we have more room aboard *Aphrodite*. I have chosen to stay in the bow cabin, finding the movement and noise peaceful, helping me to sleep at night. Lewis is using the two bench seats in the main saloon area that run down both sides of the hull. With the dining table leaf folded down and secured, Lewis has enough room to switch beds if we change tack. As the captain, Peter is staying in the aft cabin and has the luxury of his own sink. The captain's bathroom however is stuffed full with wet suits and beer, making it impossible for him to use so we all share the same bathroom (head), which is unfortunately located right outside my cabin.

With more space on the boat the cabin area is kept clean and all gear has been stowed away. Only towels or an odd shirt are left on the handrails to swing back and forth in rhythm with the ocean.

11° 42.7' S
128° 29.5' E
280° - Day 40

We have settled into the new routine with ease and have three-hour shifts each to monitor our position and check for boats. Averaging one hundred and seventeen nautical miles a day, the trade winds have been unpredictable gusting up to twenty-three knots then dropping to ten. We are all getting on extremely well and respect each other's space, enjoying the freedom of being at sea and heading into the unknown.

Yesterday we each fired the .308 and shotgun to get a feel of the weapons should we ever run into pirates along the way. The .308 had a mean kick and left our eardrums buzzing with protest well after the rifles were placed back in their gun bags and stored. I think Peter may have taken the pirate brochures I gave him a little too seriously. Maybe tomorrow we will start practicing self-defense and survival techniques?

We fill each day our own way. Peter spends much of his time writing to his family and rolling cigarettes, managing to spill most of the tobacco on the deck. Unable to afford large quantities of packet cigarettes, Peter has bought bags of tobacco and rolling papers. He has not quite mastered the delicate art of rolling his own and often resorts to the help of a plastic gadget.

Lewis seems to enjoy spending his time reading, eating and just staring out to sea, something that you can never tire of. Each set of waves, each movement of the boat is different from the last. Relaxing into a state of meditation the sound of the ocean and the wind can hold you in a trance. It is quite easy to spend the entire afternoon just sitting on the deck doing nothing.

I start each day, regardless of my shift, the same way. I have found my dreams to be most unusual since the beginning of the journey. Most nights are filled with epic stories of adventure and mystery. I am lucky to be able to remember them in detail and spend the first half-hour of my morning watch sipping a mug of black coffee and writing in my dream diary, I have entitled "Dream Time." The rest of my day I spend reading, writing, sketching on the calm days, whittling the pieces of driftwood I have gathered along the way and exercising. The latter is by no means easy on a boat at sea.

I have devised a routine where I am able to train ninety per cent of my body by utilizing parts of the yacht for dips, sit-ups, press-ups and a variety of different movements that help to keep me in shape. Rolling around on the deck trying to perform my daily exercises, I provide the afternoon entertainment for Peter and Lewis.

At each port of call, where possible, I try and run a few miles a day. After a month confined to a deck, a quarter of the size of a basketball court, my cardiovascular condition is in poor shape. Lewis has joined me on a few occasions for a jog around the harbor and also trains on the boat. Peter seems content smoking his cigarettes and watching us do all the hard work.

11° 24.7' S
126° 32.5' E
274° - Day 41

With the security of the Australian waters now far behind us, we are sailing in the Timor Sea, sixty nautical miles south of Timor, Indonesia. Unauthorized boats are prohibited to sail in the waters surrounding these islands. Unless you have a compulsory cruising permit, which we do not, yachts must stay well out of the zone. We do not know what will happen if we do cross the line. If we run into trouble with the authorities Peter will probably just shoot them!

We are making excellent time averaging one hundred and fifteen miles a day. The winds have picked up to twenty knots chopping up the surface of the ocean. We are still goose winging with the main sail to port and the pole holding the genoa far out to starboard. Catching so much wind from behind *Aphrodite* is pushed forward at a tremendous pace.

Running with the wind can be a dangerous tack. With the wind directly behind the boat becomes very unstable, with each gust the autopilot fights constantly to keep our heading true. If the wind picks up suddenly, furling and reducing sail quickly is almost impossible. To head into the wind we would have to make a one hundred and eighty degree turn to reef the main sail. If the wind starts to blow much above twenty-five knots we will take the pole down.

Assistance at any time of the day or night is only a shout away. If sails need to be reduced, changes are made at the exchange of a watch. If however it is urgent you will be wrenched from a peaceful sleep with a rough hand on your shoulder and a loud voice in your ear. Because of this impending interruption I find that I am always listening to the noise of the boat and am aware of the movements around me, even when asleep. If they should change suddenly I immediately awake to check on the situation, as does Lewis and Peter.

We have become a team and rely heavily on each other. Even if you are not on watch, you are never really off duty. Lewis has the watch before me, so he wakes me when I am on, I wake Peter as he has the watch after me.

I know it's time for my shift as I can hear Lewis thumping around on deck making his way down to my cabin to wake me. "Hey big fella, you up?"

I have no problem with an early start to the day and actually enjoy this shift the most. From 0300 - 0600 is the most peaceful time of the day. I will never tire of watching the sun rise each morning as it is always different. Normally I do not wake Peter after my watch is over because I rarely go back to sleep. Letting the person sleep in after you on this sunrise watch is becoming an unwritten rule. If you are going to stay up, unless the conditions are shitty, you let the person after you sleep in.

Making my way on deck the night is clear and calm. With no pollution in the night air the stars twinkle with an energy and brightness I have not seen before. The moon is low tonight and casting long shadows over the deck. "What we got?" I asked Lewis as I settled in for my watch.

"Six fishing trawlers and a freighter about five miles dead ahead." he said disappearing into the cabin, "If you need me give me a holler." Lewis seemed to be rundown, I do not think he is sleeping very well and the swell is unsettling his stomach.

So much for a peaceful beginning to the day I thought to myself as I noted the position of the trawlers around me. Making a mental note of their headings the VHF radio crackled into life.

"Sailing vessel, sailing vessel this is freighter, what is your heading over?"

The VHF radio is set on channel sixteen for emergencies. I quickly jumped down into the cabin and responded. "Freighter, this is sailing vessel *Aphrodite*, please go to channel nine, channel nine, over."

It is important that channel sixteen is free of chatter, once a ship has responded to a call another channel must be selected.

"Going to channel nine."

"This is sailing vessel *Aphrodite* do you read?"

"What is heading, *Aphrodite*?"

"Our heading is two hundred and seventy-four degrees at six knots, over."

"We will pass you on your starboard side, over."

The voice on the other end of the radio had a strong South African accent. Interested in where the freighter was from I continued the conversation.

"Where have you come from and what is your destination over?"

"We have come from Cape Town and are heading for Sydney, over."

"We have just come from Sydney. What have the conditions been like on your passage, over?"

"Trade winds have been steady *Aphrodite*, swell no greater than eight feet. What was weather like up Australia over?"

Telling the freighter that we had good conditions with

just a few squalls we ended the conversation wishing the other a safe and quick passage.

It is strange how lives cross paths and the difference a few words can make. I have never seen the man aboard the freighter and will probably never speak to him again, yet at sea we had been united by a common bond, a respect for one another and the ocean we sail on. Such honesty between strangers is rare. There are no boundaries out here, no walls, no prejudice, no limits, just ocean that has covered the earth from the beginning of time and has joined countries and people together for thousands of years.

Climbing back on deck I watched the freighter steam silently towards us in the night wondering who was aboard and what their lives were like. Now only one thousand feet from our starboard side I turned my attention back to the fishing boats. Trawling nets, I want to make sure I allow enough room when we pass.

Peter emerged from the cabin scratching his ass and destroying the tranquility of the moment. Lighting up a cigarette he heard the conversation with the South African and came to see what all the noise was about. "How ya doing Nev?" He said in a cloud of cigarette smoke.

Pointing out all the trawlers and their heading, I told Peter that we were going straight through the middle of the pack with plenty of room to spare. Satisfied with my decision he finished his cigarette and returned to bed.

Turning to look at the freighter steaming east and the trawlers now behind us I am left alone again to enjoy the simplicity of the night. Making my way to the stern to sit on the bench I looked up and caught a glimpse of a shooting star racing across the star filled sky. The sails are full of wind and reflecting the moonlight. The sea had picked up a little.

11° 20.1' S
124° 34.4' E
267° - Day 42

You know it is time to take the pole down when you hit ten knots over ground with twenty-four knots of wind! It's 1400 and a hot sunny day. The air temperature is eighty-two degrees Fahrenheit, the water temperature is seventy-nine degrees. We took the pole down before lunch and in doing so have lost a couple of knots. We are still howling along though, and on course for Christmas Island.

I am worried Lewis is going to get bed sores, he has not moved from the cabin roof all day and has been staring out to sea behind his dark sunglasses looking for the answers to life. Peter has just finished rolling a giant cigarette that is shaped like a trumpet, I think he spilled more tobacco on the deck than he managed to fit inside the little paper.

11° 01.0' S
117° 00.8' E
259° - Day 43

Standing on the deck feeling nothing on my skin but the drying salt water, the warmth of the morning sun and the ocean wind has brought me closer to myself than ever before, even shorts seem restricting after my morning shower. Staring out to sea I feel at peace with myself and the world around me.

It's 0800 and the day is just beginning. The shampoo that I use for washing has left my body feeling squeaky-clean. Soap does not lather well in salt water so we bought bottles of shampoo for washing. Balancing on the deck covered in bubbles, throwing a bucket over the side into the water and hauling it back up by a rope brings a whole new meaning to having a shower. We only use fresh water now for drinking and cooking. With the days getting hotter it is important we reserve as much fresh water for drinking so we do not dehydrate. The human body can last over a month in these conditions without food, without water we would perish within days.

I have never gone without eating for more than twelve hours in my entire life and usually get bad tempered after not eating for just three. So when Lewis suggested we go on a fast in an attempt to clean out our systems I was less than enthusiastic.

With our minds free of stress and everyday burdens we were going for the total cleansing package. It will be interesting to see how my body responds with only fluids for twenty-four hours. Lewis is no stranger to fasting and told me that he once went without food for a week. "That's no great accomplishment," I told him, "given a choice between eating your cooking or going without it's not a particularly hard decision to make."

Our last meal before the fast was unfortunately cooked by Lewis. Not quite as nutritious as I had hoped it consisted of beans, eggs and a runny potato mix. Even Peter who was not participating in the fast found the meal unsavory. Complaining that the mashed potatoes were too runny and not "fluffy" how he likes them and that the beans were mixed up with the eggs he was most unhappy. Making faces with each mouthful he ended up feeding most of his dinner to the fish.

10° 45.5' S
112° 06.4' E
280° - Day 44

I do not consider myself to be very spiritual and I am certainly no new age born again hippy, but there is definitely something to be said about a simple existence and the freedom you experience without stress. I know that in a year from now I will be pushing my way into a New York subway stressed to the eyeballs and to feel even remotely close to the way I am feeling now will cost me thousands of dollars for a single weekend at a health spa. This entire trip for five months with all its expenses is costing me less than fifteen hundred dollars, including beedies and beer!

With only eight hours left to go on our fast I feel remarkably well. I have been drinking fluids regularly making sure I do not dehydrate. We are howling along averaging nine knots. Even with the pole down we almost managed eleven knots over ground. The swell has picked up to ten feet and is beginning to feel more like an ocean. The waves are spread further apart and sweep up behind *Aphrodite* pushing her bow down into the trough of the wave ahead. As the wave passes under the hull the bow rises up into the sky before it drops down again into the next trough.

Aphrodite is doing a grand job and riding the waves well. You can see the pride in Peter's face as his boat handles the swell with ease. Like a father watching his son score a winning touchdown for the first time, *Aphrodite* is making him proud. Watching the waves approach us from behind I feel as though they will crash down over the deck but each time we rise up with them, riding on the surface of the ocean.

There are many dangers a sail boat has to face at sea,

but if the sails are down and the hatches battened, yachts have been known to survive the strongest of gales. With fifteen thousand pounds of lead in the keel it is not uncommon for yachts to be blown over so their mast lays flat in the water (knock down) before it rights itself. Some yachts have also performed a three hundred and sixty-degree vertical turn. A large enough wave can push a boat onto its side another will then lift the keel up into the air forcing the mast underwater. Now upside down the majority of the weight is above the surface of the water, and like a pendulum another wave can push the keel back over, causing the yacht to right itself.

Most yachts fall victim to land. In their element at sea, yachts soon lose the advantage when they go aground. Unable to escape they slowly get pounded to pieces. Freighters and other large boats are another serious danger as two hundred thousand tons of steel cannot slow down or change heading quickly. A large cargo ship will simply run over a yacht like a car squashing a bug on the highway, some have mown down yachts without ever knowing it.

Another danger with cargo ships is their load. Thousands of containers are lost each year when they are washed overboard in heavy seas. These huge metal containers often hold enough buoyancy to remain afloat just under the surface of the water. Sailing into such a container would take the keel right off the bottom of the yacht, causing it to sink immediately. The unsuspecting crew, unless on deck would drown without ever knowing what happened.

We are now out of the main shipping lanes and have not sighted another boat since the South African freighter three and a half days ago. The radio has been silent, constantly listening for others but has nothing to report. The nearest land mass now is Java, one hundred and thirty miles north. We are alone at sea.

I have not felt this removed from civilization since I was in the outback working for Northern Exploration Services. For a month Andy and I camped on the Northern Territory, Queensland border by the Gregory River. Using a Sirotem computer we plotted charts using magnetic grids in search for minerals. We were eighteen hours away from Mount Isa, a dusty mining town in the middle of nowhere and another ten hours away from McKinley, otherwise known as "Walkabout Creek" featured in the film Crocodile Dundee.

At five in the morning we would all be awakened by the generator that would roar into life and bring light to the camp. By six o'clock we would be skimming across the surface of the bush in a Bell 47 helicopter. The clear plastic dome surrounding the cockpit would give us an almost three hundred and sixty degree view of the featureless outback. Dave, the pilot, would take us far out from camp to begin our day at work and would not return to pick us up until late in the afternoon.

Walking through valleys that have probably never been seen before by man, Andy and I sweltered under the relentless sun for eight hours each day for a month. The rocky patches of red soil not covered by the needle-sharp spinifex grass was hot enough to melt the rubber soles of our boots. The only thing that interrupted the never-ending landscape were a few scattered trees and termite hills that would sometimes reach up to ten feet high. In our frustration and boredom waiting for the readings to register on the computer, we would knock the small termite hills down with rocks. The red dry soil would explode in a cloud of dust with a direct hit. Knocking down termite hills or singing was the only way we managed to stay sane on those long hot days.

The other thirteen men working in the camp were

mostly older and knew of no other life than the one in the bush. Only one week in eight would they drive on the dusty corrugated road all the way back to Mount Isa, where they would get drunk and sleep with a hooker before disappearing back in the bush again. Spending so much time alone in the middle of the most barren country in the world had taken its toll on these men. They found it hard to function in society, they had become imprisoned in the bush without ever knowing it. Most of them drank heavily every night to help them forget their loneliness. Even long after the generator had been switched off and darkness had consumed the camp, you would still hear the "tishhhh" of a beer can being opened.

Andy and I left the outback with our minds still intact. We were asked to stay on for another six months but knew we could not do it. One of the thoughts that kept us going over the last week was the cruise we were going to take on the Great Barrier Reef off Magnetic Island in Townsville.

Looking out across the ocean now, I am filled with the same sense of smallness as I felt in the middle of Australia, yet I do not feel as isolated or trapped. Even though I am confined to the small amount of space that I must share with two other men, ironically I feel a level of freedom I have not felt before. As long as the wind is in the sails and pushing us along, I know I am going somewhere and each day I am a little nearer to where I want to be.

The end of the day has been decided by the sun disappearing from sight and the stars appearing in the darkening sky. The fast is over and remarkably I am not that hungry. Peter cooked sausages tonight and for the first time on this trip I was unable to finish all of my meal. He was happy to polish off the remains of my dinner for me and suggested I should fast more often.

10° 38.7' S
110° 10.8' E
256° - Day 45

Tonight began much like every other night on this leg of our journey west but ended in near disaster. It was 2000, we had just finished washing up after another gourmet supper when Peter spotted a boat off our port side for the second time today. It looked like an old fishing trawler but we could not see any nets or supports on the deck. We tried making radio contact to this unmarked vessel but had no response. The boat was four nautical miles away. It did not present a threat so Lewis went for a nap before he would begin his 2100 shift. As the daylight disappeared we were forced to judge the direction of the boat by its motoring lights only. It seemed to be on a parallel course heading east, as we could clearly see it's red port light.

Peter started the engine as we do every night to recharge the batteries. When he came back up on deck he pointed out the boat seemed to have changed course. We could now see the bow light in the center of the starboard and port light, it was heading towards us. We were only one hundred and thirty nautical miles south of Java, Indonesia, I had a bad feeling in the pit of my stomach and thought of the brochures I had collected in Sydney. Watching the boat motor closer the feeling in my stomach told me something was wrong. It was only one and a half miles away and closing fast. I estimated its speed to be around fifteen knots.

"I have got a bad feeling about this Peter. It's not changing course. It's still heading straight towards us!"

I took the boat off autopilot and manually steered *Aphrodite* as the unknown vessel got closer. I looked at Peter, and I know the same thought was going through his mind. We were going to be rammed unless something was done immediately.

I engaged the one hundred-horse power turbo engine in gear and pushed down hard on the throttle. Nothing happened. *Aphrodite* sat idle in the water as the strange bow crashed through the waves growing nearer by the second. Peter was urgently trying to furl the genoa. We had all the sails set. With the wind in them we were unable to maneuver quickly enough to avoid collision.

The bow was now only two hundred feet away and aimed directly at us. No one was on deck and I could not see anyone in the wheelhouse. What the hell was going on? Suddenly the propeller bit into the water and *Aphrodite* responded. Peter fell back twisting his ankle on a winch as the one hundred horses we have stowed in the hull came to life. The engine was running close to full RPM. The strange vessel missed our stern by only thirty feet. The swell from the huge hull rocked *Aphrodite* as we struggled to get away. We were still unable to see anyone on board.

Still half asleep, Lewis greeted us with, "Can't a man get a moments shuteye around here?"

I changed course swinging *Aphrodite* round to put some distance between us and the strange boat. The main sail was still flying. We had no time to bring her down. The giant sail crashed one way then the other as the evening breeze caught it. Lewis, realizing what had happened grabbed the spotlight and shone it on the white canvas. "If the bastard can't hear us, he can bloody well see us now," Lewis yelled above the revving engine.

The trawler changed its course again and headed right back at us for the second time! I pushed *Aphrodite* up to eight knots. The engine was screaming in protest. We narrowly escaped collision by only twenty feet, far too close for comfort. Peter disappeared into his cabin and returned a few seconds later with his .308 rifle and a determined expression on his face. Sliding one cartridge into the breech Peter held the rifle to his shoulder and pulled the trigger. The shot filled the air around us and echoed across the empty ocean. He had aimed over the wheelhouse, a warning shot. Ejecting the spent cartridge onto the deck he slid another into the breech and said, "If the son-of-a-bitch tries it again, this one will be going in the wheel house."

I had to smile. With a week's worth of stubble and clothes that hadn't seen the inside of a washing machine for the same number of days he looked like Clint Eastwood in Pale Rider. I adjusted our course back to the original heading, keeping a careful eye on the trawler behind us that was following at a distance of about four hundred feet. Lewis shone the spotlight on the deck but we were unable to see any movement. Feeling a little more comfortable, Peter sat down with the rifle across his lap and began rolling up a cigarette to calm his nerves, stopping only to glance up to check the boat behind us. Lewis raised the genoa and I eased up on the revs but decided to keep the engine running just in case.

We were lucky. If we had not had the engine running to charge the batteries we wouldn't have had the time to respond. If the trawler hit us at fifteen knots it would have crushed the hull of *Aphrodite* causing her to sink. We were directly over the Java trench. There was over four and a half miles of water between our hull and the ocean bed. If we went down here, *Aphrodite* would sink deep to the bottom of the ocean without a trace. No one would ever know where we were or what happened to us.

The boat followed us for half an hour but did not attempt to ram us again. Most yachts do not have a one hundred horsepower engine or rifles aboard. Whatever they wanted I do not think they thought we were going to put up such a fight. Peter stowed the rifle away, much to

Lewis' relief, but has threatened to shoot anything that comes within a mile of his boat.

We are all too excited from the chase to sleep and are trying to figure out what had happened. Lewis is on watch and is taking more care scanning the horizon. With the moonlight shimmering off the surface of the ocean, spotting any other boats further than five miles away can be difficult. I get the feeling over the next few days, while we are still close to Indonesia, we will all be taking our watches more seriously.

10° 32.2' S
108° 17.0' E
264° - Day 47

Today we're joined by a fellow yachtie. It's reassuring to see someone else out here as crazy as we are. *Lisa Lee* is eight nautical miles off our port side and also heading to Christmas Island. Speaking to Roy and his wife on channel three he told me they left Yorkshire, England in 1991 and have been sailing ever since. They saw *Aphrodite* in Darwin and heard about the "incident" in the harbor. I have a feeling that our little faux pas will be following us all the way to Italy.

Don had approached the couple in Darwin looking for his passage to Brazil. Although they are heading in that direction they turned him down. When I asked them why they just said that they didn't think they would get on with him.

We are only one hundred and fifty nautical miles from Christmas Island. If the wind keeps up we should be anchored by tomorrow afternoon. We want to make sure that we still have some daylight left when we approach the anchorage. Only two hundred feet from the shore the coral bottom drops off to over one thousand two hundred feet. The anchorage can also be a little rough. There is very little protection from the elements so with a poor and exposed holding it is essential that we do not have a repeat of the Darwin incident. The tall cliffs surrounding Christmas Island and the stronger swell will not be as forgiving.

Wanting to celebrate our approach to Christmas Island I baked some muffins today. Mixing flour, oil, water, eggs, salt, raisins and baking powder in a random order and guessing quantities I was surprised when it worked. Lewis ate his ration of seven muffins within three hours and is begging me to bake some more. We are out of bread, unless we can buy some in Christmas Island I have a feeling I will be baking a few loaves in the weeks ahead.

In helping me keep my days full I have already planned the route to Fiumicino and estimated our arrival times at each port of call. I have taped these dates on the wall above the navigation table with the shift and cooking rota.

Christmas Island:	ETA August 24
Cocos Keeling:	ETA August 30
Chagos:	ETA September 16
Seychelles:	ETA September 30
Djibouti:	ETA October 18
Suez Canal:	ETA November 8
Fiumicino:	ETA November 25

I have always been a list man and believed in writing my goals down on paper. Somehow to see them written makes them more real. If they are just ideas in my head it would be easier for me to dismiss them or push them aside. I have made it a habit to tell my friends and family of my goals; having others know of my aspirations gives me a little more incentive to achieve them.

One of the drawings I sketched in Australia is a three dimensional sphere. The sphere has a maze that covers the entire surface. Each path twists and turns, meets another, becomes a dead end or just seems to go around and around. There is no beginning or end of the labyrinth that covers the sphere, such is it's shape. The quote I have written under the image reads, "Without goals in your life you may never know the right direction."

Everyone has their own dream. Everyone wants to go their own way. The sphere represents no one absolute beginning or end. There is no right way, but you have to know where you are going as there are many paths in life that will lead you the wrong way.

Before I left England Catherine talked me into seeing a psychic in Winchester with her. Catherine has always been a firm believer in spiritual guidance and influence. I however am far more pragmatic and believe in what I can see and what I know. I kept an open mind as the lady asked me to cut the deck of finely illustrated tarot cards laid on the table. After a minute of studying the cards she apologized to me and said that this was the most boring reading she had ever done. She told me that I was heading in the right direction and knew what I wanted and was already on the path to achieving it. She said that she should give me my money back because she could not tell me anything I did not already know.

I left with Catherine feeling no better or worse for the experience. She didn't ever give me my fifteen pounds back though, (that was something that I could have easily predicted!)

10° 25.1' S
106° 28.5' E
264° - Day 48

Coming into Flying Fish Cove, we have decided to anchor tonight after all. It's 1545, our ETA will be around 2200-2300. I have studied the approach thoroughly and the land marks, buoys and reef heads within the harbor. *Lisa Lee* will probably be anchored by the time we arrive. She is a faster boat and has been slowly pulling away from us over the course of the day. *Wired for Sound* is already anchored and has told *Lisa Lee* that they will guide them using their inflatable and a torch.

Wired for Sound and *Lisa Lee* have crossed paths before and know each other well. Always wanting to help a fellow sailor *Wired for Sound*, owned by a New Zealander radioed us this afternoon to offer the same courtesy. Thanking him, I said we would have some cold ones waiting for them for their trouble. Not knowing when you might need a return favor, most sailors believe in generating good karma and offer their assistance to others. Peter has no problem expressing his thanks but asked me not to do it with his beer in the future.

Wired for Sound has been anchored in the harbor for a few days and is familiar with its layout. There is one more sandy anchorage left that *Lisa Lee* will take, *Aphrodite* will then have to make the most of what is left.

Flying Fish Cove is the only anchoring point for yachts. The rest of the fifty-two square mile island is surrounded by seventy-foot cliffs. The approach seems simple enough but I have learned over the past seven weeks it is easy to become disoriented at night in unfamiliar surroundings. What seems to be a simple approach on a chart with clear markers, can be completely different in real life. With buoys, freighters, wrecks and other yachts in the harbor it doesn't take much to become disoriented. Hopefully with the help from *Wired for Sound* there shouldn't be any problems.

I cannot remember a more beautiful evening. Christmas Island greeted us with a sunset that lasted only a few minutes but will burn in my memory for a lifetime. Never before have I felt such a sense of achievement as I do right now after navigating over 1,487 nautical miles of ocean. Approaching the harbor we were able to see the masts of four other yachts rocking in the night swell. The sun left us over an hour ago and the dark mass of the island seems menacing as we slowly motor into Flying Fish Cove.

With the sails down *Aphrodite* edged her way forward. Standing at the bow I tried to make sense of the layout of the harbor and compared it to the chart I had memorized. We could just make out two people in an inflatable dingy waving a torch around about sixty feet in front of us. The buoys marked on the chart were no longer accurate. These huge steel drums that are used to secure lines of freighters as they anchor in the harbor are as black as the ocean and almost impossible to see. As dangerous as sea mines, these massive buoys would tear into *Aphrodite*'s hull, ripping through her thin fiber skin delaying our journey by weeks or possibly ending it.

Coming alongside, the man in the inflatable introduced himself as Peter, the skipper of *Wired for Sound*. Holding a can of beer in one hand and the outboard motor in the other he told us to follow his lead. Zig zagging around in front of us, with no obvious obstructions or shallow reefs in the way, I couldn't help but think he may have had more than just a few beers already. It took five minutes to be guided through the minefield of buoys to a safe anchorage on the West Side of the harbor. They welcomed us to the island then motored back to their boat. As it is illegal to come in contact with any yachts that have not been cleared by customs or immigrations, Peter asked us to keep the beer on ice until tomorrow.

Only six boat lengths from the shore the depth under our keel was still over one thousand feet, too deep for an anchor chain. Peter slowly inched *Aphrodite* closer to the rocky shore. With the swell almost as big as it was out at sea, he struggled to keep the boat under control. Edging ever closer to the rocks Peter's eyes were fixed on the depth gauge as we drew closer to the cliffs.

With a draft of five and a half feet, anything under ten feet would put us at risk of smashing *Aphrodite*'s keel against the rocky bottom as we rise and fall with each wave. The depth suddenly dropped to fifteen feet so Lewis and I quickly fed out the anchor chain. Peter disengaged the engine as the anchor dragged along the bottom, searching for a secure hold. With each wave carrying us another ten feet closer to the shore we waited nervously for the anchor to grip. Catching only one hundred and ten feet from the shore *Aphrodite* slowly swung round and faced the wind, the anchor seemed to be holding. The depth was only twelve feet under us, but enough. Not wanting to make the same mistake as Darwin, Peter put the engine in reverse and gave the anchor a test.

Aphrodite is only three boat lengths from the shore. We have decided to keep watch for the rest of the night to make sure the anchor is truly holding us steady. If the anchor drags we would be on the rocks in under twenty seconds.

It is a strange feeling to be so close to land again after ten days of just ocean. The tall cliffs that almost completely surround the island reach up into the night and seem to touch the stars. Lewis and Peter have gone to bed leaving me alone on my watch. Sitting in the dark, munching on crackers and sipping Earl Grey tea, the rocks behind me seem to be closer each time I turn to look at them. Your mind can play tricks on you when you are tired and in need of rest. The sound of the waves crashing on the rocks and the movement of the boat as it is thrown around by the rough swell is keeping me on edge. I am finding it hard to relax.

Convinced we are closer to the shore now, than when we had anchored two hours ago I have dropped a line with some diving weights on the end of it, I am able to judge by the angle of the line if we are dragging anchor or not. *Aphrodite* is thumping up and down, banging against her own anchor chain as the bow rises and falls with the swell. To steady the boat I have cut a length of rope and tied it to the chain four feet below the bow spreader. Wrapping the rope around the anchor winch, I took the slack up in the chain when *Aphrodite*'s nose dropped into the next wave. Now instead of the chain banging up and down on the deck the rope acts as a snubber, taking up the strain and lessening the jar.

Day 49 - Christmas Island

I cannot believe it! The immigration officer has just left, I have been denied the right to go ashore! Steve, the junior officer, told me he didn't think there would be a problem but would have to speak to his superior just to make sure. After radioing him from the boat his orders were clear, "Mr. Hockley is not allowed off the yacht!" Not wanting to give up I asked Steve if I could have a word with his boss.

Acting as though he owned the bloody island he said,

"You can either spend your stay on the boat or with me, meaning jail!"

"How many meals will I get?" I asked him.

"I beg you pardon?"

"If spending my time in jail, is the only way I can step on dry land, how many meals will I get?"

He did not get the humor in it and replied angrily, "I don't think you're taking this seriously young man."

"Oh, I'm taking it seriously alright," I told him, "I think the problem here is that you're taking this too seriously."

Upsetting him probably wasn't the best approach, but I was pissed off. Not willing to budge on his decision he ended it by saying that not only was I not allowed on land but I was not even to go in the water for a swim. With one last attempt I told him that I understood his position but would he be willing to at least let me come ashore for half an hour to call my girlfriend and family to let her know I was all right.

"One of the other members of crew can do that for you."

I was dealing with an asshole and no amount of reasoning was going to change his mind. Peter and Lewis went ashore to explore and search for fresh produce leaving me alone on *Aphrodite*. Before he left, Lewis said he would have a word with the immigration officer to see if he could change his mind. Peter was against this plan and kept asking Lewis not to interfere. Lewis didn't pay much attention to Peter's requests.

Left alone on *Aphrodite* I was resigned to the fact that I was stuck on the boat but decided to make the most of it. Baiting the hook and cursing the bastard in his little hut he called an immigration office, I spent the rest of the afternoon catching all the island's fish just to spite him.

Peter and Lewis returned in the late afternoon after a

day on the island. Peter thought Christmas Island was the best. Not because of its natural beauty, wildlife or history, but because he had bought eight cases of Emu Export beer for $3.50 a case! (about sixteen cents a can). This no name brand was out-of-date by a year and could have stripped the varnish off the woodwork, but it was such a bargain he didn't complain.

By 2100 we were all 'knackered,' the rough night yesterday had kept us up so we hit the bunks early and were fast asleep by 2115. At 2130 we were woken suddenly by thumping on the hull. Half asleep and dazed we thought the pirates from Java had found us and were storming the boat. It turned out to be the crew from *Lisa Lee* and *Wired for Sound* taking us up on our offer of a few beers. I told them that they were lucky Peter hadn't pulled out his shotgun and started firing as he was a little trigger-happy and it would be safer to radio first in the future. We opened up a few Emu's and tried to catch up with the others who were already well and truly pissed.

Swapping sailing stories with the other yachties it was obvious that we were by far the least experienced crew. Peter from *Wired for Sound* has been sailing for years and claimed to be a surgeon. He said he made his living by sailing to countries and working "freelance" in hospitals. I found this hard to believe looking at the man sitting across from me holding a beer in a huge calloused hand sloshing most of the contents on the deck. His girlfriend was quiet and timid for most of the night. They made an odd couple. Roy had his nephew Jason with him who was a cocky little bastard and seemed to look up to Peter (*Wired for Sound*) like his hero. Roy's wife had gracefully declined our offer and decided to stay on *Lisa Lee*. She had probably been caught on one of these "nights out" before and wanted to stay well clear. The only yachtie in the harbor that had not joined our little get together was George on *Emmy*. George was sailing alone after losing his deckhand back in Australia. Born in Germany, George was sailing around the world for the second time and seemed to be a bit of a loner. Everyone was heading for Cocos Keeling and then to Mauritius before rounding the Cape of Good Hope. George was the only one heading north from Cocos to India. It seems we are the only boat continuing west to the Seychelles and sailing up the Red Sea.

Most of the world cruisers we have met along the way have not been glamorous people but regular folk with a simple dream to explore the world by sea. I have yet to meet any sailors who were not concerned about money. Some sailors work as they go, picking up odd jobs to finance their next passage. Some are stuck in the same place trying to scrape together enough money to get them to their next destination and some are sailing on their savings, with nothing more than a boat and the clothes on their back. Cruising the world by yacht is a simple existence. In a way they are gypsies of the sea, wandering the world by means of a boat rather than by caravan. They are among the happiest people I have ever met.

Day 50 - Christmas Island

Christmas Island was first sighted in the seventeenth century and was later named on Christmas day 1643. With a population of two thousand, the island's industry is based around a phosphate mine, which was first opened in the 1870's. The phosphate is brought down the side of the island on a giant conveyor belt or on the only major road by trucks. The community is predominantly Chinese, Moslems and Malay with a few Australians.

The wind has been blowing hard at twenty-five knots all day, kicking up the dust from the island and covering

Aphrodite. The tall cliffs reach up to almost a thousand feet above sea level. The tip of this extinct volcano is covered in vegetation and hosts several rare and endangered species. Sixty-three per cent of the island has been declared a National Park. The most unusual feature of the wildlife are the Red Crabs (land crabs) that migrate annually from the upper plateau down to the shoreline to spawn and breed. Coming out of the heavy vegetation by the thousands they march to the shore covering everything in their path. Scurrying over buildings and roadways they storm the island like an army, lay their eggs in the ocean then head back inland. Giant birds are constantly circling the island. Like vultures they seem to be waiting for one of the yachts to be swept into the cliffs by the swell. Using the trade winds that hit the tall cliffs they are carried high into the blue sky as far as the naked eye can see. Aside from the gantry and mine, Christmas Island is beautiful and sits alone in the middle of nowhere.

The sound of the Moslems call to prayer is broadcast across the harbor by loud speakers waking us up at five in the morning. Every few hours they gather in the Mosque by the harbor, face Mecca and pray. Sitting on the boat alone under the warm sun, listening to the prayer fills me with peace. In a way it is nice to have this time alone when Peter and Lewis are ashore.

I have been keeping myself busy with chores when alone on the boat. Peter asked me if I could sew up part of the genoa. The stitching has been coming loose on the leech, the edge that runs diagonally from the top of the stay down to the clew. Sitting on the deck in the afternoon sun I had my trusty Minolta camera by my side. My Father bought me the camera for my birthday in New York over five years ago. It has never let me down and has captured some of the most beautiful pictures.

With five rolls of film already exposed on this

journey, I had a sixth roll in the camera with thirty-five shots already taken. With only a single exposure left on the film, I was going to wait for the sun to disappear over the western point of the island, silhouetting the palm trees and at the precise moment I would capture the feeling of the anchorage at Flying Fish Cove, and the colors that are cast across the evening sky on our last night here.

There were only three more inches left to sew when a strong gust lifted the huge sheet of canvas up off the deck throwing my camera into the air. In one swift movement I was on my feet and over the railing, jumping after my camera and the precious thirty-five images I could never hope to capture again. With my arms outstretched I watched the camera fall in slow motion into the salty water. I struck the surface only a second after my camera, and reached in after it. Grabbing the strap I held it above my head and paddled my way around to the ladder.

I quickly rewound the film and opened the back cover, praying that the water had not found a way into the film compartment. My heart sank when I saw about three table spoonfuls of seawater swishing around inside, the film and camera were ruined. Thirty-five shots taken from Turtle Head Island to Christmas Island were lost.

Lewis and Peter returned as it started to get dark. They had notified customs and immigrations of our departure time. All we need now is the final clearance from the harbormaster. Lewis did not receive any faxes from Catherine. He called her yesterday to say that I was stuck on the boat and to fax any letters she had written to the island. It is quite possible that she was in an airplane somewhere and will not even get the message until after we leave.

With the charts laid out over the table I have plotted the waypoints across the stretch of ocean to Cocos Keeling, five hundred and thirty miles away and programmed them into the auto pilot. In about five days we will reach the atoll, which is the last Australian outpost before we head deeper into the Indian Ocean, I hope they are more hospitable to illegal immigrants there than they were here, bastards!

3

Christmas Island to
Cocos Keeling

(530.5 nautical miles)

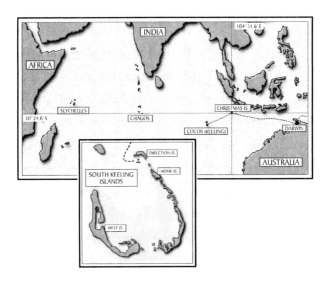

3

Christmas Island to Cocos Keeling

10° 24.6' S
104° 31.6' E
272° - Day 51

It's 2300 and a strange eerie night. The moon has yet to show it itself in the cloudless sky and everything around us seems gray. It is as though the colors have been drained from the night. There is no contrast. Even the stars seem to be quieter than usual. Visibility is extremely poor. A quiet hush has fallen over the ocean around us. We have wind in our sails but even the movement of *Aphrodite* and the noise of the bow slicing through the waves seem to be suppressed.

I have never seen flying fish before so I was surprised when about fifty of them suddenly appeared flying straight out of the ocean and into the night. Gliding up to sixty feet, they use their oversized pectoral fins as wings, spreading them out and gliding over the surface of the ocean to escape predators. Watching them silently coast over the waves they moved in formation before plopping back into the water. They only grow up to about eight inches long, but glide high enough to hit the main sail before falling down onto the deck.

Picking them up to return them to the ocean they looked at me through large confused eyes, their mouths opening and closing as if to say, "Who the hell are you?"

and "What are you doing out here?" Their pectoral fins stretch down the entire length of their silver body with a span of around ten inches. Returning the little fish to the sea I got a glimpse of their predator.

Swimming along side *Aphrodite*, they streaked through the water with a grace that you can never tire of watching. The school of dolphins took time out from feeding and decided to show off and play with me for a while. Sitting on the bowsprit with my feet dangling down into the water they swam only inches away. Seeing how close they could get without touching me is a game we have played before.

This is our first night back at sea after leaving Flying Fish Cove. We are all pleased to be on the road again and are looking forward to our next stop - Cocos Keeling. We had a little difficulty pulling up the anchor when we left Christmas Island. After a great deal of tugging and maneuvering it finally came loose but with a lump of coral attached to it weighing around one hundred pounds. The diving weights I used as a marker to see if we were dragging are still on the bottom of the harbor. When I tried to pull them up the razor sharp coral cut through the string.

Christmas Island was a little disappointing for me. Apart from not being allowed ashore and losing my camera overboard, I am upset that I never got the chance to speak to Catherine. I know she will be worried about me. It has been over two weeks since we last spoke to each other. Lewis mailed my letters to her but it will be at least ten days before she receives them.

Supplies were expensive on Christmas Island as they are flown in from Australia. Peter and Lewis did not buy anything. Cocos Keeling apparently grow their own crops and are more reasonably priced. With no fresh fruit, vegetables or bread left our evening meals for the next four days will have to get a little more inventive.

To pass the time I spend up to six hours each day carving the hard tropical woods that I have gathered along the way. With a sculpture made from a piece of wood found at each Island I already have a nice collection. There was no wood on Christmas Island suitable for carving so I will have to wait until we reach Cocos for some more materials.

Whittling in the outback over a year ago I believed that each piece of wood already held a sculpture inside. You simply have to find the right piece of wood that contains the sculpture you wish to reveal. Focused only on the image you are creating and the movements of the blade is a pure relationship between your mind and your body. Carving an old opal miner in the bush I enjoyed the connection and the dreamlike state I would find myself in. Almost like a form of meditation, I become relaxed yet focused on the image in my mind that my body was trying to reproduce.

My first sculpture on this trip was carved from a piece of wood from Mooloolaba. About eight inches long the top resembles the head of a serpent, the body spirals down and gradually transforms into the head of an Aborigine. The head then tapers into a thin blade that can be used as a letter opener. When Don first saw my masterpiece he was very impressed with my talents and claimed he had found a practical use for my sculpture other than for opening letters. Naming it the "pooper scooper" he thought himself very funny suggesting it would be ideal for unblocking the head. Rob also found himself attracted to the sculpture and on his knees, would brandish it high above his head shouting for Don's forgiveness from, "The Wood God!"

11° 13.5' S
101° 09.6' E
252° - Day 52

The weather has been superb all day. We could not ask for better sailing conditions. We're averaging five knots, the wind is steady at fifteen knots from the southeast. It's eighty-four degrees and humid. The bread I baked this afternoon was a little heavy but not bad for a first attempt. While I was in the baking mood I decided to bake some garlic bread and a pizza for supper. Using tomato paste, onions, cheese, ham and pineapple it was quite the treat. Chasing onions rolling around on the floor and trying to stop plates and cutlery sliding all over the place was hard work but worth the effort. Standing with one foot wedged under the counter and the other under the steps leading to the cockpit I spent most of the afternoon preparing the ingredients and monitoring the stove.

Lewis and Peter waited for this culinary treat both peering down into the kitchen from outside. Shouting down their individual topping preferences didn't make the task any easier. Swinging back and forth with the swell, the gimbal stove handled the job very well. Timing it wrong on two occasions, the pizza pie almost shot across the cabin when I opened the door. With "oooo's" and "ahhhh's" Peter and Lewis were enjoying the show. After three hours of mixing, rising, pounding, rising, pounding and toppings, the pizza was ready. Opening the stove for the last time it swung out towards me scorching my arm. Willing to sacrifice a burn to save the pie I hung on to the tray, determined not to drop it. Wedging it carefully on the counter between two cutting boards the boat was filled with a smell so mouth watering that all we could think about was food. Sails, boats, wind and waves were no longer important to us, it was time to eat. With the aroma of freshly baked pizza wafting up out the hatch Lewis couldn't take it any longer. "Hurry up man, we're starving out here!" Cutting the pie into slices the crust was crispy and the toppings cooked to perfection, a success!

Peter is a tough food critic and has no shame in showing his disgust or delight in any particular dish. Practically licking the plates clean not a single strand of cheese or crumb was thrown over to the fish. Washing the last mouthfuls down with Emu beer we sat in silence on the deck digesting the meal and watching the sun set in front of us. This was a perfect day at sea.

11° 49.5' S
97° 55.6' E
259° - Day 53

It has been over two weeks since I last felt fresh water on my skin, I am craving a shower. Although after a deck shower I feel clean and refreshed the salt water does not do a great job. The sea is almost as warm as the air temperature now, making the experience of washing outside not quite as refreshing as it was sailing around the colder waters of Australia. Lewis has not shaved since we left Sydney over seven weeks ago and is proudly displaying a full black beard. With no hair on the top of his head and deep creases in his forehead he looks like a pirate.

Lewis sits in the shade of the main sail wearing sweat pants, a long sleeve shirt, a hat that covers the back of his neck, dark sunglasses and a white T-shirt that he wraps around his face. He is careful not to expose himself to the sun's rays but seems to be obsessed by it. He looks ridiculous sitting on the deck under the main sail wearing so much when it's over eighty degrees.

I burnt my ass many years ago bathing nude with Catherine in the Canary Islands and found the experience to be most uncomfortable so I wear at least a pair of shorts for protection. I shaved off my beard before we reached Christmas Island, after experimenting with a goatee and moustache I have decided I feel more comfortable clean-shaven.

Peter doesn't seem too concerned about his personal hygiene much to the despair of Lewis and I. Showering only occasionally he doesn't seem at all bothered by the smell that is maturing in his cabin. Smoking up to five cigarettes an hour you can often smell Peter before you can see him. In the evening on his watch, the smoke drifts down into the humid cab making the air harder for Lewis to breathe. I have a hatch above my bed and am able to open it a few inches on the calm nights to help circulate the air out. As the nights get warmer I may start to sleep on deck.

With another couple of days to Cocos we have all decided to treat ourselves to a shower on the boat. A luxury that is seldom allowed, the shower in the head uses fresh water from the drinking tanks. Even being thrown around in the bathroom, stubbing my toe on the toilet and banging my knee on the door handle didn't lessen the blissful feeling of fresh water on my skin. The two minutes each that we were allowed soon disappeared like the soapy water down the drain.

The head is only the size of a small closet, three feet wide and five feet deep. The toilet has to be flushed manually with a hand pump, but uses seawater. The shower that hangs on the wall has a small electric pump which provides enough pressure without draining too much power from the battery. Next to the bow cabin on the port side, the head is not a place to go with a newspaper for some quite reading time. Bracing yourself against the two walls it's not a peaceful or relaxing experience. Like sitting on a bucking bronco your full concentration and energy is required for what I had normally considered to be the simplest of tasks. Lewis has repeatedly asked Peter to light a courtesy match in the head after he has used it. Failing to see the benefits of this, Peter has yet to extend us the courtesy. Most of the time we cling to a stay, and lean over the side of the boat. Making sure that you are facing downwind, it is a far more pleasurable experience peeing into the sea than it is trying to pee into the toilet. It's hard enough on a normal day, but with the boat rocking back and forth peeing in the head is like trying to hit the bulls eye of a dart board.

The sea has picked up a little with gangs of dark clouds hanging around in the blue sky waiting for us to sail under them. These squalls can dump enough rain on *Aphrodite* for a quick shower. I have stored a bar of soap on the deck for such an opportunity. We have not seen a soul since we left Christmas Island over fifty hours ago and have had no radio contact with *Wired for Sound* or *Lisa Lee*. *Lisa Lee* was scheduled to leave Christmas Island yesterday, I doubt they will catch up with us before we reach Cocos Keeling that is now one hundred and twelve miles away.

11° 52.7' S
97° 44.6' E
256° - Day 54

What a rough night that was! It's 1015 I have not slept since 0300, the beginning of the morning shift, what Lewis refers to as "the party shift." I didn't want to miss the sunrise so I have stayed up after my watch and let Peter sleep in again. The seas were a little bigger than usual. It was the first time I actually felt I was in danger since Don left us, not because of the large swell or the strong winds, but because I was almost hit in the head three times by flying fish. Landing on the deck all around me the dolphins must have been hungry last night chasing the little buggers around the ocean. Concerned that I would be knocked unconscious I kept my head low in the cockpit sipping my coffee and listening to them landing all around me.

Six landed by my feet and when the sun rose in the morning I counted another eighteen on deck. I have heard stories of sailors surviving on flying fish when supplies were low. Tasting very salty and fishy they don't supply a lot of meat, but if you get enough I guess you could make a meal out of them. As Crocodile Dundee would say, "You can live off 'em, but they taste like shit!"

Wanting to give them a proper burial, I carefully washed them off individually in a bucket of water. Tidying their long pectoral fins I lined them up on the deck like toy soldiers. Lewis came out of the cabin yawning. With a bowl of wheat biscuits he looked at me crouched over, organizing the row of dead fish and asked sarcastically, "Can I play with them after you?" After taking a few pictures I gave them back to the ocean.

The genoa that I sewed up is not holding very well. The heavy canvas is rotting and all the stitches are just pulling right through. Almost the entire length of the leech has now come loose. We will be anchored off Direction Island by tomorrow morning, and will see if they can reinforce the sail there. We have furled half of the genoa in to reduce the stress on the stitching and to slow down our speed. We want to make sure that we arrive tomorrow morning in daylight.

So far we're right on schedule. The trade winds have been as predictable as all the books said they would be.

Jimmy Cornell is a London based journalist and has written a number of excellent sailing books that provide essential information for yachts cruising the world. Knowing when and where to sail, what time of the year is dangerous and what the conditions of the sea are like, dramatically decreases your chances of getting into trouble. Speaking to Roy back at Christmas Island, he said that he has never been in a life-threatening situation and does not know many sailors who have. With so much information about the sailing seasons, one would have to be extremely unlucky or lack common sense to get into a life or death situation. Our journey will take us through some pretty rough seas and some of the strongest currents in the world that have been recorded. The Somali current that sweeps up the coast of Africa during the southwest monsoon reaches up to seven knots in the vicinity of Socotra, an island off the horn of Somalia and the seas can get nasty. We are a few weeks behind the ideal cruising time and because of this will have to expect some strong winds up the Red Sea and the Mediterranean. November through February are the worst months in the Mediterranean with violent local storms that come out of the clear sky with no warning. These gales develop quickly and can be extremely dangerous.

The schedule I have made will put us in the Mediterranean in the middle of November. If luck is on our side we will reach Italy before the gales become too frequent.

Cocos Keeling - Day 55

Now this is more like it! We're anchored by the yellow quarantine buoy and are waiting for customs and immigration to radio us back. It's 1000 and a beautiful warm sunny morning. The islands in the atoll are surrounded by reef that provides a natural barrier, keeping the strong currents and swell out of the lagoon. The water inside the atoll is calm, shallow and crystal clear, like a giant bathtub in the middle of the ocean.

The atoll was formed thousands of years ago by a volcano that was taken back by the sea. The submerged mountain rises up from the ocean bed forming a ring of islands, inside the crater the water is shallow and warm. We can easily see through the turquoise waters to the sandy bottom just twelve feet below. A variety of colorful fish and two baby white reef sharks have already come over to welcome us to paradise.

We entered the atoll at a heading of one hundred and ninety-six degrees, through the main break in the reef on the northern tip between Direction Island (Pula Luar) and Horsburgh Island (Palu Tikus). All yachts visiting the south Keeling atoll must anchor by Direction Island at the northern point. With reef and shallow waters further in, yachts are not permitted to anchor anywhere else unless they have the permission from the Marine Officer.

Cocos Keeling was first sighted in 1609 by Captain William Keeling. With a population of only five hundred and fifty, the islanders produce their own cash crops. With just one hundred white people living on Cocos the majority of the population are Malays. Most of the low twenty-seven coral islands are uninhabited. With the majority of the Malay community on Home Island, which is on the East Side of the atoll, the international airport, hospital, quarantine station and shops can be found on West Island. A ferry shoots across the six-mile stretch of shallow waters to join the islands together. Visitors are not permitted on Home Island without written permission. Strict religious dress codes have to be observed if visitors land on Home Island. Men must wear shorts and a shirt, women are required to cover up their bodies, no swimming costumes are allowed.

Each island we are able to see from the boat is completely covered in palm trees reaching up to seventy feet high. The sandy beaches and clear waters are most inviting. The immigration officer has just radioed to tell us that he cannot come over until tomorrow morning but has given us permission to anchor with the eight other yachts making it very clear that we are not to have any contact with them until tomorrow. With *Buffalo Soldier* player on the CD we are sprawled out on the deck enjoying the peaceful movement of the boat for the first time in seventeen days. We are all in great form, drinking Emu beer and cooking steak on the barbecue chatting about the journey so far and all the great things to come.

With the reef protecting us from the ocean waves we're able to fully relax and are all looking forward to a sound night of sleep. The steak was cooked to perfection and Lewis has suggested that we treat ourselves to plum pudding with custard for dessert. Peter is anxious to speak with his family and to pick up any mail that may have been sent here. Writing to his wife everyday he has a bundle of papers that he wants to post. I miss Catherine with all my heart and would like to speak to her to let her know I am well and safe. Lewis recently broke up with a long time girlfriend before this trip and is beginning to appreciate the relationship he once had. Being away from someone for so long, and having time to think about your mistakes helps you realize the value of a good relationship. Writing letters, they have remained friends and Lewis hopes that they can someday get back together again.

Not ready for a commitment was one of the reasons the relationship did not work out. I think Lewis wanted some time away to get things straight in his head. I told him that I had the same problems with Catherine a few years ago. She could not understand it when I told her that I loved her but was not ready to get married. I was committed to the relationship but simply was not ready for marriage. To attempt something too soon or even too late can be a mistake in any area of life. Like trying to sail to the Caribbean too early in the season can be disastrous. To wait in the Canary Islands just a few months before you begin the journey can make all the difference between a successful passage and failure.

Lewis agreed, but said that his delay may have cost him the relationship. I told him that if it was meant to be, a year away from her would not make a difference. The relationship I have with Catherine has actually become stronger over the last year. Being away from someone for so long you learn to appreciate them more. Joining in the conversation Peter said he has the perfect marriage. Boasting that his sexual advances have never been refused by his wife, Peter took a swig of Emu and let out an almighty belch. "She's a lucky woman." I told him. Too drunk to hear the underlying sarcasm, Peter thanked me and started to roll another cigarette.

By the end of the night we were all merrily drunk, slapping each other on the back, telling dirty jokes and bonding as men do after a couple of cases of cheap, out-of-date beer. Getting up Peter tried to make his way down to the cabin, probably to put on some Tom Jones. With *Aphrodite* almost as steady as if she was out of the water, Peter staggered back and forth as though we were at high seas. Giving up he lay down in the cockpit and fell asleep.

Even with our differences the three of us were still getting on. Knowing each other for only two months we had shared a lot together. The trust we have in each other has seen us over three and a half thousand miles and I was sure it would see us through the next seven.

Cocos Keeling - Day 56

"Permission to come aboard!" The immigration and customs officer greeted us with broad smiles and a relaxed demeanor. The young officer was filling in while the head immigration officer was away. He was radioed from Christmas Island and faxed from Darwin with instructions to deny my visitation rights.

"Listen." he said, leaning in closer, "My office is on the other side of the lagoon over five miles away. If you were to go ashore on Direction Island how would I ever know about it?"

Direction Island is uninhabited and only has a water tank, one hammock, a wooden shelter and a newly installed phone.

"As long as I don't find out, there won't be a problem."

He didn't seem to care about my visa and said to keep out of trouble and stay on the boat when the full-time officer returned. He finished the conversation by saying if anything went wrong however, he would deny what he said and would prosecute me. Watching them motor away I could see Peter was not happy with the arrangement. If something did go wrong he would still be held accountable for my actions. Lewis had the inflatable ready to go ashore and was waiting for us. As much as I wanted to go I could not put Peter in an awkward position. I told him that I would stay on the boat if he wanted me to. With the full-time officer returning in a couple of days Peter said that I could go ashore if he agrees but would appreciate it if I did not before then. After all Peter has done, allowing me to come on this journey, I could not let him down. Waving them off I settled in for another quiet day alone on the boat.

Peter and Lewis returned early this afternoon with good news. There is a man on West Island that can mend our genoa, fresh fruit and vegetables are also available. Taking the sail with them back to West Island, I asked Lewis to call Catherine and give her a fax number so she can send her letters.

Wired for Sound, Lisa Lee and *Emmy* joined us today. Sailing into the atoll late in the afternoon they are anchored in the quarantine area waiting for clearance. They called me on the radio wanting to know if I was allowed ashore, I told them that I was not. Peter and Lewis returned by the early evening bearing gifts. Lewis already had a fax from Catherine and a couple of oranges for me. Peter had found me some whittling wood, things were looking up!

Reading Catherine's letter with the sweetest orange I have ever tasted in my mouth and anchored in paradise I was the happiest man alive. Absorbing every word I devoured the letter in minutes and read it again slowly for a second time savoring her words of love. Catherine had called Peter's wife in Canberra after not hearing from me for two weeks. She said that a strange Australian man (Lewis) had left a message saying that there was a problem and I could not make it to the phone. Worried that something terrible had happened to me, Catherine called Australia to make sure everything was OK. Peter's wife had calmed her down and told her not to worry and that we were on schedule and were all fit and healthy.

Life in America was hard work for her. Spending most of her time flying with the daughter of Ron Rice to beauty pageants, film sets, sports events and photo shoots she was working around the clock. Catherine was not happy and found a lot of the people she had to work with disappointing. She said that I was the one thought that kept her going, then she would remember where I was and would cry.

I have been writing to Catherine every day. Putting

my thoughts down on paper makes it seem as though I am talking to her and she is sharing the experiences with me. Catherine has not received any letters from me since Darwin and was worried. I will ask Lewis to mail my letters to her tomorrow and fax her a single page telling her that I love her and she was all I could think about.

Peter has asked me to make a few more repairs tomorrow while they are ashore buying supplies. When *Aphrodite* dragged her anchor in Darwin and hit the other yachts, eight inches of wooden trim was ripped from the port side. Whittling the piece of wood Peter brought me will help to keep my mind busy and not to worry about Catherine.

Cocos Keeling - Day 57

I spent the early morning sitting under a pile of wood shavings carving a new piece of trim for Peter. Hanging upside down over the railing I was greeted by George who had seen me working and rowed over in his dingy to ask if I needed a hand. I thanked him and said that if he could hold the trim in place while I screwed it to the hull it would make my life a great deal easier. With the two reef sharks still circling the boat I did not want to find out if they were man eaters or not.

George was in his mid fifties and was in better shape than most men half his age. He had a lean sinewy body that has seen many years of hard work and probably many tough days at sea. George was an old salt and knows of no other life than the one with a deck under his feet. His family still lives in Germany and he makes his way back once a year to see his grown-up children and to check on his house, but he is happiest when at sea. George was anchored in Darwin the same time we were there and witnessed *Aphrodite* dragging her anchor. He admitted that he was surprised to find that we had made it as far as Cocos and wanted to know who we had recruited for navigator. I told him that it was just the three of us and thanked him for the vote of confidence. I told George about the problems we had in the early days with Don and the limited charts he left me to navigate the Red Sea. Impressed with our dogged determination to make it on our own and my handiwork on the trim he offered to lend me the charts I needed and invited me on his boat to pick them out.

Inside his thirty-eight foot sloop *Emmy*, it was apparent that George was an experienced sailor and has visited every corner of the globe on his adventures. With memories from each country surrounding the cabin, the boat was his home. Cushions that he bought from India with beautiful embroidery were laid out on the benches, pictures and carvings that he found in Africa and South America were screwed to the bulkheads. Everything had its place, not a single item was left out or not secured. An inflatable globe was suspended in the saloon area with red lines indicating the passages George has made over the years.

After Cocos, George was sailing north to India for a few months before heading west along the coast. I asked him what it was like to sail on his own for so long, he told me this was the first long passage he has made solo. He lost a member of crew in Australia, things did not work out between the two of them so George continued on his own. I asked him how he managed to keep watch at night sailing on his own. George sleeps with an alarm clock that was set to go off every half an hour, he would wake up, scan the horizon then fall back to sleep again. At times he would be so exhausted he would sleep right through the alarm and not wake up for a few hours. George caught up on his sleep when at anchor, that was why he didn't join us in Christmas Island for the party.

I picked out six charts of the Red Sea, one that covered the entire length and five that were more detailed sections of the passage. Carefully rolling them up I told George that I would take care of them and have them back to him tomorrow. Rowing me back to *Aphrodite* George said that he was looking for another member of crew to help him get to India and eventually back to Germany. He seemed impressed with my skills and asked if I would think about it.

He had no real time frame and sails when and where it pleases him. Crewing with such an experienced sailor would be a great opportunity to learn, but I told him I wanted to be back in England before the end of the year and that I was committed to Peter and Lewis. He dropped me off and said that he understood and that the offer would still stand if I changed my mind.

Sitting alone on *Aphrodite* in the calm lagoon, surrounded by a ring of lush tropical islands with the sun shining in the clear blue sky brought the colors to life around me and made the water sparkle and dance under its spell. Stripping off I slid into the crystal waters and relished the feeling of being naked. Everything was so pure, the water covering my body, the uninhabited islands, the reef fish swimming around me and the air I was breathing. I was as naked as the day I was born and felt more appreciative to be alive than I can remember. (The fact that I was swimming illegally made the experience even more enjoyable.) Laying on the deck afterwards, letting the sun dry my body with the warm breeze touching my skin I fell into a deep peaceful sleep.

The boys came back from their day on the island in the late afternoon. Lewis looked exhausted and stressed, I think he was beginning to resent having to spend so much

119

time with Peter and the endless list of chores they had to do. He brought me back another present from Home Island while they were waiting for the ferry to take them across the lagoon. It was the biggest, hairiest coconut I have ever seen. Munching on the white meat with milk dripping down my leg it suddenly came to me. I had found my next project, I was going to carve coconuts!

Cocos Keeling - Day 59

We are still anchored at Cocos Keeling waiting for the sail to be mended and the diesel fuel we have ordered. The weather has taken a turn for the worse. The clear blue sky that was unbroken yesterday is now a low laying blanket of gray clouds that seem to touch the top of the masts. The water that was a transparent turquoise blue is now dark green and covered in little choppy waves. A white breaking wall surrounds the atoll where the giant swell is beating against the reef. Last night all we could hear was the relentless pounding of the breaking waves. Out of this chaos, motoring into the reef we were joined by a wind-beaten yacht early this morning. They reported that the wind was blowing over thirty knots and the rolling swell we experienced had turned into mountains of angry sea. They had to heave-to because the conditions were so severe.

Heaving-to is a way to control the boat, practically bringing it to a standstill in strong conditions. The main sail and the genoa are flown against each other and stall the boat. I have never attempted to heave-to before, I do not know if Lewis or Peter have either, hopefully we will never have to!

I gave Lewis the charts and asked him to make photocopies on his next visit to the island. He rolled his eyes and said that I was lucky to be stuck on the boat. With only a small copier in the yacht club each chart would require up to ten separate sheets of paper and would have to be carefully tiled back together again. If overlapped by just a sixteenth of an inch a small island or reef could potentially be covered which could lead to disaster. I asked Lewis to take great care with each copy as every inch of the chart was important to us.

Lewis and Peter are going to a party tonight on the beach with the others yachties. I have a lot of work still to do with the charts that Lewis brought back this afternoon in a pile of over sixty sheets, at least it will keep me busy.

I have been in a foul mood for most of the day. We will be leaving as soon as the sail is mended and the weather clears. The thought of being stuck on *Aphrodite* for another two weeks sailing to Chagos is making me bad tempered. It will be a month by the time we reach the Salomon Islands and I will not have felt dry land under my feet, I've got "yacht" fever!

Lewis is pissed off with Peter for not letting me go ashore and is giving him a hard time. Lewis has been trying to persuade me to go ashore anyway,

"What's he going to do? Throw us both off the boat?"

It's very tempting, but if I have to spend another three months with Peter, I don't want him pissed off with me for the rest of the trip.

Cocos Keeling - Day 60

About bloody time! The immigration officer came back from his vacation today and gave me permission to go on Direction Island. I Jumped overboard and starting swimming to the sandy beach before he had even managed

121

to untie his boat from *Aphrodite*. Stepping out of the warm water onto the hot sand, feeling the grains push up between my toes I laughed out loud and started to roll around on the beach.

I felt like a child again. It was the same feeling as being stuck indoors on a sunny day doing your homework and finally being allowed to go outside to play with your friends. I was free! Free at last to roam around and explore. Free to do whatever I wanted, I was dizzy with excitement, happy to enjoy this simple pleasure again. I had almost forgotten what it felt like. Relieved to finally be on solid ground I lay on the hot sand with my feet dangling in the cool water and fell into a happy sleep.

Catherine appeared out of the warm water as naked and free as the tropical fish that surround the remote islands. The sun touched her body, gently caressing each curve as she moved toward me with a seductive grace. Her hazel eyes were cat-like, fixed on mine as she walked closer to where I lay. Her skin was tanned dark brown and her shoulder length hair was wet, shinning in the afternoon sun. Water ran down between her perfectly formed breasts onto her flat stomach resting on the nest of dark hairs below her navel. Each droplet clung to her body and sparkled like the moon reflecting off the ocean. The muscles in her legs were strong and firm her hips shapely. With each step she took her breasts swayed back and forth, her nipples stood erect, she was aroused. I could smell her as she came closer to me, the smell of a woman in love, the smell of her sex. She did not speak to me, only reached down and took my hand in hers.

Our bodies met as we stood together alone on the island. Her breasts pressed hard against my chest. Catherine reached for my mouth with hers. My hands rested on the small of her back, I closed my eyes to focus only on the feeling of her body against mine. She kissed me lightly on the lips and whispered "I love you."

"Nev, you made it!" Lewis came running up the beach waving his arms and waking me from my dream, he was genuinely happy that I was allowed to come ashore but I told him his timing stunk!

We walked along the beach chatting the whole time. Lewis told me of the girl he met yesterday that was crewing on one of the yachts. Her name was Petra, a fiery redhead from Germany. He spent most of the evening talking to her at the barbecue the night before, I could tell that he liked her. She spoke Italian fluently and only limited English. Lewis said he had a great conversation with her in Italian and they got on well together.

We reached the end of Direction Island and the soft sand gave way to rocks and coral on the windward side. The island had built up its own natural defense against the relentless ocean surf. The only thing that was preventing the island from being washed into the Indian Ocean was the reef three hundred feet away from the shore. There was no sand on the windward side of the island, the jungle grew right into the sea. Debris was pushed into the jungle by the gentle swell that rolled in from behind the reef. Coconuts, driftwood, plastic bottles, rope and old fishing nets all gathered in groups swishing back and forth with the swell. Most of the bottles were thrown overboard by the kinds of people that have no real regard for the sea or the life in it. These bottles drift across the ocean from island to island and will be one of the only permanent reminders of man in years to come.

Lewis and I tried to make our way back to the beach by heading through the middle of the island. Although only five hundred feet wide we were unable to penetrate the thick foliage. Coconuts that are washed up on these islands sprout roots into the sandy soil and grow up to a hundred feet tall. Twenty paces from the shore there were no palm trees just heavy jungle, only with a machete would we have been able to make a path.

We made our way back to the secluded beach on the lagoon side and I started to gather fresh coconuts that had fallen onto the sand. The flesh inside would provide us with snacks on the long voyage we had to Chagos and the shells would give me more materials for carving.

Petra saw us on the beach and came over to introduce herself. She looked as though she was in her early thirties. Her fiery hair and freckled face gave her a simple beauty that most men would find attractive, especially those who have been at sea for a few months. Wearing a sarong over her bathing suit she had a large figure and powerful looking thighs, almost dwarfing Lewis'.

Leaving them alone on the beach I headed off in the other direction to explore the shelter and signs hanging up around it. Visiting yachts over the years have nailed signs to a palm tree that has become a kind of guest book for Direction Island. A collection of pieces of driftwood from scratchy carvings, to finely chiseled engraved signs are the island's only memory of all the sailors that have visited them. Boats from Sweden, Canada, Australia, America, England, France and New Zealand all left a story behind in the images and letters that mark each piece of wood.

The wind is blowing at twenty-five knots, Peter and Lewis will pick up the genoa tomorrow and the following day we will leave. By the time we raise the canvas for Chagos we will be four days behind schedule. We cannot afford to spend too much time in Cocos, as much as we would all like to. I have a feeling we will pay for it later if we get too far behind schedule.

Cocos Keeling - Day 61

Peter and Lewis have gone to pick up supplies and the genoa from West Island. I am only allowed on Direction Island so have managed to avoid the chores of gathering water, diesel and food. I have plotted our next course to Chagos over fifteen hundred miles away, this is our longest leg across the Indian Ocean and will take us around two weeks.

The collection of atolls lie between the fifth and eighth parallel south of the Equator. Diego Garcia is the largest island in Chagos Archipelagoes and is strictly off limits to yachts. The island has been made available to the United States military as a defense post and may only be approached in a serious emergency. The other fifty-five islands are all uninhabited and are patrolled by British customs.

The Salomon atoll is north of Diego Garcia. With a sheltered anchorage inside the lagoon it is the most convenient for our passage west. Permission to anchor up to three months is allowed by the authorities. A fee of $55 is the only charge, no visa is required.

It's funny how quickly we adapt to the environment around us. We have been anchored in Cocos for six days and have settled in to a comfortable routine. The thought of sailing into the middle of the Indian Ocean tomorrow fills me with uncertainty and apprehension all over again. The unknown is a natural human fear. Often we will put up with a bad situation rather than face something that we have not experienced before. Opportunities are lost every day because fear of change prevents us from moving on. Relationships, careers and personal growth have all suffered because of this affliction. I did not fly to America on May 6th 1993 because the fear of change was too great for me. Instead I went to Australia with a friend to overcome that fear and to build the confidence in myself to face it.

In the past eighteen months I have learned that although I will always fear change, not to achieve my goals or experience the things that I want to, far exceeds the fear of trying. Everything that we need to overcome any fear, we already possess within ourselves. Learning how to find that inner strength often takes time and courage. Some people turn to others for help, but inevitably it still comes from within you. It is a gift that cannot be given but others may help you unwrap.

I spent the rest of the day on the beach sketching under the shade of the corrugated shelter on an old picnic bench. The drawing is of a hardback book opened to the center. At the top of the left page it reads "Life," on the top of the right page it reads "The Future." The left-hand side of the book is complete. The pages have drop shadows and fine detail illustrating depth. The right hand side of the book has only a few lines indicating where the pages will be drawn. A two dimensional picture of a hand is on the left side of the finished page and becomes three dimensional as it reaches across the fold of the book holding a pencil and drawing the right side. The writing above the picture of the hand reads, "Art, like life gives us the opportunity to draw our own conclusions. The hardest challenge however, is discovering what we truly desire. Once we have established this, it is not unrealistic to believe we can accomplish anything." As the text bleeds onto the unfinished left-hand page it becomes sketchy, as though it were still be written.

Each page of the book represents another day in a life. The hand represents the person who is living that life, and the pencil represents the materials we each have to change our life and the ability to draw whatever we want. Life is unwritten and like the drawing we can decide where we want to go.

I now have the confidence to try just about anything. The people that helped me realize this have changed the direction and quality of my life forever. Complete strangers, like Neville Grey in Townsville, to my family and friends have all played a part in the role of making me believe in myself and the choices I have made. We will raise the anchor after sunrise tomorrow and leave the friends we have made here behind, sailing alone to Chagos as the other yachts head to Mauritius.

Remarkably the newly installed phone on Direction Island that stands alone in a clearing of palm trees actually works. Phone cards should be sold on West Island but are unavailable as the phone officially is not supposed to be turned on yet.

I was the first to use it so when I gave the operator the telephone ID number, she had no record of it.

"I am sorry sir." The lady said, "This phone does not exist on my records." "Well," I told her "I assure you it is here."

When I had managed to finally convince her that I was on Cocos Keeling and the phone was actually working she dialed Catherine's number in Daytona Beach, Florida. The phone rang five times, I had almost given up, thinking that she was in California when she answered. It was three in the morning and Catherine had landed the night before after flying in from Hawaii. She was totally exhausted and had only been asleep for a few hours. I apologized for calling so early and said that I could call her again later from the Seychelles, in about a month. "Don't you dare hang up!" She screamed down the phone.

"You awake now honey?" I teased her.

We spoke for ten minutes trying to cram everything in as though it would be the last time we were going to speak to each other. Talking for just a short time it felt as though we had never been apart, the last eighteen months were erased and we were back together again. At the end of the call Catherine blew me a kiss down the phone and said goodbye. Each time we spoke we were one step closer to being back together. The next time I would speak to Catherine I will be in the Seychelles on the western side of the Indian Ocean.

I walked out of the shade of the palm trees and into the late afternoon sun. Looking across the bay and seeing *Aphrodite* anchored a hundred yards from the beach, knowing where she would be taking me, I knew without a doubt I was the luckiest man alive.

4

Cocos Keeling to Chagos

(1,530 nautical miles)

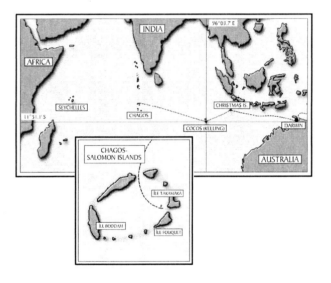

4

Cocos Keeling to Chagos

11° 51.1' S
96° 03.7' E
277° - Day 62

We left Cocos Keeling at 0700 with the morning sun casting long shadows across the empty beach. When we cleared Direction Island we raised our sails for the first time in a week and headed west with the sunrays. Lewis went below to kill the engine and we sat in silence, listening to the harmonic groans and creaks of *Aphrodite* coming back to life again after seven days of rest. It didn't take her long to warm up and stretch her wings. Both sails were raised high and the fifteen-knot breeze soon pushed us over the horizon.

The ocean has been left unsettled by the storm that has long since blown away. The waves are larger than before and will take many days to quiet. Like a quarrel between two lovers, the wind has flustered the ocean leaving her agitated and moody. Like Catherine she needs a little time to brood before she'll settle down again.

We are only fifty miles from Cocos but already feel a world away, consumed by the wind, the ocean and the skies. We are enjoying the freedom of again being at sea, the only rules out here are the ones made by Mother Nature.

The Salomon Islands are over fifteen hundred miles

away. To keep our cross track error down I have plotted each waypoint only one hundred miles apart. An alarm sounds each time one is reached, the autopilot then needs to be directed to the next. We have fifteen waypoints set until Chagos.

The genoa is full of wind and holding well against the fifteen-knot breeze. The sail repairer did a good job and stitched a length of red material down the entire leech to support the rotting canvas. When the sail is furled around the stay it looks like a giant forty-foot candy cane hanging from the top of the mast. It's not the most aesthetically appealing repair job I have seen, but as long as it holds up that's all that matters.

Motoring out from Direction Island we were greeted by a large cargo ship that had dropped anchor in the night. Just inside the atoll the huge rusty steel body seemed out of place and offensive in the tropical paradise. Essential to the survival of the five hundred people living in the south Keeling Islands, the cargo ship will unload the supplies onto a flat barge before motoring it to West Island. It'll take a few days and many trips to complete the task.

The fresh fruit and vegetables we bought in Cocos have been rationed three ways. We have four tomatoes, a cabbage, three bananas and two oranges each for the next 2,580 nautical miles - one month! The bananas are already starting to spoil and will need to be eaten in the next day, the tomatoes, if kept in the dark should last a week or two. The cabbages and oranges have a longer shelf life and if rationed properly should see us to Chagos. There are no markets in Chagos, the islands are uninhabited, so it'll be another ten days until we reach the Seychelles and can stock up supplies. Never again will I take fresh produce for granted.

To supplement my diet I bought some multi-vitamin tablets back in Darwin but have still found that I lack certain nutrients my body requires. My nails over the last two weeks have been slowly turning bright white, I fear it is due to lack of calcium. The cartons of UHT we have stored in the galley seemed like a good substitute for fresh milk as it would not require refrigeration, but unfortunately this sterilized milk tastes quite vile and is difficult to drink without retching. The limited fruit we bought in Cocos will help to supplement our bodies but will only last a few weeks.

Peter is looking much healthier than when I first met him. Away from the stress of running his business and the temptations of chocolate and other sweets, the diet of mainly pasta, as much as he complains about it seems to be agreeing with him. The long hot days and the constant motion of *Aphrodite* is slowly burning the fat from his body. He looks as though he has lost at least ten to fifteen pounds. He smokes endlessly and spends the first couple of minutes before his early morning watch hacking and coughing. His endless chain smoking is really beginning to piss off Lewis, already they have had a number of arguments about Peter's personal hygiene. It's a recurring problem between the two of them. Although I am just as repulsed by Peter's lack of cleanliness I have been unwontedly given the role as mediator.

Lewis and I have the opposite problem to Peter and do not wish to lose excessive amounts of weight. We try and eat enough calories to sustain our bodies and provide us with enough energy. We loaded up on crackers before we left Australia and snack on them throughout the course of the day. Spreading vegimite on them, a potent yeast extract or peanut butter and honey provides a simple snack that is relatively nutritious and filling.

It's Lewis's turn to cook tonight, which probably means pasta or an experimental dish of some sort, which Peter usually ends up throwing to the fish.

11° 22.3' S
94° 13.5' E
330° - Day 63

Rain all day. The winds have been steadily blowing harder peaking at twenty-seven knots and constantly changing direction. The waves seem even more confused now than they did yesterday. We are making good time but the ride is rough. I managed to have a fresh water shower during one of the heavier squalls but considered wearing my harness. With soapy feet on a wet deck I was sliding all over the place, it was not a pretty sight. Peter and Lewis looked on from were they sat in the cockpit, sipping coffee and watching me dance around on deck. Twice I almost fell overboard when *Aphrodite* was hit with a combination of waves, still my skin feels better for it.

We have made it a rule that a harness must be worn on the night watches at all times. With bigger seas, stumbling over the railing and falling into the empty ocean, far from the shipping lanes would mean certain death. Searching for someone in the night, not knowing when they fell overboard is a terrifying thought.

The temperature is getting hotter as we head towards the Equator. It's eighty degrees and humid. Although the skies were gray with heavy squalls scattered all around us, I spent most of the day on deck finishing my first carving out of coconut shell. Using a pencil I outlined the shape of a tropical reef fish I saw in Cocos before I began chipping at the hard shell. After eight hours of cutting, scratching and carving the sculpture was complete. I have attached a strand of leather to the dorsal fin and hung the fish with the other sculptures in my cabin. Swinging back and forth with the swell, the different types of wood banging against each other sound like a wind chime.

Sailing to Chagos, away from civilization, we feel

more alone and vulnerable than ever before. We have gathered our passports and some emergency supplies and placed them in the grab bag with the EPIRB. Should anything happen and we are forced to abandon ship in the life raft, our lives will depend upon the contents. Taped into a recess in the saloon wall, it can be easily reached in an emergency and must not be forgotten. I have my own personal grab-bag containing my sketchbook, logbook, family photos and letters that are the only material objects that hold any value to me. I keep it in my cabin wrapped in two old plastic bags. These few objects are priceless thoughts, moments and feelings that could never be replaced. Everything that I am is depicted in the contents of the bag. The drawings, quotes, my writing and photographs are all a part of me and tell a story.

The sea is black as ink with only the white horses dancing atop each wave to distinguish the coming swell. There are a few windows in the clouds showing the stars, otherwise the skies are low and menacing. I only have another hour on my shift before I wake Peter at 0300. He served up beans on toast tonight, I am dreading going into his cabin to wake him!

11° 08.7' S
91° 54.2' E
300° - Day 65

The skies have cleared and with it the wind. The sea is like a millpond without a ripple to disturb the glassy surface. We have been motoring for the last eight hours to make headway. It is hard to believe that everything in the middle of the ocean can be so calm. The opposing winds of the northern and southern hemisphere meet at the Equator and cancel each other out, leaving a region of light or no wind known as the doldrums. We are six hundred and sixty miles south of the Equator and expect to have no wind as we get nearer, but not now. I have planned to cross the Equator around longitude 51°00'E. Sailing northwest from the Seychelles before we cross over to the Northern Hemisphere, we will avoid the strong easterly currents and hopefully have the Somali current up the coast of Africa helping us along.

It's the perfect day to catch up on chores and to tidy the boat after three days of rough seas. The air is heavy and moist turning the cabin into a giant steam room. We have decided to air everything out by bringing the cushions, sheets and pillows up on deck. I spent a couple of hours in the morning washing the clothes and towels I have used over the last few weeks. Using seawater and a little washing powder we do our laundry in the same bucket we shower with. All my clothes are so dried out and saturated with salt I can practically stand them up on deck. They have not been washed in fresh water for four weeks, it'll be another three at least before we reach the Seychelles and I will have the luxury of putting them in a washing machine. *Aphrodite* is littered with clothes hanging off the boom, pegged to the railing and stays. If we had any wind we reckon we would probably get another knot or two out of the old girl with so much cloth up!

I have not stopped sweating all day. Even in the shade it must be well over ninety degrees. With no wind blowing over the water the heat hangs in the air, squeezing the water from our bodies. I should drink more, but the water in the tanks tastes stale and is not very refreshing. It's only bearable if I mix a few drops of lemon juice with each glass.

Peter and Lewis are both laying down in the cockpit, too tired to talk or argue. They have not been getting on very well and the difference in their characters is beginning to cause problems. The day started with an argument about the "unwritten rule." At 0600 sharp Peter woke Lewis for his shift. Lewis complained that he's being cheated out of a much-needed lay in.

"But it's the unwritten rule." Lewis kept saying.

Lewis felt that it was only fair that he should be allowed to sleep in as I allow Peter to rest and Lewis allows me to rest. Lewis has asked Peter to extend him the same courtesy. Peter claims to know nothing of this "unwritten rule" and kept referring to the rota taped to the cabin wall that clearly stipulates when a shift begins and ends. Not wanting to get involved I stayed out of the argument.

The constant hammering of the diesel engine is driving us all mad, we have at least another week and a half before we reach Chagos, at times I wonder if we will make it before killing each other off.

09° 58.6' S
89° 14.5' E
288° - Day 66

The wind has picked up enough for us to kill the engine but is playing silly buggers, swinging ninety degrees in seconds with no warning. Influenced by the dark squalls that are bruising the sky and spread to the horizon, the sails struggle to catch the unpredictable rush of wind and flap noisily each time a squall passes. We can only sit on deck and wait for the next squall to hit us, it would be impossible for us to avoid them. We have to take what's coming and hope the wind will not be too severe. The dark patches of water silently sweeping across the ocean surface indicate the coming wind. Watching the invisible force driving down on us we are able to judge the length of the wind and estimate its force.

We only have part of the main up and have furled the genoa to form half a candy cane. Our speed varies from six knots to two. We want to save as much fuel as possible and will only use the engine if the wind dies all together. Frustrated by the conditions and each other we spend the days doing our own thing. The relentless crashing of the sails and constant rocking of *Aphrodite* as she is hit then released by each squall is worse than the thumping engine, we're all tense and short tempered and have retreated into our own worlds.

We had not seen or heard of another living soul in the past week until today. Circling above us like a vulture, an Albatross has been trying to rest his wings by landing on top of the mast. Each time the giant bird tries to settle, the antenna wobbles and scares him away again. Such is his need for rest he has not given up and has been circling the boat all day, we can all sympathize with him.

07° 50.0' S
81° 36.0' E
290° - Day 68

The last couple of days have almost put us back on schedule. The wind has been picked up to twenty-five knots and with it so have our spirits. *Aphrodite*'s been crashing through the swell and the sails have been in need of constant trimming keeping us busy and off each other's back. The skies are bright blue and clear of squalls. The only clouds are on the horizon that we're never able to reach. We went one hundred and forty-nine miles yesterday, close to our record in a twenty-four hour period. The water temperature is eighty-two degrees Fahrenheit, only nine degrees lower than the air temperature. The entire deck is wet from the waves that keep breaking over the bow. The sound of just the wind and water again, is as pleasurable to our ears as a symphony orchestra, or Tom Jones in Peter's case.

Catherine mailed me a tape in Australia entitled *Chant - The Benedictine Monks of Santo Domingo de Silos*. This one-hour tape is filled with Gregorian chants that saturate the air with emotion when played. Catherine wrote a little note with the tape that I still keep in the case, it reads: "I hope you like this and it makes you feel groovy!" The chants seem to resonate from the cabin and into the disturbed tropical air making the experience around us seem more meaningful.

The ride is rough but not unpleasant. *Aphrodite* crashes through the waves sending spray far out to each side. The movement of the boat and the ocean seems to be slowed down. The only indication of the wind speed is the LED speed over ground display and the towels pegged to the railing flapping frantically. Everything else, the swell beneath us and the movement of the boat is like a film being played at half speed. Each movement is deliberate and full of power. *Aphrodite* is crashing through the waves one by one with the force of the wind in her sails that have been blowing for centuries. Each stay, each sheet is holding fast against the pressure of the trade winds blowing at their best. If one single sheet or stay were to fail under the stress, the harmony and balance we now have with nature would crash down around us. The sails need to be watched and adjusted constantly to maintain the balance. Our cross-track error is ten miles as we have been sailing with the wind. In another five miles or so we will adjust our course to bring us back to our ideal heading.

The dark lumps of Albatross shit that were left on the deck from our visiting friend the other night have washed off. After hours of trying to land on top of the mast without success, he eventually settled on the railing. Perched on the back of the boat he caught a free ride before leaving us at sunup. He seemed quite comfortable with our presence only a few feet away and did not mind Lewis shining the spotlight on him to take a photograph. We thought he would have had the decency to face the other way, so when he relieved himself it would fall harmlessly in the water instead of piling up on Peter's boat. Too exhausted to move he just sat there looking out to sea like Lewis does under the shade of the main sail.

For breakfast, Peter threw a chunk of my homemade bread on the deck for him. Landing just under the bird with a heavy thump, the Albatross looked down at it and flew away, probably deciding if he ate it he would not be able to takeoff again for a few hours. Circling *Aphrodite* once as if to thank us for the free ride, the bird caught the wind under his giant wings and was gone, leaving the three of us alone again.

06° 54.0' S
78° 26.5' E
300° - Day 70

Three hundred and fifty miles to go, no wind and motoring. I have finished carving my second coconut fish and have decided to try something a little more challenging. Using an unbroken shell I have sculptured five dolphins swimming in a circle. All the excess shell has been carved away so each dolphin swims alone with only a few points of contact with the other dolphins to hold the sculpture together. Once it is complete a candle can be placed in the center, which will cast light through the holes projecting shadows of each dolphin on the wall. The flickering flame will give the appearance of them swimming. I have spent two days so far shaping each dolphin and will spend another day adding detail.

I am at my happiest when creating and letting my mind wander through thoughts and ideas that I would otherwise never think of. Dreaming of America and all the things I want to achieve, the world I am in now and New York City could not be farther apart. I do not know how my grand ideas will become reality as there will be many obstacles in the way. All I know is that it is the right direction for me and I am excited about beginning my life there. I have never really excelled in any one thing before but have managed with pure determination alone to experience and achieve more than most my age. When I set a goal for myself I do not quit until I have achieved that goal. If I had quit back in Sydney I would not be sitting in the middle of the Indian Ocean right now carving a coconut and sailing towards Africa!

When I went to high School in Rochester, Minnesota I was awarded a T-shirt by the weightlifting coach, not because I was the biggest or the strongest, he awarded it for sheer determination and effort. I wore that shirt until it became too small and faded to wear any longer, it represented so much to me. You don't have to be the best at something to be a winner. Five years later I entered the Mr. South Coast of England bodybuilding competition and came third in my weight class. Again I did not win, but standing on stage in front of hundreds of people I achieved something that I set out to do five years earlier. America is the next challenge and however long it will take, or however hard it gets I will not stop until I am settled there.

Having so much time to think about what I want has made it easier for me to visualize where I want to go and how I am going to get there. Imagining myself in the place I want to be, filling in every piece of detail like one of the old paint-by-number drawings I used to color in, makes it easier for me to believe that I am going to get there. Seeing my future, no matter how impossible or unrealistic others may tell me it is, makes it achievable.

It's only when you put yourself in a difficult or challenging situation will you ever really understand just how strong you really are and what you are capable of. To go through life only taking the easy path you will never truly discover yourself and what you are capable of.

06° 05.7' S
74° 57.4' E
310° - Day 72

No two days on this leg have been the same. The conditions vary from minute to minute and with them so do our attitudes and personalities. The wind has died down leaving us only one hundred and eighty miles from Chagos, but days away. Our supplies are getting low, each day it seems we are exhausting another food group, today we ran out of cordial and potatoes and have used up the last of my muesli. The cupboards that were full when we left Darwin are now more than half empty, there are just a few tins left to roll back and forth with the swell, we have used sixty per cent of our diesel and still have over twelve hundred miles to go. We could motor through the last two waypoints but it would leave us with very little fuel for the stretch of ocean to the Seychelles, without fuel it would be practically impossible to sail into the enclosed marina at Mahé. We are all far too proud to allow ourselves to be towed into the anchorage and would rather suffer now than have the embarrassment of being pulled behind the harbormaster like a broken down car. It would feel like a defeat to be assisted on any leg on our journey, it is important for all of us to reach Italy on our own.

I would like to have the ability not to allow myself to be so influenced by the environment. To remain in control of your emotions when everything else changes around you is one of the qualities I would like to possess. We are all uptight again as it feels we are not making any progress, our morale drops with the wind and we are left drifting and bad tempered, Lewis and Peter have both spoken to me about the other. Lewis finds Peter's attitude and habits narrow minded and annoying, while Peter says Lewis is stubborn and difficult. Asking me to talk with Lewis, Peter said that he respects me more and may listen to what I have to say. I would rather not get caught up in the middle of it and can understand both points of view to a degree.

Lewis and I talk on the stern deck, a place we now like to call "the beer garden." Joking around like a double act on the long windless days, it is a way to sharpen our wits and pass the time. There are no termite hills to knock down out here so we use sound effects and elaborate arm movements to tell a story that normally turns into some kind of serious destruction. Illustrating something breaking on the boat or falling overboard is how the story ends up. Peter smiles at our jesting but I think it is more out of sympathy than humor. Peter is like the straight man in the act. Never joining in and certainly never cracking a joke. I don't think he has yet to make Lewis and I laugh intentionally.

Peter had the camcorder out yesterday and was taping the ocean. While he was panning the empty sea around us, you can hear me in the background making gale noises replicating one hundred knots of wind, Lewis was in the beer garden holding on to one of the stays for dear life.

"Oh my God," Lewis shouted, "hold on for ya lives mates, there's a storm coming!"

In a broken voice, to give the impression of hurricane strength winds Lewis and I were having a great laugh. Peter continued recording the sea and did not make any remark on our theatrical skills. After a few minutes of staggering around on deck and fighting the imagined elements we collapsed in the cockpit laughing and exhausted from the effort. During our entire performance Peter not once joined in the fun or acknowledged what we were doing, he just stared at us, smoking a cigarette with the confused expression on his face we have both come to know so well.

Peter has not shared his thoughts about the trip and seems distant from Lewis and me. It's hard to engage him in conversation and often I get frustrated by always making the effort. I get the feeling he finds it hard to express himself. I come from a loud family and to be heard it was always necessary to raise your voice above the others to make a point. With everyone contending for attention I soon learned that unless you speak up in life you may never be heard.

Peter, a quiet man, has yet to really let himself go. The only time I have ever heard him strongly voice his opinion was when he has had a few too many "tinnies." Finally achieving a life long dream to sail around the world, he does not seem as ecstatic as I would imagine him to be, maybe it's not what he had expected, maybe he's just missing his family or maybe he just thinks Lewis and I are both nutters!

05° 25.4' S
72° 51.8' E
290° - Day 74

Thirty miles from Chagos, now we're going too fast!

It's 2400 and a clear beautiful night full of fresh trade winds blowing from the southeast at twenty knots. There will not be any lights in the Salomon Islands and the chart that we are using has not been updated since the eighteenth century! Sailing into the dark lagoon at night, with so many coral heads hiding just under the surface would be foolish. We have brought the main down and are sailing with only the wind in part of the furled genoa in an attempt to slow our speed. Such is the life at sea that one has to live by the rules of nature and cannot rush her or make demands.

The beginning of the day was full with squalls, dumping rain onto the deck of *Aphrodite* every half an hour. Placing a container at the base of the mast, I was able to catch eight liters of fresh water as it ran down the mainsail, along the boom and dripped onto the deck. Waiting for the salt to wash off the sail before I bottled the water, each mouthful tasted as pure as nature intended it to taste. Compared to the stale tasting water we have swilling around in the tanks, the rainwater is like a sweet nectar.

Working by the Gregory River in the outback, I drank straight from the freshwater spring. Scooping it up in my aluminum billymug I soon became used to the sweet taste of naturally filtered water. When I returned to Townsville a month later, my senses were so heightened that I could actually smell and taste the chlorine in the tap water.

The phosphorescence are twinkling in our wake tonight like the reflection of the millions of stars in the clear night. These microscopic organisms glow bright yellow when stimulated and dance in the water leaving a trail behind *Aphrodite* like a star shooting across the sky.

I have estimated our arrival to be around 0700, we will enter the atoll on the north side when the sun has made its appearance to guide us across the lagoon.

The Salomon Islands - Chagos, Day - 75

The loom of the sun is beginning to take over the night. The glow from the east has spread across the sky chasing the darkness further west. As the light cast across the ocean the low laying Salomon Islands showed themselves for the first time only a few miles off our bow.

At a heading of 172° we entered the atoll under motor. We will be anchoring by Île Takamaka on the eastern side of the atoll four miles away. It's ninety degrees Fahrenheit with only a few wispy cirrus clouds high above us to mark the blue sky. Like a private pool the water inside the lagoon is calm and eighty-six degrees. Lewis was watching for coral heads by standing on the bow railing peering down into the clear water. I have been scanning the ten islands circling us for signs of other yachts but there are none, we are the only people here.

Dropping anchor off the sandy beach I have never imagined anywhere as beautiful. Untouched by man, most of the islands in Chagos have never been harmed or desecrated. So far from mainland, Chagos Archipelago is out of reach from the ruinous hands of tourism. With no population to rely on tourist dollars, these islands sit unnoticed by the world.

As soon as the anchor had been fastened Lewis and I were busy pumping up the inflatable to go ashore. Looking up every now and then to check the islands were still there, it was like a dream and we both wanted to touch it before we would wake. After two long weeks of being surrounded by water these islands were like a mirage, we were craving land, the reverse of what you would normally see in a desert. With no harbor master, immigration or quarantine officers to clear us, we wasted no time and sped across the one hundred feet of water to Île Takamaka. Peter insisted that he wanted to stay on the boat in case the

146

anchor dragged and would go ashore later.

We were jubilant to be on land again, I was craving it more than Lewis after only two days on Direction Island. As happy as we were to experience it together we both soon went our own ways. With only a few days to anchor we all needed some time alone, perhaps that is why Peter stayed on the boat. Lewis walked along the southern edge of the island while I walked west. On the chart a small symbol for a ruin was marked on this island a few hundred feet into the dense jungle, I set out to find it.

Feeling like Indiana Jones I scouted the edge of the island for any trace of an old path or signs of the ancient ruins. Two hundred yards up the beach I found an opening that led to a small clearing. Walking into the jungle was like entering a cave. Although the clearing was perhaps fifty feet wide, no light penetrated the heavy canopy of palm trees eighty feet above. In the furthest corner of the clearing stood a manmade water filter. With layers of rocks, grit and fine sand, presumably the yachts that anchor here for a few months at a time would filter seawater for drinking. A circle of burnt ash indicates where trash is disposed of. A few charred baked bean tins are the only remains from passing visitors.

My shirt soon became soaked with sweat as I continued to fight my way further into the heart of the island, at points having to get on my hands and knees to find a way through the unrelenting wall of thick vegetation. Everything was sweaty and damp and the floor was covered in a spongy layer of rotting vegetation. Fifty paces from the water the jungle suddenly gave way to grass and bushes. Much like Direction Island, Île Takamaka had built up its own natural defense against the elements by surrounding itself with a wall of palm trees and heavy vegetation. Walking into the clearing and feeling the sun on my face again was like discovering a

lost world, I was sure this would be where I would find my
ruins. The clearing was the size of a football field with
only a few clumps of trees and bushes to break the open
space. Searching the ground for clues I heard a noise
behind me and turned to find two chickens scratching
around in the grass feeding!

"What the hell are you guys doing here?" I asked out
loud. They were as surprised to see me as I was them and
after looking up at me, and then at each other they quickly
scrambled for cover. By the time I thought about how nice
it would be to have chicken on the barbecue they had
disappeared into the vegetation leaving me feeling hungry
and thinking of Kentucky Fried Chicken.

Heading east, away from the sun I made my way
across the island to the windward side facing the ocean. I
came to the far side of the clearing with no ruins in site
and decided to keep on walking. Pushing my way back
into the dark jungle was like walking out of an air-
conditioned building into a hot summer's day. It took me
half an hour to reach the water on the eastern side of the
island. I should have remembered Direction Island back in
Cocos. The windward side of Île Takamaka was a contrast
to the quite serene lagoon side. The ocean washed into the
jungle pushing in driftwood and coconuts. Two hundred
yards out the surf was pounding hard against the reef with
all its strength.

Wading out into the water I was waist deep before I
was able to make my way around the trees to head back to
the boat. With each step I stumbled against broken coral
and roots buried under the three feet of water. I had only
managed to walk about twenty feet when something
touched my leg. I froze, waiting to see what it was when it
hit me again. Climbing up onto the nearest tree I pulled
myself out of the water and peered down to see what was
attacking me. As the sand settled from my footsteps I saw

what it was, bloody coconuts! Some Indiana Jones I was! I was about to step back into the water again when something caught my eye only fifteen feet from where I was crouched.

The movement of this predator made it unmistakable. Hunting for prey the Grey Reef Shark glided only a few feet away from where I was crouched. Seven feet long its streamline body swam silently past like a missile searching for a target. With a single flick of its tail, it was gone leaving me very thankful for the coconuts.

Not wanting to risk wading in the water again with the shark around, it took me an hour to fight my way back through the sweaty jungle to the west side of the island, I never did find the ruins.

When I finally broke out of the bushes onto the sand, I collapsed on the beach exhausted from the effort of fighting my way through the jungle. Covered in twigs, leaves and insects I threw my clothes in a pile and floated naked in the warm salty water to cool myself. At the far end of the beach *Aphrodite* was a beautiful sight anchored alone in the atoll, protected by the reef surrounding her. Her raised stern, long bowsprit, slender lines and mid cockpit gives her a buccaneering look. I gathered my clothes and walked back towards her.

Peter picked me up from the beach and said he was concerned because I was gone for so long. I told him about the shark and the struggle I had through the jungle to get back.

"You be careful, you have no idea what's in there," he said.

I was touched by Peter's display of concern, it was the first time he has shown any toward me, although I was not sure if it was for my safety or if he was more worried about the thought of sailing to the Seychelles with just Lewis. He was in a good mood, he seemed at rest now we were anchored and was enjoying a beer, Lewis and I set up the barbecue for supper.

We are now all able to fully relax for the first time in months. Peter and Lewis had a lot of work to do in Cocos gathering water, fuel, fixing the genoa and buying supplies. As there is nothing in Chagos except coconut trees and a couple of chickens we have nothing to do but rest, sleep and enjoy the peace that surrounds us.

We cooked the last pieces of meat we had stored in the freezer on the grill. Savoring each mouthful we knew we would not be eating meat again for a few weeks, for Peter this was a terrifying thought.

I have decided to sleep outside tonight as it is still well over ninety degrees in the cabin. Arranging my blankets and pillows in the 'beer garden' I lay naked on the deck looking up into the clear sky counting the shooting stars that seemed to be endlessly whizzing through space. It's nights like these I miss Catherine the most. When you can share special moments with someone you love, somehow it makes the experience more remarkable.

The Salomon Islands - Chagos, Day - 76

I spent the morning with Peter snorkeling around the reef in search of meat. Peter is already starting to panic at the thought of living solely off pasta for a fortnight and is hunting desperately for fish with his spear gun. Although we were completely surrounded by huge, colorful meaty fish, we were unable to spear even one. I decided that after lunch I would try catching them with the rod. Lewis spent the morning alone, I think he was missing his redheaded friend back in Cocos.

Rowing out in the duck to the edge of the reef I

dropped anchor and settled in for a restful afternoon of sleeping and fishing. Laying down in the inflatable was like sleeping on a waterbed. The tiny ripples that swept across the lagoon rocked me into a deep sleep in minutes. Drifting in and out of consciousness for what felt like a fifteen-minute power nap turned out to be a two-hour snooze. It was the same feeling as I had sleeping on Coogee Beach outside Sydney in the late afternoon with the warm sun covering my body like a blanket. Although I was aware of the noises and movement around me my body was completely at rest.

Bringing me out of my meditative-like state Lewis shouted out from *Aphrodite* that a storm was coming over. He had an uncanny knack for waking me at what seemed to be the most inconvenient times. Angry that my sleep had been interrupted and I was past the point of return I looked up to see what he was shouting about. Sure enough, rolling across the sky towards us, in a line of giant gray cumulus clouds was a fast approaching storm. Coming from the southeast, the weather was rapidly bearing down on our secluded haven.

Deciding to call it a day I reeled in my line and tried to pull up the anchor. Tugging and heaving from every possible direction it was stuck fast. The wind had picked up to twenty knots in under a few minutes and was blowing harder by the second. I wanted to get the dinghy back to *Aphrodite* and secured as soon as possible. Floating in the lagoon the inflatable was exposed to the full force of the winds. Another few minutes of yanking on the anchor rope did not prove a thing, so I decided to leave it. Using the water container as a buoy I untied the rope from the dinghy and fastened it to the plastic container before rowing back.

Just as soon as I had reached *Aphrodite* the wind speed was gusting over thirty knots. The orange sheet of canvas that we had draped over the boom was threatening to rip itself free from the railing. We quickly brought down the canopy and secured everything on deck. The tiny ripples of water across the atoll soon turned into small chop as the wind lashed out at everything in its path.

Aphrodite's anchor was holding well so we all just sat on the deck looking up at the giant rolling clouds pass us close overhead. This was the second time that we had been at anchor when there was a storm. We were safe by Direction Island the last time and had lucked out again.

The storm blew past in under an hour and continued northwest. I pitied anyone out at sea in its path. Lucky I had managed to untie the inflatable otherwise she would have been torn from her anchor rope and tossed away like a plastic bag.

Swimming out with a knife and mask to the bottle I used as a buoy, I dove down the thirty feet to the reef. My first two attempts were beyond feeble. I had only managed to reach the bottom before the air in my lungs ran out. On my third attempt I hyperventilated, forcing all the carbon dioxide from my system before saturating my lungs with oxygen. I reached the anchor with about twenty seconds of air to spare. The anchor was jammed under a ledge of coral so I managed to fold the four arms up to free it. It took all my strength to swim back to *Aphrodite* holding twenty-five pounds of iron that was trying to drag me down to the bottom.

For the first time since we left Darwin we all spent the afternoon together, bathing in the reef, lounging on the beach and discussing our next leg to the Seychelles. The books we have read and the people we have met that have sailed there said that Mahé is a bureaucratic nightmare. Compared to the freedom and lack of authorities we have experienced here in Chagos the authorities in the Seychelles require crew lists and ship's papers in triplicate.

Health, customs, immigration and security officials will want to board us before we are given permission to anchor. The entomological department also requires all yachts to be sprayed on arrival.

The Seychelles will be the first country we will reach that requires clearance since leaving Australia. Papers need to filled out upon arrival, two days before departure, a day before departure and on the day that you actually leave one must visit the security office for a final check to make sure all papers are in order and fees paid. I get the feeling our happy-go-sailing days will soon be over.

Sadly we must leave tomorrow. Although we could all use a couple more days to fully recover, we are four days behind schedule and want to make up the time before we reach the Bab el Mandab (Gates of Sorrow) - the southern entrance to the Red Sea. I hope the naming of the entrance to this infamous passage is not going to be a reflection on our decision to sail it.

The Salomon Islands - Chagos, Day - 77

I guess we won't be leaving after all! We just had a visit from the British Marines and have been 'ordered' to a barbecue! We were about to pull up anchor when Lewis spotted a Naval ship outside the atoll. Deciding to stick around to see who our new neighbors were, we sat under the canopy and watched a camouflaged dinghy full of men in jungle greens racing towards us. Pulling up along side, eight smiling faces looked up at us, two of them women! "Alright there mates, permission t'come aboard?" One of them said.

Doing their monthly rounds of the islands, the Navy had spotted our mast in the lagoon and decided to come over and see if we needed anything. Alan came aboard while the others sped off in the dinghy to check the islands. Accepting one of Peter's beers he was a friendly chap and seemed more interested in our traveling stories than the ship's papers. Carefully stamping our passports with the British Indian Ocean Territory ensign, Alan seemed to appreciate the importance of having this meeting documented in our travels. In years to come our passports will be a printed reminder of all the countries we had visited, few people in the world can boast a British Indian Ocean Territory stamp in their book.

Like a true Brit, Alan polished off his beer in record time and gladly accepted another. He had been posted to work in Diego Garcia for ten months and only had another four weeks left to serve, he said he was looking forward to going back home to see his wife and family again, we all made noises of understanding, thinking about our families and loved ones on the other side of the world. Alan's home was in Plymouth, only a three-hour drive along the coast from Southampton. I told Alan that my older brother Steve went to Plymouth Polytechnic for an engineering degree, and lived there for a few years. Sitting on the deck waiting for the others to pick him up he asked if we would like to join them for lunch later in the day on Île Boddam. We told him that we were planning on leaving, but thanked him all the same.

"It'll be a shame to have all that meat and fresh vegetables go to waste," he said knowing that for sailors the lure of fresh food was irresistible.

The three of us looked at each other and then thought about the pitiful rations we had left for the next ten days and decided one more day wouldn't make a difference.

"Good, then" Alan said, "I'll see you at 1200 sharp by the old manager's office."

When the camouflaged dinghy came to pick Alan up, one of the women asked us if we had any medical problems that needed seeing to.

Smiling at the opportunity I said, "Well, now you come to mention it, I think we could all use a good seeing to."

The men in the dinghy all fell about laughing at the remark and the doctor, probably used to hearing such comments from the men she works with everyday smiled and said, "I'll see what I can do for you."

Blowing her a kiss and waving goodbye we watched the dinghy race off across the lagoon powered by two, eighty horsepower outboards.

As we prepared for lunch, we were as excited as if we were going to our senior prom. Our mouths started to water just thinking about all the fresh food the Navy would have flown in to Diego Garcia. We put on our best salt-stained shirts and combed out our matted hair, setting off for Île Boddam with empty stomachs and wide-open mouths. I don't think the Navy had any idea just what they were in for.

The trip across the lagoon took twenty minutes in our little inflatable with the fifteen horsepower Evinrude running close to full throttle the entire time. Even over the exhaust of the outboard and a hundred yards from the beach Peter's keen sense of smell picked up the aroma of sizzling steak. He homed in on it and cranked the throttle fully round, pointing the inflatable to the plume of smoke rising out from the palm trees. It was like watching an old Tom and Jerry cartoon where Tom followed his nose towards a scent that floated through the house.

There were a few old shacks from the original settlement on the beach and two giant brick barbecues that were constructed by the Americans, there was even a volleyball net strung across two palm trees. Alan came over and asked why we were so late. The barbecue was over and most of the supplies had been eaten, we had forgotten to adjust our clocks to local time! Alan told us not to fret, he was kind enough to save us some of the rations.

We met people from London, Scotland, Wales, Plymouth, Texas and Alabama, everyone wanted to know where we had come from and how long we had been sailing, most of what we said was responded to in the same way, "God, you're lucky bastards!"

We chatted politely for a few minutes but slowly began to edge our way closer to the food. We approached the barbecue like we were walking into a religious ceremony and gathered around the grill in awe. Heaps of steak, burgers and sausages dripping in fat and blood were stacked over the glowing coals, it was a beautiful sight and they were all ours! We each grabbed four burgers and piled them high with fresh onions, lettuce, tomatoes, cheese and sandwiched them together inside a fluffy white bun, once we had finished the appetizer we returned with clean plates for steak and sausages and returned to our benches to continue feeding.

While we were busy cramming more meat into our bodies Alan told us stories of Chagos and the sailors he had come across during his rounds. Not too long ago he rescued an elderly couple that were shipwrecked for a month on one of the islands. As the couple approached the atoll a fire broke out in the galley, the man left the helm to help his wife put it out, by the time the fire was extinguished the yacht was caught on the reef and finally sunk. The couple managed to salvage a few supplies from the wreckage but were left alone on the island until the Navy saw the smoke from their fire a month later.

As the other Marines gathered round we shared our stories and experiences of the trip, everyone seemed to envy our lifestyle. As we finished our meal Alan told us that whatever was left over from lunch we were more than welcome to take back with us.

Waiting for everyone else to finish snacking on the remains felt like an eternity, looking around the beach we watched our rations for the next week and a half slowly disappear in front of our eyes. Lewis was looking longingly at something, when I turned to see what it was I almost shouted in protest. One of the Americans had picked up a ripe tomato the size of a small apple and ate it in three bites. Something that would have lasted me a few days had disappeared in seconds down the throat of that greedy bastard! We had to stop this orgy before all our food was gone. Peter was the first to take action and bagged up fifty burgers and forty sausages and placed them in a separate cooler. Lewis and I managed to gather some fruit and buns but most of it had already been eaten. Satisfied that our stash was safe we rejoined the others on the beach.

It was hard to soak in who we were partying with. M16's were leaning up against the ruined hut and high-powered camouflaged boats were pulled up on the beach. The United States defense post for the Indian Ocean was only two hundred miles south, three thousand marines were ready to act at a moment's notice.

The group of ten men and two women were all wearing the same standard issue green shirts and camouflaged shorts. Only one woman stood out of the crowd. Her name was Molly, she was from Texas and was parading around the beach in a colorful two piece bathing costume that didn't leave much to the imagination.

She seemed to be far too glamorous and fragile to be in the American Navy and didn't look like she had the strength to even pickup one of the M-16's let alone fire it. It has been over eleven weeks since I have had a conversation with a woman and decided that I would say hi to her, as we were not introduced earlier.

She was beautiful and had a contagious laugh and easy manner that made it enjoyable to talk to her. Standing in the warm water up to our waists away from the others, we talked about Chagos and how beautiful the islands were. This was Molly's first time out of Diego Garcia, she did not want to leave.

I could not stop looking at her. Her long blond hair, bright blue eyes, tanned smooth skin and gorgeous body had captivated me. I had been in the company of Lewis and Peter for months, resting my eyes on her was like a breath of fresh air. I felt a twang of guilt as I stood flirting with her. I was sure Catherine would understand my harmless advances towards a beautiful woman in tropical paradise, as long as I didn't entertain my thoughts I was all right.

Molly collected postcards and asked me if I would send her some from the countries we were sailing to. She wanted to give me her address (the ol' chat up lines still worked!), so we started to walk back to the beach to get her bag when a T-bone steak splashed in the water only a few feet from where we were standing followed by half a coconut, we were being bombarded with food!

Threatened by my advances towards Molly, Alan was trying to drive me away by throwing anything at me he could get his hands on. I couldn't believe it, a British Naval officer had just tried to hit me with a steak! The fact that he was married and was going home in a few weeks didn't matter, I was trespassing on what he thought was his territory. Surrounded by men in camouflage I realized that they didn't like me chatting up one of theirs. Everyone was laughing about it, but not wanting to upset a man who owns an M-16, I told Molly I would get her address later and went to look at the ruins with Lewis and Peter.

The island manager lived on Île Boddam with a small

community of workers for fifty years. The village has been deserted now since the 1930's. Many of the buildings still stand but are completely consumed by the jungle that has taken back the land that was once worked by the copra slaves from Madagascar and Africa. The old settlement consisted of no more than a dozen or so houses.

The first house we came to was hiding behind the trees and bushes, only part of the roof could be seen. Most of the old wooden tiles had long since blown away leaving the inside of the house exposed to the elements. The wood paneling had rotted away leaving just a spindly frame to hold the house together. Inside the house the floorboards creaked and groaned as we walked around from room to room. The old house had history and some of the bare rooms made me feel uneasy, I shuddered involuntarily and became covered in goose pimples when I walked down the main hallway to the back rooms. The smell of rot, the dark stained paneling and the shadows of branches and leaves moving around the room as the wind blew in the trees above spooked me, I left the house feeling uneasy. We walked further into the jungle and came across what must have been the center of the settlement.

A stone church with steps leading up to a twelve foot arched doorway stood amidst the palm trees. All that was left of this once sacred building were four walls. Grass was growing out of the cracks in the floor where the row of pews once stood. The jungle surrounding the building grew right up to the outside walls, the white plaster that once coated the church was now discolored and cracked. There were no signs that a roof ever existed, just a huge gaping hole that looked up into the blue sky. Giant rusty hinges hung onto the doorframe frozen in time. Roots were slowly prying the bricks and mortar apart. Years from now the church and village will only be a pile of overgrown stones. The other houses were all rotting and bare, the small village, once full of life was now empty and dead.

We made our way back to the beach, the party was coming to an end and the marines were packing up their equipment getting ready to leave. Molly gave me her address and asked me to keep in touch. Alan apologized for throwing the steak at me and said that he was only messing around and didn't mean anything by it. We took a group photograph of everyone before we climbed back in our little inflatable dinghy. With mountains of free food donated by the British Navy, we headed off across the lagoon back to our precious *Aphrodite*. Although we paid Alan fifty-five dollars for anchoring at the islands we certainly got our money's worth out of the British navy. We had more burgers and sausages than our little box freezer could hold. Reluctant to let any of the precious new cargo go to waste we decided to have a barbecue and consume what we were unable to store.

The waypoints are programmed into the autopilot and ready to take us to the Seychelles. The naval ship has already steamed away from the atoll. We heard from Alan one last time on channel sixteen wishing *Aphrodite* a safe passage. I radioed back, thanking him for the steak and told him to give my best to Molly, I didn't get a reply.

Leaving Sydney harbor
July 6th, 1994

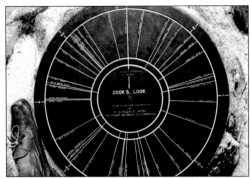

Cook's Lookout, the highest point on Lizard Island

The windy Great Barrier Reef, Cook's Lookout

Anchored at Lizard Island, Peter
and Don still aboard

The Great Barrier reef

My first carving

Our first stormy night

Mangrove tree at Stanley Island with
Aphrodite at anchor

Palm Tree Island, Lewis
shopping for lunch

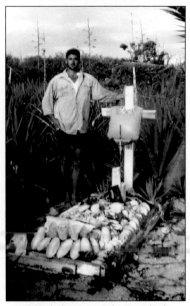

Unmarked grave on Palm Tree Island

Goodbye to Rob (back right)
and Don (front right) in Darwin

Peter on watch for pirates in the Timor Sea, south of Indonesia

Peter and Lewis adjusting to the routine
in the Indian Ocean

Christmas Island

Sunset over Christmas Island

Enjoying my morning shower

Another new beginning

Lewis covering up

Old friends come to visit

Quarantine - Direction Island, Cocos Keeling

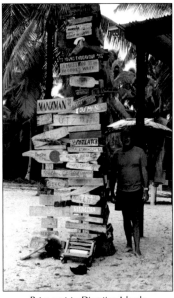

Peter next to Direction Islands
"visitors book"

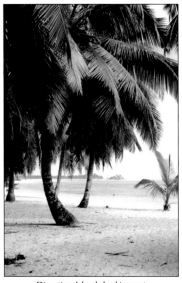

Direction Island, looking out
across the lagoon

My next project

Carved from a coconut

Sunrise over Cocos Keeling

The Indian Ocean at its best

Anchored safely in the Salomon Islands, Chagos

Lewis off to explore Île Takamaka

Fish number 2

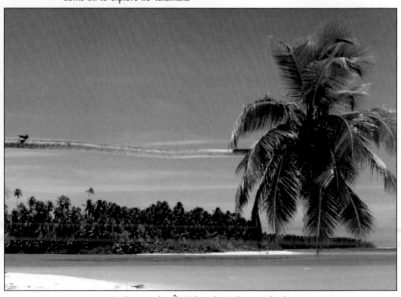

Bird on a palm, Île Takamaka, Salomon Islands

Île Takamaka, Chagos

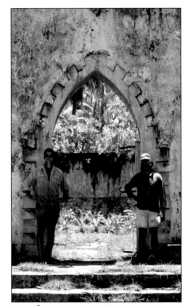

Luncheon with the Royal Navy on Île Boddam

Plotting the next leg to the Seychelles

Île Boddam, the old settlement

Swimming dolphins sculpture

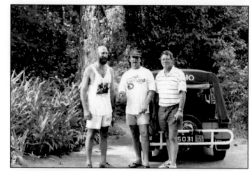

Our friend Brian showing his plot in paradise, Seychelles

The basket lady in Djibouti town center

The streets of Djibouti

The local market in Djibouti

Following fish

King Tut in the Cairo museum

"The crew" on shore leave

Keops pyramid

Smoking Sheesha with Muhammad

The Great Sphinx

Sunrise over Lake Timsah, Ismalia

Suez army building a bridge across the 500 foot canal

Cold and wet in the
Mediterranean

Anchored safely in Fuimicino

5

Chagos to Seychelles

(1,050 nautical miles)

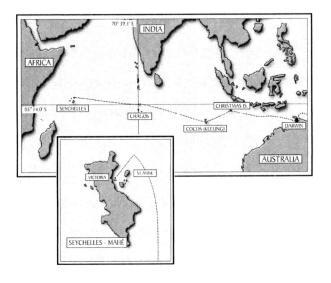

5

Chagos to Seychelles

05° 14.0' S
70° 39.1' E
265° - Day 78

We have sailed right off the edge of the tiny Salomon
Islands chart and have again returned to the Indian Ocean.
Once in pristine condition this giant chart is now like one
of my old schoolbooks - dog-eared and covered in pencil
marks. Each dot of lead that makes a trail from east to west
tells a story. Like a Morse code message the dots and
dashes are a reminder of the passages we have sailed. The
scale of the chart is so huge that the dots practically sit on
top of one another. The dull pencil lead markings each
cover an area of a couple of square miles.

Returning to the larger chart is like stepping back
from a situation and seeing it for what it really is. When
you use the smaller more detailed charts it is easy to forget
where you are, you become focused on only what is
around you and lose sight of the big picture. Looking at a
tiny spec of pencil lead in the middle of a huge folding
sheet of paper makes you realize just how small and
vulnerable you really are. It is very gratifying to see the
little pencil dots trailing across the sheet. Each one
represents another tiny goal reached, the islands we sail to
are the immediate goals and the chart I pull out every now
and then of the west coast of Italy is the ultimate goal. This

chart is still in pristine condition, it has never been used before, it still seems so far away I cannot ever imagine using it.

Just by looking at the coordinates marked across the Indian Ocean you can figure out who was on watch. Peter puts down more of a scribble than a dot, like he's filling in a multiple-choice box. Lewis uses the bow divider to mark our latitude and longitude and I use the parallel ruler to draw faint vertical and horizontal lines. Where the two lines crossover marks our position.

I have been accused many times in the past of being somewhat fastidious. Everything I do I am extremely particular about, I like things to be a certain way, if they are not quite right I must fix them. My neatness and order though, did help me to find work while in Australia. I was quickly promoted through the ranks of the popular steakhouse, Duke's Bistro outside Sydney because of my compulsiveness.

Working as a dishwasher to raise some extra money for my sailing adventure I was stationed at the front of the kitchen where the waitresses would dump piles of greasy plates, cutlery and glasses on my aluminum table. It was my job to stack the dirty dishes onto plastic trays and slide them into the dishwasher. A few minutes later I would raise the opposite door and slide the scalding hot tray out the other side. On top of recycling the used tableware back to the crowds of people waiting to be fed outside, I would have to keep the salad bar stocked and the meat lockers full. I was told that I was the only dishwasher in the history of Duke's Bistro to ever keep on top of the chores. Not only was there never a pile of dirty dishes stacked on my table for more than a few minutes the area was kept spotless, no pieces of meat stuck to the wall or sauce spattered across the tiles. It was not that I was any faster than the others, I just prided myself on my workstation, it did not matter that I was only washing dishes. The owner and chef of Duke's Bistro, Ian Butler noticed my potential and promoted me to prepare the appetizers after just a couple of weeks. I had my own table in the middle of the kitchen where all the action was.

Preparing Kilpatrick and Monet oyster, prawn cocktails, side salads, pate and desserts, I was in my element. I was so organized that I had time to carve the slices of carrots into shapes or join them together by cutting slots to form a sphere. My talents did not go unnoticed and customers soon congratulated the chef that put together their wonderfully displayed side orders. One lady said that she almost could not bring herself to eat the tiny carrot sculptures. Again Ian promoted me, I became his assistant, a great honor. I was on the front line, the most dangerous part of any kitchen, at times the stress was so great, pots were hurled across the room in frustration. I always held my own and kept up with the endless stream of steaks that were pushed in front of me. Ian would only like to say things once.

"Medium-rare with mushroom no sour cream, well-done with pepper, sour cream, rare, medium with pepper and mushroom..."

To ask him to repeat an order would mean another unfortunate pot would be chucked across the kitchen, I soon learned how to listen.

I think my attention to detail is what has helped me over the last few months. Navigating isn't hard, you just need to be careful and thorough. I think the real test of my navigational abilities will soon become apparent. So far I have only had to point *Aphrodite* in the direction of an island, I have yet to meander my way through reefs or sandbars. The Red Sea is full of obstacles, here anything less than perfect will not do, I have my work cut out for me.

The light gusts of wind from the north have helped us

very little today. In an effort to catch every breath we have put up the spinnaker. This huge lightweight sail can only be flown in gentle conditions. With calm seas and light wind the giant sail has captured enough breeze to add a knot to our speed.

We are only two hundred and forty nautical miles from the Maldives, a chain of over a thousand tiny islands scattered from the Arabian Sea all the way down to the Equator. We spotted Peros Banhos, the largest atoll in the Chagos group. It'll be the last land we see for over a week. We are all praying this passage will not be a repeat of our last. I would rather have stormy weather and high seas than the dead calm of no wind and the long days that accompany them.

05° 17.0' S
67° 56.2' E
245° - Day 81

The sky this afternoon was consumed by a giant squall that floated silently across the blue sky and as luck would have it right over *Aphrodite*. The clouds were dark purple and black like an angry bruise, we could not run from it, only sit, watch and wait to see how bad the winds were going to be. Moments before it struck I suggested we reef the main, lucky really, because only seconds later the wind was over thirty knots and we would have been in a world of trouble.

The weather has been predictable only by its inconsistencies, no wind, wind from the southeast, wind from the northwest, one thing does remain consistent however, the relentless heat. The mercury is touching one hundred degrees and I have spent the last two nights sleeping on deck in the evening. Our spirits are low and the Indian Ocean seems bigger than it has ever felt before.

Peter is keeping himself busy, trying not to worry about the little fuel we have left in the tanks and the nine hundred miles of endless ocean to the Seychelles. Lewis is keeping to himself, and I feel rundown. My nails are completely white now. They are so bright it looks as though I am wearing white nail polish. I think I will make a visit to the hospital in the Seychelles for a checkup.

Temporarily lifting our spirits and breaking the wearisome day we spotted a dozen whales at lunchtime. Munching on his last tomato that we salvaged from the jaws of the American Navy, Lewis saw them a mile off our port side. Appearing in unison out of the gentle rolling ocean they were heading north. Towers of white spray filled the blue sky as they surfaced and exhaled. As we bobbed along west it became apparent that our paths would cross a few hundred yards ahead of our current position.

"Survive the Savage Sea part two." I said out loud breaking the silence.

"Oh, don't say that Neville." Peter said. He went below to start the engine.

"They're not pigeons you know." Lewis said around a mouthful of crackers. "You can't shoo them away!"

"It's my boat and I'm going to turn the engine on if I want to!"

"Sure waste all our fuel, that's a better idea!" Lewis said sarcastically.

Things are starting to fall apart. In three days we had barely covered two hundred miles, the boat has become our prison, it feels like a life sentence. Our only chance for parole is wind and right now there isn't any.

"Maybe it's a good omen?" I said to try and change the subject. "I have a good feeling about those whales, I think the wind's going to pick up now."

Lewis and Peter just stared at me as though I had

finally lost it. I put my head back down and continued carving my coconut. Lost it, what do they know?

05° 17.6' S
67° 45.3' E
267° - Day 82

The whales never did hit us, maybe Peter revving the engine did scare them off after all, but that no longer matters. It's just like old times again. The wind is back to greet us from the southeast pushing us along at five knots, I was right after all. Never again will they doubt my wisdom, I made them both say, "Nev knows all."

The twelve yachts that Alan said were anchored in the Salomon group before us are now probably in the Gulf of Aden or safely anchored in Mauritius. We feel alone, as we have not sighted or had contact with another yachtie since Cocos twenty days ago, it doesn't feel right.

The only sign of human existence was a river of trash we spotted floating in the currents of the ocean around one hundred feet wide. Everything from soccer balls, plastic containers of different sizes, oil drums to great tree trunks were caught in the drift. We had to change our heading a few times otherwise the debris would have crashed into the hull. God only knows where it all came from or where it'll end up.

05° 37.1' S
64° 35.7' E
262° - Day 85

Absurdly the clocks go back an hour today. Winding the hand back on my diving watch seems ridiculous to me.

Nowhere has time mattered less, time is only measured now by the distance we have covered. I think it's Saturday, it feels like a Saturday, but I am only guessing. The days are becoming increasingly difficult to distinguish one from the next. The morning sunrises and the evening sunsets seem to come and go, only mealtimes and watches break the monotony of time. I do have an extra hour on my shift though, I was not planning on going anywhere so it doesn't really matter.

I am thankful for the twelve coconuts I have stashed in the hull, without them I do not know what I would do all day, I think that is part of the reason Lewis and Peter are not getting on very well, they have too much time on their hands to argue. Even though my hands are covered in cuts and calluses through chipping away at the hard coconut shells and gripping onto my little penknife I still enjoy creating my sculptures out of the shells.

The alarm has been going off all night as there is not enough wind to even make a single knot. If *Aphrodite* stops moving, the autopilot is unable to steer as there is no resistance on the rudder and emits a high pitched beep as a warning. We only have sixty liters of diesel left and another seventy for emergencies, we are cursing ourselves for not thinking of asking Alan for some diesel back in Chagos. For the time being we are drifting and have had enough. The days are so hot I am training at night during my watches, it helps the three hours go by faster and keeps me awake.

Peter laid down some more rules yesterday, although he was speaking to both of us they were obviously directed at Lewis. No laying down during the night watches and all clothes have to be stowed away and not left laying around in the cabin. Peter has caught Lewis a number of times laying down on the evening watches and is concerned that he may fall asleep. Lewis assured him that he may appear

173

to be relaxed, but is awake and always alert. Lewis also argued that he does not have a cabin to hang his clothes up in and that Peter's cabin was a mess and the rule should not only apply to him.

"While we are on the subject can we talk about personal hygiene?" Lewis added angrily.

Oh shit, here we go! It was inevitable that it was going to come up eventually. Peter looked hurt at the remark and asked what he meant by it.

"You should be a little more considerate and shower more often, sometimes you're really on the nose!"

"I shower!" Peter retorted.

"Not every day you don't and the cigarettes you smoke are stinking out the cabin. I only think it's fair that if we're making rules we should all be able to have a say as we're all affected by them."

"Well you snore!" Peter exclaimed, trying to even the score.

"What the hell am I supposed to do about that? At least you can pick up a bar of soap a little more often or smoke up on deck and not in the cockpit."

"What do you think Neville?" Peter asked, "Do I stink?"

"Well sometimes there is a bit of an odor." I said (the understatement of the century. There was no need to upset anyone more than was necessary). We were all pissed off with the weather and were taking it out on each other, if we were not careful what was said it could cause irreversible damage to our relationship, restraint was in order.

The argument was eventually resolved by Lewis saying that he would keep the cabin area cleaner and would not lay down during the night watches, which he thought was ridiculous. Peter said he would shower more often and would smoke on the stern bench in the evenings, which I could see he resented as it was his boat and he probably felt he should be able to do what he pleases. Although all the issues had been addressed it feels like we have become divided. I chipped in and said that I would make an effort to clean away all the coconut shavings at the end of the day.

Having an odd number crew will eventually lead to segregation. There will always be someone who does not quite fit in. Lewis and I get on well, I can tolerate Peter but we have nothing in common. Lewis can tolerate Peter to a degree and Peter seems to have taken a dislike to Lewis. The afternoon debate was ended by Peter saying that in the future his decision will be final and he wants less "talk-back."

I felt as if it was a little too late to start laying down the law. If at the very beginning Peter had made his position clear there would not have been any problems. After three months it's hard to suddenly introduce new rules and expect others to immediately follow them.

I am trying to remain as neutral as possible, as much as I am annoyed with Peter's habits, personality and attitude I still find myself admiring him. He is living proof that a dream can be achieved against all odds. Peter left high school at the age of thirteen and never graduated with his schoolmates. He worked on a cattle farm for eight years until he was twenty-one. He is not a bright man but has been dedicated to a life that he has built for himself and his family. I have known men over the years that have wasted their talents and squandered away opportunities because they never made the effort. Peter was a man that made his own opportunities, and is living out a lifelong dream, something that very few of us can ever boast. I think Lewis should try and give him a little more slack and remember where he is and who brought him here.

05° 45.0' S
61° 15.0' E
270° - Day 86

Our friend the wind is a back again greeting us from the southeast blowing a consistent twenty knots. The sky is gray and full of rain.

This is the first good breeze we have had since we left Chagos, so when we were forced to bring down all the sails it pissed us off. We had been hearing a knocking noise from under the hull all morning, as the wind picked up and our speed increased the knocking turned into a banging and the steering began to play tricks on us. The autopilot was protesting and the ram was working overtime to try and keep us on coarse.

With the sails down we all peered over the railing to try and see what the source of the problem was. Everything seemed to be intact but the rudder was jammed solid. I volunteered to jump over and have a look.

The water was eighty-seven degrees and disappeared under my feet to the middle of the earth. It is strange sensation to swim in an ocean so deep, I imagined sea creatures coming up from the depths and dragging me down to the ocean bed. The sunlight broke through the clouds and struck the surface of the sea, penetrating the water and refracting deep into the heart of the Indian Ocean. Strangely it looked as though the light was coming from below rather than from above. I dove down as deep as I could, to see what it would feel like. The air bubbles that dribbled from the corner of my mouth shimmered and danced all the way to the surface as the sunlight reflected off them. As I watched them I imagined what it felt like to be an African only three hundred years ago, dumped from a galleon slave ship with heavy shackles and weights tied to my legs, watching the hull of the ship disappear and fade as you were pulled deeper and deeper to your death. The pressure, the cold, the blackness that would take you by the ankles and suffocate your body. That thought alone made me shudder and filled me with terror, I kicked my legs and pulled hard with my arms to get back to daylight.

The water got warmer closer to the surface and the pressure eased. I could see the distorted faces of Lewis and Peter gazing over the deck watching me, probably wondering what I was doing. I broke the surface exhaling like the whales we saw a few nights ago and filled my lungs with fresh air.

"Well, can you see the problem?" Peter asked.

"Don't know yet, haven't looked."

Swimming around to the rudder the problem was obvious, the drive shaft had come right out of the transmission. Roughly the size and weight of an olympic barbell, the drive shaft was close to sliding right out of *Aphrodite* and dropping to the bottom like one of the many doomed African slaves years ago. The only thing preventing this catastrophe was the propeller at the end of the shaft that was hitting the rudder. The noise we heard was the propeller smacking into the fiberglass as the water forced the blades to turn. If we lost the drive shaft we would be without an engine and at the complete mercy of the currents and winds approaching the reef surrounding the Seychelles.

I shouted to Lewis and Peter to go inside the engine compartment to have a look. Pushing from the outside we managed to slide the prop shaft back though the housing into the engine compartment. Peter then secured the shaft back into place with a bolt and some 'loctite' to prevent it from happening again.

It's 0200, I have just checked the prop shaft, it is

holding well. I have two hours left on my watch before I can go to bed. The wind is howling at thirty-three knots and the rain is coming down in bucketfuls. I have gathered as much fresh water as I can and have taken three freshwater showers! The rain is blown by the strong wind and comes down in sheets, it is so heavy that I can only see forty feet around *Aphrodite*, the world beyond is hidden by the rain and darkness.

The radar is spinning in its case to scan the ocean but is little help. The storm is so heavy it looks like an island in the middle of the green illuminated screen, we are sailing blind. Any ships within a three-mile radius will not show up.

We had radio contact with a cargo vessel early today, the first for weeks. The skipper sounded like Gandhi, the cargo was being taken to Sri Lanka, the tear drop island off the southeast coast of India. They had steamed around The Cape of Good Hope from Brazil and had reasonable weather along the way. We were not in a major shipping lane but should expect more traffic now we are closer to Africa. Freighters coming from the Red Sea or around the Cape of Good Hope may well cross our path.

05° 44.0' S
56° 12.2' E
321° - Day 88

I am filled with anxiety once again. We have only one hundred miles to go, our arrival in the Seychelles will mark the end of our passage across the Indian Ocean and the beginning of our journey north towards the Mediterranean Sea. We had radio contact earlier with a yacht from the Seychelles fishing around the reef who warned us of the one hundred dollars a day harbor fee. If he's right we will only be staying a couple of days to refuel before we head out, let's hope he's wrong because we all need some time away from *Aphrodite* and each other.

It's a fabulous day with clear blue skies, a refreshing breeze from the southeast and a twenty-pound tuna for lunch! The silver lure I threw over the back of the boat had done a good job. I fed out a hundred feet of line in the morning and forgot about it. It was not until Lewis started yelling and pointing to the rubber cord holding the line to the railing that I even noticed. The black elastic was stretched almost to the point of breaking, jerking back and forth as the fish on the end of the line struggled to get away. The ten minutes of reeling in the tuna by hand on a large plastic reel was hard work but worth the effort. It was such a momentous occasion, being the first "proper" fish we have caught so far, Peter recorded it all on video.

Lewis helped me cut the giant carcass into fillets. The dark meat was as red and tender as the steaks Ian cooked on the grill back in Duke's Bistro. We froze most of it, the rest we will eat for lunch in a few minutes and barbecue tomorrow on the grill when we are anchored in Mahé.

04° 47.2' S
55° 34.2' E
019° - Day 89

It's Monday morning, October 3rd, 1994. We have another four hours before we will step on dry land, but we can already see the reputed site of the Garden of Eden framed by blue sky in front of us. We have the yellow Q flag flying from the spreader and have already made radio contact with the authorities to warn them of our arrival. To enter the anchorage we are approaching the island from the south and will sail up its fifteen-mile length before we round the tiny island of St. Anne to head south into the enclosed harbor.

I have been up for most of the night. My watch was from 0300-0600 but I was too excited to sleep and decided to stay up with Peter as we approached the island to keep him company. There are numerous boats of all shapes and sizes around the islands, most of them fishing. A motor vessel full of tourists cut across our bow, if we hadn't changed our heading by thirty degrees it would have been a close call. The bastard hadn't even seen us until he past. He radioed to apologize.

"Pardon monsieur, I deed not see your vessel!"

An airplane dropped out of the clear blue sky and seemed to land right in the harbor as it disappeared out of sight behind the mountains, probably loaded with more tourists. I think Adam and Eve would be most upset if they could see their paradise on earth now.

Although the tourist industry is said to be kept under control to preserve the unique wildlife and unspoiled forests of these islands, it's hard to imagine, surrounded by so many people, that it hasn't had a destructive effect. Maybe I'm just not used to civilization after fifty-one days of relative seclusion.

Along with the spectacular reefs and scenery, the giant land tortoise, tropical birds, unique wildlife and the Coco de Mer palms are the main attractions for tourists. The population is eighty-five thousand, the Seychellois are a mixture of African, Asian and European origin. French and English are the official languages but Créole is spoken by most.

The Coco de Mer palms have been said to be over eight hundred years old. The giant Coco de Mer nut is the largest seed in the vegetable kingdom and can only be found in the Seychelles. Many years ago, when sailors found these strange looking coconuts washed up on far away shores it was thought they came from the ocean. To add to the enigmatical quality of the Coco de Mer nut, they resemble the sex of a women and have mystical qualities associated with them. The two halves of the nut join together to produce perfectly formed buttocks. Coarse coconut hair and folds in the middle of the nut make the resemblance to a woman's sex unmistakable.

We should be anchored by lunchtime but have the authorities to look forward to first. All our paperwork has been collected and is ready for approval. Our firearms, spearguns and ammunition have been pulled out of storage as customs will insist that they are housed in a lock-up during our stay.

Victoria on Mahé, is the capital of the Seychelles where the majority of the population resides. The surrounding one hundred and fifteen islands, including one of the world's largest atolls, Aldabra, are scattered over a thirty-mile radius.

The yacht club in Victoria is said to be well equipped for cruisers, with hot showers, a bar and lunch buffet. A yacht anchored in Victoria heard our conversation with the authorities and radioed to warn us of the reef approaching the anchorage. A million-dollar catamaran sank after hitting it a few weeks ago.

Peter is going through his usual pre-authority jitters. Drinking his Emu beers he seems nervous waiting for the harbormaster to guide us into the quarantine area. We had a little difficulty figuring out where we were supposed to go. After three attempts we were told to stay where we were, they we sending someone out to get us!

When the immigration and customs officers came aboard wearing clean pressed uniforms buttoned to the neck we knew they meant business. Their white starched shirts stood out in contrast to their dark jackets and even darker skin, these were African men. Unlike our friend

Alan from Chagos, we felt that offering a beer to these chaps may not be considered proper and decided a soda or water would be more appropriate. We sat around the table in the saloon going over passports, the ships documents and crew lists. Peter was having a difficult time filling out the forms that the officers were piling up for him to sign and complete. His hands were shaking to the point where they were unable to read his writing. The officers kept asking him to translate his scribbles, this only made him more nervous and his writing more erratic. Finally Peter gave up and asked me if I would finish completing all the forms for him, he made me captain of *Aphrodite* and went up to the cockpit for some fresh air and a cigarette to calm his nerves.

When all the crew lists and immigration documents had finally been approved the customs officer asked us if we had any weapons on board. As we laid our arsenal on the table it was obvious by their reaction that they had not expecting such a supply of arms. The shotgun and .308 rifle were stored in expensive leather gunbags and each had a hundred rounds of ammunition, the two spearguns had powerful elastic bands and the three foot spears had razor sharp trident tips attached to the ends of them. They must have thought we were mercenaries preparing a coup.

Shifting nervously from one foot to the other the customs officer carefully unzipped the .308 bag as if it contained a venomous snake that might strike at him if he was careless. He reached inside and slowly pulled out the rifle, the other officers shuffled in closer to get a better look. Handling the rifle with exaggerated care he looked as nervous as Lewis did when he first saw them in Darwin.

"Ees eet lowded?" He asked.

"No, no it's not," Peter stammered. "The ammunition is in the boxes."

The temperature inside the cabin was ninety-five

degrees. Peter, Lewis and myself were sweating buckets in the heat. The officers, in the full uniforms did not seem at all bothered by the sauna-like atmosphere and continued to handle the rifle without even breaking a sweat. We tediously documented all the weapons, the make, model and identification numbers. They insisted in taking all the individual cartridges out of the boxes and counting each round carefully. The last box had four cartridges missing.

"Where are deese boolets?" The customs man ordered.

"Well 'er, we 'er shot off a few rounds." Peter was close to fainting under the questioning.

"Why?"

"Testing the rifles." I stepped in. "When we left Australian waters we each fired a round. We have kept the spent cartridges." The last thing we wanted to tell them was that we had fired our high-powered rifle at a fishing boat in the Timor Sea that we had suspected were pirates.

All the weapons were gathered and placed in the customs boat that was carefully guarded by a third man. I had a strange feeling that Peter would never see his rifles again.

"We would like to search da boat now please."

This was getting ridiculous. I admit we looked like bandits, dirty and unshaven but did we really need to be searched? Arguing would have only delayed it and would have made us look guilty so we let them get on with it.

We watched the three officers conduct their "extensive" search for more weapons or drugs, no pillow or cushion was left unturned, no cupboard was not glanced in, after two minutes of looking in the saloon area they continued the search for our stash of illegal contraband in Peter's cabin. One of the officers found a Rambo style hunting knife in the closet. His face broke into a huge white smile as if he had caught us red handed and the months of training he had endured to become a customs officer had paid off.

"Why do you have dis?" He asked feeling the edge of the blade with his thumb.

"It's just a knife." Peter shrugged.

"Please keep da knife on da boat, or we will have it confiscated!"

We watched the customs boat motor away with our arsenal of guns. Neville John Grey in Townsville had told me that he never carried weapons on board simply because it's always a pain in the ass each time you anchor in foreign countries. He preferred to have a couple of flare guns that are permitted without a license and can be just as effective at close range. George told me back in Cocos that he threw his shotgun in the Red Sea because he couldn't bear to go through the administrative bullshit again. I doubt very much Peter would be willing to part with his rifles though.

With final clearance approved we motored into the enclosed marina and dropped anchor, on the second attempt it bit deep into the muddy bottom and held fast. We began our pre-launch ritual of blowing up the inflatable and attaching the outboard that we keep fastened to the stern railing, covering the main sail, putting up the canopy over the boom to shade the cockpit, dropping the ladder over the side, tying up the fenders, storing away all the winch handles and clearing the deck of any rope. As the holding is secure we will all be going ashore.

After replacing a blown bulb up the mast, Lewis is going to mark our arrival on the West Side of the Indian Ocean by doing a celebratory dive off the top set of spreaders into the harbor.

Djibouti, our next port of call in Africa, has become a milestone for Lewis and I as it marks the end of one major leg in our journey and the beginning of another, the Red Sea. Substituting the words from Eric Clapton's *Alberta* with Djibouti or isn't it a "Djiboutiful" day, Lewis and I have quite the laugh integrating the word into our conversations. Yelling Djibouti across the harbor at the top of his lungs and diving off the mast thirty-feet above the dirty harbor water Peter thought was a "stupid move" but recorded it anyway. The loud slap as Lewis struck the water belly first marked our arrival. We had made it across the Indian Ocean.

The Seychelles, Mahé - Day 90

At first light we made a beeline straight to the post office to collect the valuable mail we were all praying had been sent by family and friends. We each had a couple of letters, Peter from his family, Lewis from his and his ex-girlfriend, me from my parents and Andy but nothing from Catherine! As much as I loved the letters that were sent, the one person that I needed to hear from the most had not written. I checked with the lady behind the counter for a second time to make sure that it was not being held under the name of the yacht, a common practice for sailors, but she just smiled sympathetically and shook her head. By my desperation she understood what I was searching for.

We stood on the steps of the post office for five minutes and quickly read the letters that had been sent. We would all read the letters again, probably more than once, this was just a quick fix until we got back to the boat. I was half way through Andy's letter when I was tapped on the shoulder.

"Hey, asshole, wanna fight?"

I was so shocked I just turned and looked at the man with a puzzled expression on my face, did I hear him right?

"I said wanna fight?"

185

I did hear him right, what the hell was this? I have been on dry land for less than a day and some black guy looking like Frank Bruno wants to fight me? I ignored his request and kept reading my letters, thinking that probably he would lose interest and wander off.

"Wanna fight?!"

Realizing that the quiet approach was not going to work I thanked him for the offer and told him that I was reading a letter from a dear friend and that I did not want to fight.

The poor bloke looked quite upset when I turned him down and wandered off muttering to himself, probably to search for a more reactive opponent.

Ninety per cent of the Seychellois live on Mahé, as we walked through Victoria it was obvious that most of the locals relied heavily on the tourist dollars that come in each year. The small town center was filled with stores selling African carvings, beautiful seashells, t-shirts, beachwear and of course the Coco de Mer nut. It seemed that everywhere we turned the Coco de Mer was mooning at us. From real nuts the size of watermelons to tiny key ring replicas, the Coco de Mer is unique to the Seychelles and is taken full advantage of in all the holiday memorabilia.

Peter and I made our way into the supermarket in search of food while Lewis went off to explore the other shops. Walking around the rows of empty shelves it became immediately apparent that our list which included plum pudding, custard, muesli, rice cakes and peanut butter was a little optimistic and would have to be rethought. There was very little fresh produce, and what was there was rotten. The area seemed to be busy with local women waiting for something. Maybe a fresh order was coming in? Peter and I decided to hang around to see what delights would be brought out for us.

The ladies obviously knew the drill and positioned themselves to get ready. The man wheeled a shopping cart into a clear area and promptly stepped away. It reminded me of a scrummage when I was used to play rugby at Mountbatten secondary school in England, only much fiercer. The ladies shoved and pushed each other aside to get the best selection. When the scrummage was over and the ladies had left we peered inside the now almost empty shopping cart. Only a few onions remained, onions! All that for a just few onions?

We left the supermarket empty-handed and met Lewis outside. Munching on a giant juicy cucumber, Lewis seemed to have had better luck in his quest for fresh produce than we did. He told us he found a market down one of the side roads where there seemed to be plenty of fruit and vegetables. Peter had had enough and said he was heading back to the boat, I think he was missing his family and wanted to read their letters in private, Lewis and I marched off down Market Street.

The market was set up in a dirt clearing off the side of the road. Wooden tables were piled high with mounds of cabbages, lettuce, cucumbers and other green vegetables that spilled over onto the dusty floor. One table was covered in blood and giant fish heads. The flies liked this table the most and a black cloud seemed to hover over it like a rainsquall. Trying to feed off the congealed blood and entrails left on the stained table, the flies fought over each other and the palm tree leaves that swatted them away every few seconds. The dry air was saturated with hundreds of different scents. Vegetables, herbs, spices, teas, blood and the unmistakable stench of rotting food all mingled together to fill the enclosed area.

Lewis and I were like two kids in a candy shop. Although it was too late to buy any large quantities of food we treated ourselves to a cabbage, a cucumber and two tomatoes for supper. We were going to wait until the last day to buy our supplies, if we bought too much now it would only spoil by the time we leave.

As we walked back through the quiet streets of Victoria the locals were packing up their t-shirts, nuts, beach towels and heading for home. The woodcarvings that were being carefully wrapped in towels and placed in a wicker basket caught my attention. Although all these sculptures were mass produced to appeal to the average tourist and probably far removed from their original designs, they still resonate strength and emotions to me. The hunters, unity bowls, elephants and masks each tell a story. The sculptures represent a particular tribe and their guardians, religion, social and spiritual beliefs. The carvings were sent over from Kenya and probably only originally purchased for pennies.

"Hey American, you like? I give you good price!" The man packing them away saw me looking and reeled me in for a sale, he had no idea what he was in for.

"How much for this one?" I asked, pointing to the charging bull.

The elephant was magnificent. The bull's ears were flared and it's giant ivory tusks on either side of his trunk were held out like a lance ready to spear his assailant. The detail in the carving was superb, the skin showed the creases and cracks of the old bull's dry hide, the knuckles of his bony spine ran along the elephants back and the expression in the bull's eyes captured his anger.

"I give you this for," he hesitated as if to figure out how much I could afford and how gullible I would be, "two thousand rupee!"

He picked it up and handed it to me, a popular technique. If I had it in my hands it was as if I had accepted the deal.

"Look at the detail master, that is good price," he added.

It probably would have cost twice that if I bought it in New York at one of the ethnic stores in the village, but this was Africa and barter was allowed.

"Two thousand rupee?" I put the back of my hand to my forehead and rolled my eyes in their sockets, swaying on my feet as if the price was so unbelievably high I was going to faint. His black face opened up into a huge white smile, I was playing the game and the theatrics were appreciated.

Bartering is an art and like a chess game takes time, patience and skill to win over your opponent.

I put the sculpture down on the table with exaggerated care as if it were so expensive I could not risk damaging it and slowly backed away from the table.

"I am just a poor traveling man and cannot afford that, but thank you."

As I turned to walk away he picked it up and handed it to me again. "How much you pay?"

I studied the sculpture carefully, turning it in my hands making 'mmmm' noises as I thought out my next move.

"Two hundred rupee," that was about forty dollars.

He imitated my fainting, "You do not understand master, this is hand carved, it takes many, many weeks to create such a masterpiece, I give it to you for eighteen hundred, there take it, it's yours!"

Before I went to the stall I put four hundred rupee in my front pocket and left the rest in my wallet. I took the handful of crumpled bills out of my pocket. "This is all I have," I told him shrugging.

Again he stopped me, "One thousand rupee!"

"If I had it I would buy it my friend, but this is all I have," holding the notes out towards him like bait, I was using his trick now. I went to put the money back in my pocket.

"Here, it is yours!" he said, huffing and tutting as if I

had just robbed him. He was closing up for the day and it was always good to make that one last sale. I doubt very much I could have bought it for four hundred SR at the beginning of the day.

Lewis and I walked back towards the yacht club with our shopping and my new prized possession. The night air was warm and dusty, the bars were already open and serving cool beer to the tourists sitting on the balcony eating their hamburgers with fries. Life seemed hard for the locals here. Unemployment is said to be high and efforts are being made to raise the standard of living. The local copra and cinnamon industries have declined in recent years, the Seychelles economy now relies heavily on the tourist industry. Major hotels have already been built in Mahé. I fear it will only be a matter of time before the tourist industry is not so well monitored and takes over like so many of the once unspoiled tropical islands in the Caribbean or Pacific.

It was already dark by the time Lewis and I arrived back at the club. On the third call we managed to get Peter on the VHF radio on channel sixteen and asked him to collect us from the jetty.

By the look of him when he collected us it was obvious that he had already drank his way through most of the last Emu beers. He seemed upset that we had asked him to collect us and wanted to make it a rule that if we got back after a certain time he would not be responsible for collecting us.

"Peter, it's only eight o'clock, what's the problem?" I asked.

"I just feel as though I am the one that is always making the effort, and I am fed up with it!"

The Seychelles, Mahé - Day 91

We all have a lot of work ahead of us to stock the boat with fresh supplies for the trip up the coast of Africa to Djiboutiful! Along with a few minor repairs, the next three days will be full with cleaning and preparations. Lewis is in good form as he has already spoken to his parents and checked on his dog Monte, and Peter seems more relaxed now that he has spoken to his family. I have left a message for Catherine and am waiting for her to call and fax her letters. I seem to spend most of my time thinking about her. If only we could talk for just a few minutes I know it would put my mind at rest.

I am looking forward to starting this day with a run, it's been over three months since I have exercised my legs. Wearing just a pair of running shorts and my trainers I headed off in the early morning before the sun was too high in the sky. Just half a mile from the yacht club it became painfully clear to me just how much my endurance has suffered over the last three months. Wheezing and holding the painful stitch on my side I persevered and continued east along the shore, heading toward the international airport that was built twenty-two years ago. Even though it was early, the temperature was already well over eighty degrees and rapidly getting hotter.

The island's mountains were covered in a thick blanket of green vegetation. At the base of the hills was a turquoise lagoon that was formed when a road was built on re-claimed land by the army. The still water inside the lagoon is joined to the ocean on the other side of the road by giant corrugated drainage pipes. Fisherman that used to live on the ocean shore now have to paddle across the lagoon in their kayaks and under the road through the pipes to begin their day of fishing.

When I returned from my run I felt rejuvenated and

ready to begin the day of chores. The five miles had spent the tension that had been building up inside of me. *Aphrodite*, as much as she is loved had become our prison on the long passages. This was my time, and I was going to use it well.

The freshwater shower I had after my run ranks close to the top of my list of pleasurable experiences. It had been almost two months since I last had the luxury of a proper shower without worrying about dropping the soap and chasing it around the deck or losing the shower bucket! I felt reborn when I walked out of the men's changing room, the salt that had coated my body for weeks and matted my hair was washed away leaving me feeling ten pounds lighter.

Our morning was full and there was not much time to rest and take in the scenery or chat with the locals. By the early afternoon Peter had organized the fuel while Lewis and I had bought the first batch of food supplies. We spent most of the morning in the supermarkets and bought whatever tinned or boxed foods were available. We wanted some potatoes but discovered that they are not grown locally and are flown in from Africa. We arranged with one of the stalls to buy their sack of spuds when the supplies came in. A bag of fresh potatoes will last us through to the Mediterranean and would complement the heaps of burgers we still have left, when the meat was gone they will be a welcome change or addition to our pasta dishes.

After buying two reggae tapes from a music store that only seemed to sell illegal copies made from originals my funds were almost completely exhausted. All the money that I had reserved for the second half of the trip I spent in Darwin on my share of the EPIRB. Lewis said that he would lend me whatever I needed for the rest of the journey. I promised that as soon as I got back to England I would mail him a check.

My savings account has just over two thousand pounds in it. I am trying to reserve that money so I can buy my ticket to America and start a new life. If I spent too much of it now I may find myself with barely enough money to cover the flight, let alone set myself up in a new country. It's strange, I have under one hundred dollars on me, only another couple of thousand to my name. I sold my car to raise the money I needed to leave England and travel around Australia. I do not own an apartment, I am unemployed and my future is filled with uncertainty, yet I have never been happier.

Before I started traveling I wasted hours of my life each week, worrying about how much money I was making, how much money I wanted to make and all the things I could buy with that money. I would still like to have certain things, and more money in the bank for a rainy day but the difference now is that I do not worry about it, it seems like such a waste of my time when I have more important things to think about and discover. Someone once told me, in life eighty per cent of what you worry about never happens. Fifteen per cent of what you worry about happens but is never as bad as you thought it would be. Only five per cent of what you worry about actually happens and worrying about it never helped it from not happening. In a way it seems like the more money you have the less freedom you get, quite the opposite to what most people think.

When we got back to the yacht club the harbormaster told me I had a fax from Catherine and that she would call me tomorrow morning at nine. There were five wonderful pages for me to read, this was what was most important to me. I read them in minutes. She was working hard but could not wait to see me again and to begin our lives together. Knowing that she missed me and was miserable without me made me feel a lot better.

I spent the rest of the afternoon with Lewis and Peter standing in the inflatable scrubbing down the hull of *Aphrodite*, washing her decks and polishing the chrome railing. The tobacco stains had been scrubbed from the cockpit and the coconut shavings washed from the deck. By the time we finished the white and blue fiberglass gleamed under the sunlight and the chrome sparkled like stars. Peter looked happy as *Aphrodite* was once again restored to her former beauty, the cabin area however was not quite as well kept.

Strands of tobacco had collected in piles in most of the corners of the galley, I told Peter that he should carefully gather them together as I was sure he could roll at least half a dozen cigarettes from them, by the look on his face he was actually considering it! The white ceiling above the stove was coated in black soot from the meth that is used to heat the burners. The wooden floor in the galley was scratched and dented by falling tin cans and pots. Even though most of the cabin area was newly installed not long before the trip it already looked lived in and worn out. Peter said that when his wife sees the state of the boat in Italy, she's going to flip out.

Peter had spent a great deal of money getting the boat ready for the journey, he had new floors put in, the hull sprayed, a new turbo diesel installed, new navigational equipment, cushions, trim and a new main sail. Peter is not one to do things by halves, I think that is why he is so successful in business. He was advised to wait until after the journey before he sprayed the hull, to do it before was like spraying a car before you drove around Australia for two years. That was not good enough for Peter, if he was going to live out a lifelong dream he wanted to do it in style. He told me that the boat is not insured, to insure a yacht for world cruising costs many thousands of dollars, if *Aphrodite* went down Peter would have no compensation. He also explained to me an interesting Australian law that prohibits anyone from owning their yacht or power boat exclusively. The Australian government owns a small percentage of every sea faring vessel in Australia. If there was ever the need for the use of Peter's precious *Aphrodite* by Australia he would have to hand her over.

After two very sweaty hours of cleaning, scraping, stacking, dusting, waxing and polishing the main cabin area was once again declared fit for living in, the captain's quarters however, needed a little more attention. Lewis and I left that up to Peter as he seemed to be immune to the unmistakable odor of sweaty armpits, stale farts, beer and tobacco. We wished him luck and watched him disappear into darkness. I offered to tie a harness around his waist.

"If you get into trouble Peter, pull hard on the rope twice and Lewis and I will drag you back to safety." He did not laugh at the joke.

By the end of the day we had all had enough of each other's company and needed time alone. Peter stayed on the boat, Lewis went for a walk and I decided to go for another jog before it got dark. When I returned an hour later I met Lewis in the yacht club, he introduced me to his new friend. Brian was wearing a white T-shirt with the word 'Scotland' printed proudly on the front in large colorful lettering.

"Don't yoo find it just a wee bit hot t'be runnin' around outside t'day lad?"

Brian introduced himself with a thick Scottish accent, he had large tattooed forearms that reminded me of Bluto in Popeye. He bought me a beer and asked me to join them. Brian was a 'brickie' and was visiting the Seychelles looking for his plot in paradise. Working in construction, he spent his time between Africa, Mauritius and the Seychelles.

"Aye, they're beautiful islands ye know, I kanny wait t'settle doon here."

We talked for most of the evening, Peter joined us after he had finished fumigating his cabin, we were all in a better mood because of the few hours we had away from each other. When Brian asked us if we had any difficulties spending so much time together on such a small boat we all just looked at each other.

"It's like yoo all got married or something don't ye think?"

When it was time for Brian to leave he offered to take us all on a 'wee trip' around the island tomorrow and arranged to meet us outside the yacht club at nine thirty.

The Seychelles, Mahé - Day 92

Catherine called at five minutes past nine. She was fighting with Sterling trying to make her eat her supper. Every third or forth word was interrupted by Catherine telling her to 'put that down', 'sit round to the table' or 'do not make me count to three, one, two...'" She admitted to me that she had never reached three before, just the threat alone and the thought of the terrible 'three' was enough to make her sit up straight and keep her elbows off the table. Catherine had her hands full and sounded tired.

Because Catherine was giving me her attention, Sterling soon wanted to speak to me and kept insisting that she had something 'really important' to tell me. Catherine would not surrender to her demands and said that she would meet me soon enough when I came to visit. The conversation was hurried and Catherine soon had to go., "I love you," she said, Sterling made a loud 'ooooo' noise in the background and started to sing, "Catherine and Neville sittin' in a tree, K. I. S. S. I. N. G., first comes love then comes marriage..."

"I love you too, speak to you tomorrow?"

"I will call you the same time."

Brian picked us up in his rented Mini Moke and we headed south along the eastern side of the island. As we passed the airport Brian pointed out Ringo Star's private jet.

"He comes here a lot ye know. Wilbur Smith is also in the Seychelles right now on Cerf Island!"

Half a mile past the airport Brian pointed to the lagoon on the other side of the road where the sea once met the mainland. An old, one hundred and fifty foot schooner had become grounded many years ago and was permanently imprisoned when the army reclaimed the land by building the road. Her three white masts stood out against the dark vegetation and pointed towards the sky like a shrine. Her reflection in the flat green waters of the lagoon gave her an eerie appearance of a ghost ship. Now shielded from the swell the giant yacht sits sheltered from the sea she once battled with. Her proud and sturdy lines revealed a boat that had probably crossed many oceans but was now rotting in the mud. She would never feel the wind in her rigging or sail in the open ocean again. It was as though her soul would never be able to escape and would remain trapped in the shallow water for eternity. For a sailor there is no sight more disturbing than that of a once great ship disabled and grounded, it was the end of a life.

We drove in silence along the coast for another five minutes before Brian swung the Moke onto a road that led into the heart of the island. The tiny car that was little more than an engine and four seats bolted to a chassis trundled along struggling to make the grade as we drove into the jungle. There are only a few major roads in Mahé, one that circles the island at the base of the mountains and a couple that run over the mountains through the heart of the jungle.

Brian was the perfect tour guide. He seemed to enjoy sharing his knowledge of the Seychelles and to have someone to talk to. The highest point on Mahé is just under three thousand feet, the middle of the island is a series of valleys filled with vegetation. Small houses and shacks are nestled away amongst the trees and peer out like hiding animals. Eventually we got off the main road and drove up a dirt road into the jungle. The vegetation grew right up to the tire tracks on both sides and the Mini Moke just managed to squeeze through in a couple of places. The dusty road kept winding its way through the jungle and eventually came to a small clearing.

The area was littered with rubbish and junk but Brian had grand ideas about building a luxury home that would someday overlook the western side of the island and the sparkling ocean below. An old white Ford Cortina, stripped and rusted, sat on its suspension. The wheels were inside the car along with most of the engine. A corrugated sheet of rusty steel was supported by a rickety frame of branches and provided the only shelter in the clearing. We were watched the entire time we were there by a skinny brown cow that was chained to a palm tree and was hiding behind a pile of trash. Beyond the clearing the jungle took over again with walls of green vegetation reaching over one hundred feet above the dry soil. It must have taken many days to clear just this small area, I did not envy Brian and the task he had of clearing the jungle to lay a foundation to build his new home.

For lunch we stopped off at one of the swanky hotels on the coast for lunch and pretended we were guests and swam in their pool for the rest of the afternoon. On the way back to the yacht club we drove past what looked to be like an architectural dig. Brian said the government had claimed they had found an old pirate map that indicated that treasure was buried on the site. Most of the locals that

Brian has spoken to said it was a load of crap and was just a ploy to drum up interest in the islands, get free publicity and increase tourist dollars, he said that they have been digging for a few weeks and have yet to find any treasure.

We were dropped off at the marina and arranged to see Brian tomorrow for lunch and have promised to give him a tour of *Aphrodite* before we leave. When we got back to *Aphrodite* I gathered my drawing materials and sat on the end of the marina to spend some time alone and sketch.

It was one of those perfect tropical evenings, the sky glowed bright red with a final spectacular burst of color before the sun disappears to the west. The gentle breeze blew down from the mountains, stirring the ancient Coco de Mer palm, rustling the leaves and cooling the night air. The yacht club was quietly buzzing with the chatter of locals and sailors ending the day with a cold beer from the bar. I felt as content as I have ever felt before, sitting alone on the marina with my sketchbook on my lap and my feet swinging over the end of the pontoon.

My most recent addition to my sketchbook is one of my best. The quote reads, "Discovering who you are takes a lot longer than you think." The image is of an old man holding between his thumb and forefinger a puzzle piece. He is focusing on it with all his effort. The deep creases in his forehead and weathered face tell a story of a man that has traveled down a long and tiring road and has almost reached the end of his journey. The old man is made up of thousands of pieces of puzzle. Each piece has been carefully studied and then put into place to form another part of himself. The old man has almost finished but time is no longer on his side, the top of his head and part of the left side of his face still needs to be pieced together. Studying the last few pieces, the man has spent a lifetime trying to figure out who he is and what he wants. His one last wish is that he discovers himself before it is too late, he knows that he will never have another chance.

The Seychelles, Mahé - Day 93

As we leave tomorrow morning we have already gained clearance from immigration and will collect our weapons from customs tonight. They made such a fuss about us having the rifles when we arrived but cannot be bothered to deliver them back to the boat and have asked us to collect them.

I made a trip to the hospital after breakfast to have my nails looked at, Lewis came along to keep me company and to spend as much time away from Peter as possible. The more time Lewis and I spend together the better we seem to get on, quite the opposite to Peter. Over the last three months I am happy to call Lewis my friend, we have shared a great deal together. Peter is a good man but he is just so different from Lewis and me, it is hard work spending any great amount of time with him.

When we got to the hospital I was scolded by a very big and serious nurse that I was not drinking enough water and that my nails had turned white because I had serious calcium deficiency. "Drink more!" she demanded, pointing at me like I was a disobedient child. She took pity on me and gave me a handful of calcium pills before sending me on my way.

I returned to the boat to see if Peter needed a hand with anything while Lewis decided to spend the rest of the day by himself. Peter was upset with Lewis for wandering off and complained to me about him for the rest of the afternoon.

Brian came aboard for lunch and seemed to enjoy the

tour around *Aphrodite*. He stood at the helm and looked out across the harbor, imagining what it would feel like to be at sea. By mid afternoon Brian had left and Lewis was still nowhere to be seen. Peter and I walked to the customs office at 1600 to collect the weapons. When the officer pulled them out of the locker and put the bags on the table Peter's face turned bright red with anger.

"What the hell did you do to them?" he shouted.

The officer did not reply and just looked at Peter with a blank expression.

"Look at the cases they're all covered in glue and tape, do you know how much they cost?"

"You can clean them with a bit of polish man, it's no problem," the officer said with shrug.

The .308 rifle and shotgun case had been wrapped in duct tape to prevent anyone from removing the weapons. Peter was quite upset and argued with the officer for ten minutes, I waited outside.

I spent the rest of the evening laying down in the cockpit reading Catherine's fax for the sixth time. I fell asleep by nine o'clock with the sheets of paper on my chest.

The Seychelles, Mahé - Day 94

Lewis and I walked to the markets early to collect our sack of spuds. The locals were just setting up, getting ready for another day in paradise. Lewis was well rested and in good form after having a day to himself and away from Peter. He had spent it wandering around town talking to the locals, I envied him. We met our buddy at the stall and picked up his only bag of potatoes. He had hidden the sack under his table, afraid that if the locals saw it he would not have been able to hold them for us. Because they are flown in from Africa, potatoes seem to be a prized vegetable in the Seychelles. Walking back to the yacht club with a sack of potatoes slung over my shoulder and a sack of onions over Lewis', we had the locals staring at us with envy, we were both relieved to get them back to the boat.

I saw 'Frank Bruno' outside the post office again as we carted the heavy bags back to the marina. He was shouting at a family of tourists this time. The two small children cowered behind their parents legs as mom and dad looked at the man with the same confused expression I had. I wanted to tell them not to worry and that it was not personal but the bags were heavy and we were leaving in half an hour.

We threw the sacks in the captain's head, that was the only dark space left on the boat large enough to hold them. All the cupboards were loaded with fresh supplies and the water and fuel tanks full to the brim, we were set to go.

With final clearance we motored out of the marina and joined half a dozen fishing boats heading to sea, we were the only one bound for Djibouti.

6
Seychelles to Djibouti

(1,672.5 nautical miles)

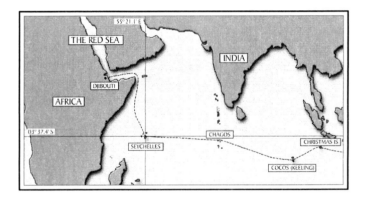

6

Seychelles to Djibouti

03° 37.4' S
55° 21.1' E
310° - Day 95

This is the longest leg on our journey. Over sixteen
hundred miles away, around the Horn of Africa, nestled at
the very western end of the Gulf of Aden, is Djibouti. This
passage will take us out of the Indian Ocean and into new
and unpredictable waters. Over the last six weeks we have
all come to know the Indian Ocean well, apart from the
days of unsettled wind, she has been good to us, the trade
winds have been fair and the sailing conditions almost
perfect. Our first ocean crossing experience has been a
success. Leaving her waters behind and venturing into the
new is making me unsettled and nervous.

Every sea has its own personality and reputation. With
careful planning the Indian Ocean offers steady trade
winds and ideal cruising conditions. The Gulf of Aden,
although almost five hundred miles in length will feel like
a harbor after the last seven weeks in the expanse of ocean.
The one thousand three hundred miles of Red Sea to Port
Suez will undoubtedly be the most challenging leg of our
entire journey, we all know this and are prepared for the
worst. Reaching the Mediterranean after battling against
the northerly winds of the Red Sea will make the final
twelve hundred miles to Italy a time to relax and wind

down. Although the Mediterranean has a reputation of blowing hard or not at all, being so close to our final destination will make it feel like the journey is over. We have been lucky so far, but I am sensing somewhere along the way we will have to pay for our good fortune and suffer just a little.

It seems the further along this journey we travel the harder and more challenging everything is becoming, we will need to rely on each other more than ever before. The cyclone that has been building strength two hundred miles south of us is making me anxious and we only have another couple of weeks before the northwest monsoon prevails. It is important we are in the Gulf of Aden before the wind changes, but we have the doldrums to contend with first. We have anticipated sailing through this dead zone and have filled our diesel tanks to the brim, the last thing we want to do is motor up the coast of Africa but we do not have the luxury of time and need to press on.

The other sailors we met and a few of the locals all warned us of the weather they thought we would experience. Everyone had an opinion, some said there would be gale force winds while others swore we would have no wind at all, I guess there is only one way we are going to find out. We are nearing the Equator, and for now still have favorable winds, for every day that we do I will be thanking whoever is responsible.

The light breeze is heavy with humidity and the sea is calm. We are keeping a much closer eye on the barometer now that the seasons are close to changing. The weather fax hasn't been any use to us what so ever. We have been unable to get a clear reading since we left Australia. Although it hasn't really been necessary so far, it may prove to be invaluable in the weeks ahead.

Aphrodite looks as clean as she did when we left Middle Harbor Yacht Club in Sydney three months ago.

We scrubbed the hull and deck, greased the winches, stored away our supplies, serviced the engine, washed our laundry and cleaned, dusted and polished the cabin. I managed to speak with Catherine for a few precious minutes before we left today. She never did manage to fax her second letter so I will have to live off the sound of her voice for a few weeks.

02° 15.1' S
55° 17.4' E
304° - Day 96

O'Yaba is singing his heart out below with, *How good it is to be here.* The two tapes are alternated and are a welcome change from Tom Jones or Neil Diamond, I don't think its quite Peter's choice though. The fresh food we bought at the markets is making lunchtime a culinary feast and supplying our bodies with the much-needed nutrients and vitamins they craved. Bowls full with cabbage, rice, cheese, raisins, cucumbers, tomatoes and a sprinkle of herbs and olive oil are the perfect way to spend the early hours of the afternoon. The three of us sit under the shade of the main sail, munch on cabbage leaves, look out across the empty ocean and chat idly.

I think we have all come to accept our differences as nothing has been said about the most recent bouts of arguments and disagreements we had in port. We all know what has to be done and we all share at least one thing in common. No matter how difficult the relationship gets between the three of us the toast we made in Darwin remains our common bond.

We are only one hundred and thirty-five miles from the Equator where we will pass over the middle of the earth and cross over into the Northern Hemisphere. For

Peter and Lewis they will be leaving their half of the world and entering mine.

O'Yaba is doing a grand job summing up how we feel.

> Oh, how good it is to be here,
> Oh, how good it is to be here,
> Another day, la la la la la la,
> Oh, how good it is to be here,
> Oh, how good it is to be here...

We are averaging three to four knots in a six to ten knot breeze. The spinnaker is holding well and ballooning out in front of *Aphrodite* leading the way. We are still heading northwest as it's important that we take advantage of the Somali current that runs up the coast of Africa. Crossing the Equator at 51° 00' and catching the current, that may reach speeds of up to seven knots near Socatra Island, will help us to round Somalia and enter the Gulf before the new monsoon begins. Some yachts have recorded up to one hundred and seventy miles in a day with the current under their keel.

To make sure I drink more water, as ordered by the nurse, I bought some bottles of orange squash to add to each glass of stale tank water. The sun is hotter and appears bigger than it has been before. The heat feels like two giant hands wrapping around my body and wringing each drop of water out of me like a damp cloth. The wind is light and is providing little relief against the heat.

The dolphins swam with me during my watch tonight. They are becoming like old friends, I was happy to see them. For half an hour they surfed off our bow waves that pushed them in front of *Aphrodite*. Swimming under my feet they looked up at me with grinning faces, whistling and chirping as if trying to tell me something, they seemed happy to see me too. The family of fifteen dolphins played for half an hour, showing off and enjoying my attention.

They left me so suddenly, as though they were frightened and knew of some danger that I did not. As quickly as they had greeted me they disappeared in a blink of an eye leaving me feeling lonelier in the night without them. I strained my eyes, looking out into the dark ocean but there was no danger, no ships, no land, just water and black sky littered with a million stars.

Sitting on the very nose of *Aphrodite* with my feet skimming only inches away from the water and feeling the soft, warm wind over my body felt like I was dreaming. I imagined I was flying across the surface of the ocean in the night, gliding silently over the waves like a flying fish, it is a moment I shall never forget.

00° 55.2' S
52° 20.7' E
306° - Day 97

I dreamt last night we crossed the Equator, there was a checkpoint with an armed guard manning a barricade, he was holding an M-16 across his chest and put his hand out ordering us to stop. I wound down the window and stuck my head out to greet him. He asked to see our papers and looked inside suspiciously. He shone a flashlight in each of our faces to check we matched the pictures in the passports and finally waved us through using the barrel of his gun. As we passed under the barricade the spinnaker got snagged and tore, Peter started to yell and scream at the guard for not raising the pole high enough.

We have had the spinnaker up solidly for the last two days. The six-knot breeze is like a whisper across the ocean but has been consistent in helping us average three to four knots. We are just a stone's throw away from the Equator, if the winds stays with us we will crossover late tonight or early tomorrow morning. We have decided to mark this momentous occasion by bringing the sails down, jumping into the water and swimming across to the top half of the world. I have been secretly preparing for the celebration by putting my creative skills to good use and making party hats for each of us to wear for the celebratory dinner.

Lewis is brewing up another unique concoction for supper. He is mixing in a whole variety of spices and herbs into the tomato sauce. Peter has just finished yelling at him as he felt it was disgusting not only because Lewis was mixing in so many ingredients, but that he was tasting the sauce off the same spoon he was using for stirring. Lewis argued that the bubbling sauce would kill any germs and told Peter to lighten up. Peter whilst smoking, farting and generally oozing unpleasant odors from every pore continued to complain that it was not sanitary for Lewis to eat off the same spoon. I found it all rather ironic and could not help smiling to myself listening to the two of them argue like an old married couple.

00° 38.3' N
50° 41.0' E
356° - Day 99

We have made it to the top half of the world! We crossed over to the Northern Hemisphere at 2055 last night. We chickened out and decided pulling the sails down to jump overboard was not such a wonderful idea after all. The wind was filling them at five knots and the night around us was black, save for the stars in the sky. The party was not quite as wild as we all thought it would be. There was no red line dividing north from south, no mermaids to greet us and King Neptune never even made an appearance. The only indication that we had crossed over was the green glowing LED screen, which showed all zeros for our latitude. Disgusted by the anticlimax I went to bed early to catch a few hours of sleep before my watch. Peter stayed up to keep Lewis company and to smoke a couple more cigarettes, much to Lewis's disappointment.

Our nose is pointing due north for the first time since we sailed up the East Coast of Australia. We are racing to find the Somali current we have read so much about. It's only 1000 and already we have had a gift from King Neptune, a beautiful thirty pound Tuna. We have fresh muffins baking in the gimbal stove for a celebratory snack, and now fresh fish for lunch. Tonight I will bake a pizza and we all wash it down with a few glasses of wine. Not a bad first day in the northern world.

It's ninety-seven degrees with only a light wind blowing at four knots from the southwest to cool the tropical air. The surface of the ocean is rolling and gentle, lifting up and down like the chest of a sleeping giant. Although the Intertropical Convergence Zone (ITCZ) otherwise known as the doldrums, has a reputation for long calms, the region of no wind depends upon where you are crossing the Equator and the time of year. The charts indicate that an area of around three hundred miles may be affected where we are. The tropical storm season in the Arabian Sea has already begun and will continue through late November. We are sailing only a few hundred miles past this region and may well expect some rough weather as we approach the Gulf of Aden. Right now, as if sensing our desperation, the wind has taken pity on *Aphrodite* and has stayed with us.

Just before we sat down in the beer garden for our party I handed the hats out to Peter and Lewis who did not quite know what to make of them. Because of the limited raw materials on the boat I had to improvise. The top quarter of old plastic soda bottles served as the foundation for the hats. I garnished the tops with strips of tin foil that I stuffed down the nozzles and the white screw tops became the noses and eyes for the faces I drew on the sides. I punctured two holes in the base of the hats and threaded a piece of string through to act as an adjustable chin strap.

Peter set up the camcorder on the cabin roof under the splash deck and supported it with a few towels to record the party.

"Is that on now?" Lewis asked.

"Stuff me dead!" Peter complained still trying to fasten the party hat to his head.

"It's running? Oh shit my hair!" I joined in.

It was already turned on and recording our little soiree. Peter made his way to the beer garden complaining and cursing as he tried to secure half a coke bottle to the top of his head. Tom Jones was playing "I'm not responsible."

"The pizza looks great there big fella." Lewis said.

"Yea, the guy was half an hour late so we got it for free!"

The freshly baked pizza smelled delicious and was complimented by a chilled bottle of Rosemount Estate Chardonnay we bought specially for the occasion. When Peter had settled down I uncorked the wine and poured it into our little plastic mugs. Before Lewis and I even had a chance to raise our cups to make a toast Peter was gulping his down.

"Don't wait for us, just get it down ya." I said. "We're supposed to clink glasses and cross arms aren't we?"

We were having a great time laughing and joking about one another. The camera was holding well on the roof but wobbled occasionally with the swell.

"The camera man's drunk!" Lewis shouted. "Hey, King Neptune, steady that camera!"

"Who's going to win the crazy hat competition?" I asked.

We both looked at Peter and burst out laughing. He looked ridiculous. The string under his chin had pushed his ears out and the hat made his head look like a giant pineapple. His serious face made him look even sillier.

We munched on the pizza and joked the whole time.

"We do this every night by-the-way." I said to King Neptune. "It's not just because we've crossed the Equator. Some nights we even swap hats!"

"When customs come on board, we put our hats on." Lewis continued.

"That's right, they don't have any problems clearing us."

Peter did not make a contribution to the show and just sat there quietly while Lewis and I carried on. Eventually I think he had enough as he made a final toast and shut us down.

Later that evening when all the dishes had been cleaned away and shorts loosened to accommodate the pizza and wine we had swishing around in our stomachs we decided to end the party with one of our favorite songs.

"Welcome to Tom Jones Karaoke night, Catherine, this one's for you!"

With Tom Jones leading the way we cleared our throats and sang, "The greatest gifts in life are free."

Love is like candy on a shelf,
If you would like a taste then help yourself,
The sweetest things are there for you,
Help yourself, take a few,
That's what I want you to do.

213

We're always told repeatedly,
The greatest gifts in life are free,
I'm rich with love a millionaire,
I've so much, it's unfair,
Why don't you take a share...

Getting carried away as usual I turned my baseball cap around on my head and began rapping to the tune. Lewis joined in but Peter seemed to be upset by our sacrilegious behavior.

We all knew the words by heart but couldn't pull it off. Completely out of sync with Tom and even more out of tune we laughed at our feeble attempt and gave up, only picking up a few of the lines when we were not rolling around in hysterics.

02° 47.8' N
49° 47.3' E
343° - Day 100

I feel as though I have changed my life by the direction I am heading in and in doing so have become somebody new. From the moment I first stepped on the deck of *Aphrodite* I began the transformation. Now, one hundred days later I feel like a different man, each day brings new experiences, and with each experience comes change. The experiences we have in our life effect our actions, as our actions define who we are, experiences have the power to change who we are. The power of a single thought that becomes a decision can have a profound influence on your life, it can change everything you have ever believed to be true.

In one hundred days we have sailed over seven

thousand miles because of a single decision made by each of us. One hundred days ago I wouldn't have felt confident in navigating my way out of Sydney harbor. Today I have just finished plotting our route up the Red Sea. Using six different charts I have managed to find our way up to the entrance of the Suez Canal. After we're piloted through the one hundred and one miles of canal we have only one more leg, Port Said to Fiumicino. This will mark the end of our adventure together. Peter asked me if he could plot the coordinates for the last leg. I get the impression that it's beginning to dawn on him that he will be the one responsible for navigating *Aphrodite* back to Australia.

I left Peter alone in the cabin scratching his head and gnawing the end of the pencil as he figured out the last leg of our journey.

04° 29.4' N
50° 05.4' E
027° - Day 101

The sea was dead calm this morning, almost as if it was preparing itself for something. The heat is suffocating as there is no wind to cool it. The endless thumping of the diesel engine and the halyard hitting the boom are the only sounds echoing across the flat empty ocean.

The temperature inside the cabin is over a hundred degrees. Barry, the barometer is holding steady in the fine weather region and the skies are completely clear of clouds. We are motoring up the coast of Kenya, about a hundred miles off to our port side but far from sight. The horizon to the west is hazy and out of focus. The sands from the deserts of Africa are blown up to thirty miles off the dry coast. The winds are known as the *Kharif* and can sometimes reach gale force during the night. We only have a single knot of current with us but it should strengthen as we head further north.

I'm taking advantage of these calm conditions and have started a new sculpture using a coconut from Cocos Keeling and the puzzle nut seeds I found on the beach in the Seychelles. Puzzle nuts fall from their trees and split open on the ground. Inside the large seeds of different shapes fit perfectly together to form a sphere roughly the size of a clenched fist. Some of the nuts contain up to thirteen giant seeds that make an intricate three-dimensional puzzle. Carving random sized holes out of the unbroken coconut shell I placed the individual seeds inside and glued the nine sections back together again to form a sphere contained inside the coconut casing. The complete puzzle nut now appears to have been placed within the coconut as it can freely move around inside, yet it is not obvious as to how the nut found its way in there. The contrast between the hard dark coconut shell and softer puzzle nut seeds inside make an interesting and intriguing carving.

08° 12.9' N
51° 03.9' E
043° - Day 102

I have a feeling our long lonely passages are a thing of the past, we have spotted four cargo ships already today. Last night on my watch a freighter loaded to the eyeballs with containers passed us half a mile away. Like an old lady behind the wheel of a giant Cadillac I was perplexed as to how the captain managed to see his way over the stacked containers. It's the closest I've been to one of these giant ships, it seemed to block the stars out of the night, it was unnerving. I have a feeling we will be getting a great deal closer in the weeks to come. Africa is only sixty miles off to our port side but still blanketed in a cloud of sand and African dust that just hangs in the air.

Today it's Catherine's birthday. I have spent most of it writing to her and thinking about where we will be this time next year. The two constants that have stayed with me over the last few years has been my desire to live in America and to share my life with Catherine. These two thoughts are so strong I have no doubt that they will become a reality for me.

For the first time I feel ready to begin the next chapter of my life. I am ready to move to America and I am ready to spend the rest of my life with Catherine. I think about her each day and love her more with each memory she has given me.

The winds are starting to blow from the northeast. We are on a mission, trying to round the horn before it gets nasty. The Somali current has picked up to three knots under our belly and is helping us along. Lewis and Peter are still having difficulties. Today they were disagreeing about the way Peter runs his business! The two argued for a couple of hours, no agreement was reached and nothing was accomplished by the debate. I listened to the two of them voice their views, but kept well out of the way. This was not my battle.

10° 48.6' N
51° 51.2' E
012° - Day 103

Only one hundred miles to go before we start to head west. I know we will all feel more at ease when we are in the relative security of the Gulf of Aden but the engine is on high revs. Even though there is a fifteen-knot breeze coming from the north and four knots of current from the south, all the sails are down and we are motoring!

As the wind is coming from the north we would have to sail on an unfavorable tack, Peter does not want to do this and only wants to sail when the wind is coming from a convenient direction. We are howling along at a constant six knots over ground but Lewis and I would much rather kill the engine and sail. As Lewis and Peter do not see eye to eye I had to tactfully persuade our captain that if we sailed it would only put us a few miles off course. Peter eventually agreed but only on the condition that if the wind drops to under ten knots he will start the engine again.

We have not sighted any freighters today only dolphins and thousands of crabs! Carpeting the sea around us they were coming up from the ocean bed saturating the water and drifting in the current. They reminded me of the crabs I used to catch off the jetty in England as a kid. I spent hours dangling my orange line into the water, carefully pulling them up as they clung greedily to the bacon rind hooked on the end. Even when they were out of the water and in the bucket some of them would still refuse to let go. After a few hours my plastic beach bucket shaped like a castle would be full with dozens of crabs pissed off that I was holding them prisoner. Sitting on top of each other, about five layers deep, they would jostle for position and try to climb out. Occasionally one would break free and make a dash for it. With its pincers held high it would scuttle sideways across the concrete surface, dividing the tourists like Moses in the Red Sea as it ran for freedom. Catching the little buggers took skill and speed.

At the end of the day, when the tourists were herded off the ferryboat with their deck chairs, coolers, towels and screaming kids I would let all my crabs free. Spilling the bucket over onto the jetty, up to fifty crabs would stampede in every directional with snapping pincers causing mass panic amongst the sunburnt families heading home after a day at the seaside. Adults, children and the family pets would all flee from these relatively harmless shellfish like they were a herd of charging bulls. Screaming and yelling would fill the air at Mudeford Quay as the daily rabble dashed for their cars.

As we sail through the cluster, *Aphrodite* gently pushes the floating crabs aside with her bow waves. We don't have any bacon rind on board and Peter is doing a load of laundry in the bucket so the crabs are safe today.

12° 07.8' N
50° 51.3' E
280° - Day 104

Today we have rounded the horn and are heading west to Djibouti, four hundred and fifty miles away at the far end of the gulf. Amazingly we have experienced nothing but calm waters and beautiful clear skies all day. With all the hype and anticipation of rounding the most easterly point of Africa I feel as though we have been cheated. I can hear my fathers words now, "Neville, you're a jammy bugger!"

We've been lucky so far and have yet to experience a storm. Although a few of the squalls we have encountered along the way have been severe, they were short lived and lasted no more than half an hour. Part of me would like to have the experience of sailing in a storm just once, a storm I can tell my grandchildren about, with mountainous waves and wind so powerful it can blow you off your feet.

Although I have traveled and had many experiences, my life has been free from hardship and suffering. I do not know what it feels like to be pushed to the limits, to have your very existence challenged, or to experience the feeling of true danger. I feel as though I have always been sheltered, I would like to one day feel the full force of life for myself. To survive a life threatening situation is like having a new lease on life, you become more appreciative, everything would be instantly put into perspective. Only when something has been almost taken from you can you ever truly appreciate it, I want to take nothing for granted, I want to appreciate everything.

In the letter I received from Andy back in the Seychelles he describes the accident that almost killed him when he fell through a skylight of a fire damaged warehouse. Only two months after he had flown back to England the accident happened that changed his life and attitude forever. After falling twenty feet head first, Andy broke both his wrists, elbows and shoulders before his head struck the concrete floor and left him in a coma for three days. Doctors were not sure that he was going to make it and prepared his family for the worst, but being the determined son-of-a-bitch that he is, Andy fought with all his effort and survived the accident, proving many of the doctors wrong.

The letter is written in a much softer and calmer way than the opinionated Andy I knew and traveled with for a year. He is not as determined to make a point as he once was and knowing how fragile life is has made him a stronger person.

Apart from the ten freighters we have already sighted, the day has been quiet and peaceful. Peter was the first to see Africa this morning and has been taping the coast of Somalia ever since. We must have at least half an hour of Peter panning the barren and lonely coastline saying, "It's all just really, really high sheer cliffs, sheer cliffs as far as the eye can see, sheer cliffs, very very high!" Another few minutes of panning left to right and he repeats the same sentence all over again. Even the way he breathes, the short heavy breaths as his tar filled lungs try to inflate is beginning to annoy me.

Lewis is sitting under the sail in his usual spot spying on the freighters as they motor past. A man on the bridge of one of the freighter was watching Lewis watching him through his binoculars, as we drew parallel they waved at each other through the magnified lens, the man was smiling. It's reassuring to know they are aware of us.

The "sheer cliffs" to port are over five thousand feet high and appeared out of the clouds at 0630 this morning. We are only eight miles off the coast and have officially left the Indian Ocean. The water is noticeably dirtier here but I showered never the less. Lewis came up with the brilliant idea of using an old window-cleaning bottle for a post-shower, freshwater spray. Once you have showered with salt water and shampoo, we are each allowed half a cup of fresh water. Adjusting the nozzle to a fine mist, half a cup is enough to rinse the salt off your entire body without using excessive amounts of tank water. It's only a simple luxury but one that we all wish we had thought of three months ago, as washing continually with salt water has covered parts of our body in tiny red spots. It does feel funny though to be standing on the deck naked, spraying yourself for five minutes with what looks to be window cleaner. Lewis was the first to use the spray bottle and didn't rinse out all the window cleaning fluid, he's complaining now that his skin squeaks when he rubs it.

The full moon tonight is high in the starry sky and bright enough to read and write by. Its reflection is dancing off the little waves, covering the surface of water in glitter. We are sailing along the "sheer cliffs" of Somalia along the southern edge of the Gulf. To the north, Yemen is in conflict, we were advised by one of the freighters to steer clear of this country.

The unsettled relationship between North and South Yemen has remained high since the two united in 1990.

Aden is the former capital of South Yemen and a more convenient stop for yachts heading north up the Red Sea. The harbor offers very little comfort for cruising yachts and formalities are said to be complicated. Djibouti, although not quite as convenient offers a safer anchorage and has better facilities, we should arrive there in under a week.

11° 42.0' N
47° 09.8' E
260° - Day 106

Our first visitor from Africa joined us today. Searching the cabin as if he owned the boat he ignored our presence while buzzing around the galley. Making a complete nuisance of himself over lunchtime, we repeatedly caught him munching on our cabbage leaves and slurping the cola off the top of our soda bottles. If you shooed him away he dive-bombed at your head in protest before settling in again for another free feed. Peter ended the fly's life by swatting it with the back of his notebook. The burial service was a simple one that consisted of Peter flicking the spattered remains over the railing. The crime scene is marked on the back of his book by a little red stain of fly guts.

We are two hundred and forty miles from Djibouti, the sailing conditions are perfect with the wind blowing us deeper into the Gulf. I woke this morning from a dream that was so weird, it left me with a strange feeling that has stayed with me all day. The dream probably lasted only a few seconds but seemed to begin the moment I shut my eyes and continued for the six hours I slept.

Scene one began with me wandering around a monastery looking for a shower. The stone hallways were dark and each footstep echoed along the empty passages as I searched for the changing room, I never found one. In scene two I found myself outside on a warm and sunny day on the side of a mountain. Standing on the green grass I watched a deer run in terror as a lion chased it around the edge of the cliff. The lion swung at the deer, and with one powerful blow killed it in mid air, it fell lifeless to the ground with its hind legs twitching. The lion returned to his owner who was sitting in front of a TV playing a video game where a dot bounced left to right on a screen. Each player had to return the dot to the other side by moving a bar up and down. By the time I reached them the lion had picked up a remote and was playing against him. The man looked up at me and said with a wink, "He's a hell of a lion, but I can still beat him at tennis." The lion looked at me with two black pits where his eyes should have been, he was blind. I looked up and saw a lady watching us from the road wearing high-heeled running shoes.

11° 36.3' N
43° 12.1' E
184° - Day 109

It's Sunday afternoon, the 23rd of October, we are in the Gulf of Tadjoura and can clearly see the port of Djibouti ahead. Unlike the tropical islands in the Indian Ocean, Djibouti is a working port with heavy traffic and dirty waters. Two massive cranes stand erect in the harbor, ready to unload more cargo from the ships that endlessly steam down from Port Suez. There are two giant freighters waiting patiently for their heavy loads to be unburdened from their backs. Boats of different shapes and sizes are anchored around the large harbor, some are rotting at their anchorage with gaping wounds in their sides, barely managing to stay afloat, while others like the two French warships sit menacingly at the entrance of the harbor with their guns uncovered. Thick black smoke is billowing up from the eastern end of the port and scaring the blue sky, everything looks dirty and oily, it's not a pretty sight.

The country of Djibouti is little more than a port in the Tadjoura gulf. The population of around 580,000 are mainly Afars and Issas, although there are also a large percentage of refugees from the neighboring countries of Ethiopia and Somalia. Before Djibouti was occupied by the French it was little more than grazing land for nomadic tribes. In 1862 the French acquired the rights to settle in Djibouti to counter the presence of the British in Aden. In 1888 construction of the port and town began along with the Addis Ababa-Djibouti railway that provides Ethiopia with an outlet to the sea. The French eventually gave Djibouti independence on June 26th, 1977 due to increasing acts of terrorism by the Issas. Arabic is the official language but French is widely spoken as France still provides aid to the country and has maintained a military presence due to its agreement with Djibouti.

We have spoken to the Capitainerie on channel twelve and received our instructions. The master of the vessel is required to motor over to immigration in the commercial harbor to present passports and fill out the papers. Peter has given me this title and seems to be more relaxed knowing that he will not be responsible for filling out the forms and dealing with the authorities. I think he's intimidated by all the paper work and would much rather stay on the boat and drink beer instead.

Djibouti - Day 110

Djiboutiful! We are anchored at the Club Nautique de Djibouti and have already gained clearance from customs and immigration. Lewis and I met a tuna fisherman last night from Ethiopia. "King Solomon" let us tie our dinghy up to his fishing boat in the commercial port while we went to look for the immigration office. He introduced himself by pointing to my feet and saying, "I like your shoes!" My Téva sandals had caught his attention and he wanted a pair. At the very least he said when we come back tomorrow we must bring him a present for using his boat as a pontoon. I told him that we would.

I presented "King Solomon" today with a can of Tuna for his help. Our new friend understood the humor and his giant black belly rolled up and down as he snorted and laughed at the joke.

We cleared customs and immigration in a few minutes. We shoved our passports under the glass window with twenty-seven dollars, the man kept the money but shoved the passports back without even looking at them, as if to say "What the bloody hell do I want to look at these for?" We tried to explain to him the importance of having our visit to Djibouti documented. I don't think he understood what we were telling him but stamped our passports anyway, I think just to get rid of us. Customs and immigration really do not seem to give a shit about our presence here. They have not inspected *Aphrodite* and customs told us to just keep the rifles and morphine we have on the boat out of sight.

Thankfully we only have a few chores while we are here. Lewis and I will meet Solomon again tomorrow and his friend, apparently he has some cheap diesel he can sell to us, Peter will take care of the fresh water. The sack of potatoes and onions we bought in the Seychelles are lasting very well along with the burgers and sausages donated by the British Navy. The only food we will need to buy are our own private rations.

After breakfast we motored over to the yacht club to

do some laundry and scout around. A dozen or so African kids were already fishing with hand lines next to the pontoon. The fish they were catching were little more than a couple of inches long, this was not for fun, they were fishing for food. When the older boy caught one his younger brother, no older than four, took it off the hook and beat its head against the concrete floor to kill it. When the fish stopped moving the little boy put it with the others they had caught, they had three so far. I came back an hour later, the boy was still crouching on the waters edge, holding the line and concentrating on the little fish swimming around the hook, almost trying to will them to bite it, his brother was urinating in the water next to him.

We walked into town and were almost immediately surrounded by children begging for food. Their tiny hands clutched imaginary meals and in a gesture of eating they cried "Mangé, mangé." It was disturbing to have so many children look at you with large sorrowful eyes hoping you were the one that might feed them today. We had no Djibouti franc and no food, all we could do was shrug helplessly and say "I'm sorry." The children followed us for a few hundred yards, tugging on our shirts and begging to be fed.

In the center of the town there were fewer beggars and the people walking around seemed to be busy going about their business. The older buildings surrounding the little park in the middle of the square had a definite European style to them as they were designed and constructed by the French. We went to the bank and each exchanged a handful of American dollars to Djibouti franc, then made our way to the post office to mail letters and make phone calls. The post office was busy with Monday lunchtime customers. We waited in line with the locals to mail the letters to our families and make calls from the telephone booths. I left a thirty second message for Catherine giving her the yacht club's fax and phone number, the call cost me eight hundred and seventy-five Djibouti francs, about five dollars! I was surrounded the entire time by locals waiting to be served so the message was hurried and noisy. Peter and Lewis both made calls to their family, Lewis made his quick but Peter was on the phone for quite a few minutes, it must have cost him a small fortune. While we waited for him outside, we were greeted by the older children that walked past, they shouted "Welcome to Djibouti!" each time they saw us.

We took a crowded bus that leaned heavily to one side to the markets. The young men waved and shouted at us when we passed, each time they yelled, "Welcome to Djibouti!" We were the only white people on the bus which everyone thought was hysterical for some reason. The bus was already stuffed full but the driver kept stopping for others to hang onto the side. The more people that clung to the windows the more the bus tilted over. By the time we reached the markets the tires on the passengers side were rubbing against the wheel arches and the whole bus seemed dangerously close to toppling over.

The market was bustling with locals going about their everyday chores. The fruit and vegetable stands were well stocked but most of the food seemed to be rotting and going to waste. Old ladies sat on the mud floor that was packed as hard as concrete with a few pieces of good fruit laid out on a rag hoping to make a sale. The square was so busy they shielded their merchandise from the stampeding feet that filled the market. We left empty-handed, none of us were prepared to risk eating the food that had been kicked around on the floor or half eaten by flies.

We headed back to the club by foot and walked past stalls selling fake Ray Bans, Lacoste polo shirts and Nike t-shirts. The stalls looked like they were all about to fall to the ground in a pile of rusty corrugated iron at any moment. White sheets were draped in front of each stall to keep the flies out and to shade the occupant from the sun. We walked along the narrow street gracefully turning down the requests to browse the merchandise as we passed each store.

The children were waiting for us when we returned to the little shopping center. With an encouraging push from their parents the children were sent running over to us. We left the group of children outside the supermarket and walked inside. The quality of food was far better than the open markets but cost almost three times the price. We each bought our own supplies. The children were waiting for us with open hands when we returned. Lewis and I bought a packet of chocolate biscuits to hand out. At first it was obvious they wanted money but with a nod of approval from their parents the children accepted the snacks but took the biscuits back to their parents for even distribution. Peter was getting quite annoyed by the constant aggravation and kept waving his arm trying to get rid of them and telling them to "Rack off." I found his lack of compassion unnecessarily cruel, he didn't share out any of his rations.

We dined at the yacht club tonight and met a few of the sailors that will be our neighbors going up the Red Sea. *Impulse* is being sailed by four South African men all in their mid to late twenties. They will be leaving tomorrow and are bound for Spain. There is a couple from England, living in the smallest yacht I have seen so far cruising the world. Their thirty-four foot sloop, *Day-Glo* is stranded in Djibouti due to engine problems - they don't have one! They would love to join the convoy north but have been stranded in Djibouti for two months and do not know when they will be able to leave. They were towed into the harbor by the authorities when their engine failed in the Indian Ocean, they are waiting for parts they cannot afford and are hoping friends back home can bail them out. A few yachts left yesterday to start the voyage north, most of the remaining seven yachts will be leaving next week, they will be the last to attempt the passage this season.

We ordered steak in the restaurant that seemed to take forever to come. We made jokes that they were chasing a cow around the desert, when we were finally served Peter sent his back because it was not cooked right, not once, not twice but three times! Each time the waiter handed him the plate, Peter examined the piece of meat before pushing the plate away from him in disgust. The littlest things about the man I find most infuriating. I am all for getting what you want but we aren't in Sydney or New York, this is Djibouti and a certain amount of leniency or understanding is called for. Lewis was just as amazed with Peter's attitude, by the time Peter was finally satisfied with his meal Lewis and I were ordering coffee.

After dinner we sat in the lounge area and talked to the crew of *Impulse* and an Australian couple sailing the forty-foot sloop *Bianca*. While we discussed the passage up the Red Sea, Peter fell asleep on the sofa in the most unflattering position. His stubbly chin was resting on his chest, his mouth hanging open and his legs spread wide apart. His 'family jewels' had escaped from his shorts and were hanging out of his right leg hole! Lewis and I apologized on Peter's behalf and told everyone that he was doing a load of white laundry and judging by his lack of constraint hadn't collected his underwear from the dryer, it was not a pretty sight!

Djibouti - Day 111

I had an interesting last day in Djibouti, the walk from the yacht club into town was an event in itself. A mile from the club I was confronted by soldiers armed with machine guns who demanded that I cross to the other side of the street. The government building they were guarding was inhabited by the President who apparently does not like people walking on his grass! Further down the road, on the safe side of the street, old ladies were lighting up their fires in preparation for the lunchtime rush. These "open air restaurants" were little more than a fire in the street with a circle of old milk crates for customers. They were the third world's version of the hotdog and kebab vendors you would find on the street corners of New York City. Instead of a grill, old paint tins and frying pans with no handles were used for cooking, I was tempted to try the local cuisine for experience value only, but decided better of it as I hadn't had a Hepatitis A, Typhoid or Tetanus booster before the trip. The only precaution I had taken was buying a can of insect repellent, the same make I used in the bush to keep the flies away. The men in the camp called the spray "Fuck-Off" because that's what we told the flies to do if they ignored the repugnant smell we coated our exposed parts with.

I made my way through town and was greeted by the children who knew my face and put their hands out for chocolate cookies. I bought myself a Coke and a packet of cookies to hand out. I caught the local bus to the market and decided to keep on going. Another five stops out of town the scenery got even more desperate. The refugees from Ethiopia and Somalia were living outside the city in makeshift homes constructed out of sheets of iron and blankets, no one shouted "Welcome to Djibouti" to greet me. The dusty street that seemed to be the main road coming in and out of Djibouti was littered with old ladies standing next to the road behind foldaway tables selling, what looked like grass. I walked up to the nearest table and smiled at the lady who returned the greeting with rotting, stained and crocked teeth. I asked her what the plant was. She motioned that you eat it and chew on the leaves like tobacco, she called it "Cat" I bought a bundle and thought I would give it a go.

On the way back through town I picked out a postcard for Catherine that had a picture of a camel on it. Unfortunately the selection was rather limited and consisted mainly of camels, goats, cows and donkeys. I had to remind myself where I was and that I would not find any postcards with "Beach Bums" on the front showing girls in skimpy bikinis, although I was hoping to get lucky.

By the time I reached the square it was lunchtime so I bought some bread and made myself comfortable on one of the benches. Before I managed to start eating a man walked up and pointed to the grass in my bag.

"Do you chew?" I asked him, on the hope he understood English.

He smiled at me showing a huge juicy ball of green leaves in his mouth, "You like, is good yes!" the man asked.

"What is it?" I asked the man, hoping to get a better description of the plant.

"Cat."

"How do you spell it?"

"Khath, you chew it, it makes you free your spirit."

Muhammad's eyes were blood shot and glassy, I told him that in America people smoke stuff like this to "free their spirit." He smiled and nodded as if to agree with this logic. We talked under the shade of a tree and chewed Khath together, making patterns on the dusty ground when we spit out lumps of soggy grass. Muhammad was a far better shot than I was.

After "lunch" I said goodbye to my chewing partner and decided to make my way back to the club. I noticed an old lady sitting on the dusty ground outside the supermarket, she was weaving brightly colored bowls and plates from wicker. The detail and patterns for each basket were wonderful, I bought a set of small bowls for my parents and a larger fruit dish for my brother and his wife, I can worry about how I am going to get all this home when we reach Italy.

I met Lewis at the club and we motored off to the commercial side of the harbor to meet Solomon and negotiate a deal with his friend for some diesel. We filled our tanks and bought an additional five, ten-gallon plastic drums. We had enough diesel now to see us through to the Suez and on to Italy. We were prepared for the worst and ready to go. Before we said goodbye to Solomon I gave him a T-shirt I had picked up in Australia.

When I crewed on *Bird of Dawning,* the sixty-five foot cruiser I helped take up the coast of Australia, the skipper gave me a T-shirt. It had a cartoon image of the boat that was bursting with large bosomed, topless ladies fishing with men holding a girl in one hand and a beer in the other! Solomon said he liked this gift more than the tin of tuna.

7

Djibouti to Port Suez

(1,310 nautical miles)

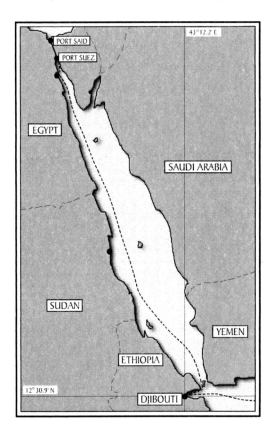

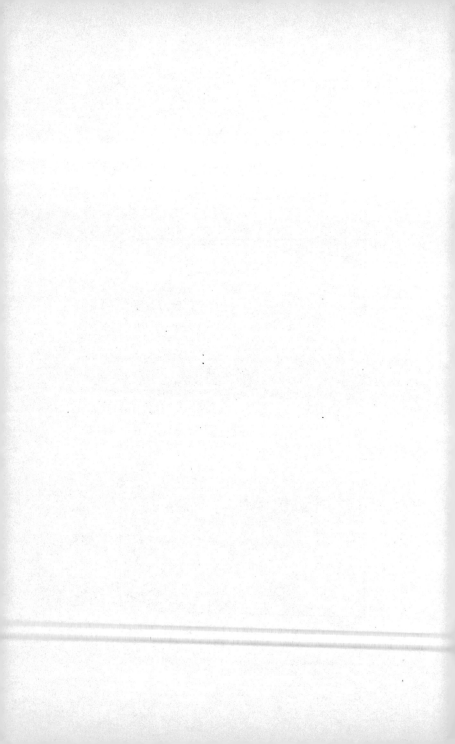

7

Djibouti to Port Suez

12° 30.9' N
43° 12.2' E
62° - Day 112

With our new Djibouti courtesy flag flying from the
spreader we have set out for the Gates of Sorrow six days
behind schedule but ready for the Red Sea. It's 1600
hours, the wind is in our favor and we look like a new
crew, clean-shaven, haircuts and almost as fresh and eager
as we were back in Sydney. Yesterday Lewis shaved off
his beard, it was a mammoth task that took him most of the
afternoon and a whole array of instruments. After hours of
pruning and clipping he finally reached his jaw line that
hadn't seen the light of day since Mooloolaba. Peter's
haircut is very smart and short, he looks like he's a little
boy ready for his first day at school.

The barbershop looked like it was the oldest in
Djibouti and was probably first opened in 1888 and didn't
appear to have been remodeled since. The three old
fashioned chairs were rundown by use, the floor around
each one was worn by years of shuffling feet, the cushions
were split, the mirrors were cracked and the barber looked
old enough to be the original owner. The only training he
probably ever received was the "short back and sides"
diploma, (which I did not see hanging from the wall). I
asked for a "numero trois" and had my entire head buzzed

with a razor, I felt this was the safest approach and would at least give Keith, my trusty barber back in Southampton, an even palette to work with. Since the age of three I have entrusted Keith with my scalp, he has cut my hair for twenty years and has never let me down. I am confident when I return to England he will be able to fix whatever damage has been done.

Peter is the happiest I have seen him for weeks as he has stocked up on cigarettes and is now ready to battle the northerly winds.

"How many cartons did you buy there Peter?" I asked.

"Oh, about twenty-two. At eight dollars a carton you can't go wrong!" Peter added as he sucked another one down.

"That's a bargain!" Lewis said with a grin.

"It's almost enough to make you want to start smoking eh Lou?" I said.

"I don't know about that!"

"I won't be able to give up for a while anyway." Peter said with a cough.

We have taken two cartons away from Peter's stash and stored them for "backseesh." We have read that the authorities through the Suez Canal respond favorably to packets of cigarettes, Marlboro are the preferred brand. The right "donation" will help to ensure a quick and easy passage, without them your trip could be mysteriously delayed. Cigarettes are like a currency and the bigger the ship the larger the payment. The freighters that pass through the Suez reportedly pay by the ton. The larger freighters weighing in at three hundred thousand tons pay $4 -$5 per ton and dozens of cartons of Marlboro.

Lewis and I have been eating right out of the Nutella jar we treated ourselves to back in Djibouti. The thick chocolate spread should last us for most of the Red Sea but unfortunately most of it is already gone. Rather than spreading it thinly onto our crackers we have been taking turns spooning great heaps of runny chocolate out of the jar and eating it like yogurt, so much for delaying gratification!

With a full stomach swishing with digesting chocolate, I have been studying the chart and the narrow passage we will be taking into the Red Sea. It's a little intimidating. Tiny islands bridge the twenty-mile gap between Yemen and Djibouti and each of them must be passed on the correct side and at a safe distance. Some yachts have reported being shot at because the currents brought them too close to restricted areas. Due to the heavy traffic, a separation zone is in operation and divides northbound from southbound. Northbound vessels must pass to the starboard side, yet maintain a safe distance from the restricted islands and the waters surrounding them.

We will pass through the Gates of Sorrow around dawn tomorrow. It is important that we clear the headland of Ras Bir by at least ten miles and sail east past the Musha Islands. It will be extremely dangerous to attempt the passage to the west as rebels have been known to molest vessels that pass too close to the Djibouti coastline. When we reach the Gates of Sorrow we must keep a safe distance west of Perim Island as yachts have been used for target practice if they venture too close. Once we have cleared the entrance we will sail toward Tair Island then continue north to the Hanish and Zubair Islands, which belong to Yemen and are en route to Jabal. If the weather is not in our favor, anchoring at these islands is tolerated but landing is prohibited. If the wind and currents are with us we will press on.

12° 47.9' N
43° 16.9' E
339° - Day 113

We passed through the Gates of Sorrow in the early hours of the morning and in doing so have begun our journey up the Red Sea. We are howling along averaging nine knots over ground, the wind is steady at twenty-four knots from the northeast and the current is in our favor at three knots. It's 0800 and heavy traffic has been continuously steaming down from the north all night. So far we have spotted one oil rig, twenty freighters and we have just been joined by a battleship. Needless to say with so much company during the night I was unable to sleep and am in dire need of a power nap.

The French battleship has just cleared our stern by no more than half a mile. To our starboard side is Perim Island. If they start shooting at us at least we'll have the support of the French on our side. The missile launchers and turret guns mounted onto the cold gray deck are uncovered and pointing menacingly to the north. Its gray streamlined body is slicing through the waves at twenty-five knots like the dorsal fin of a shark.

The Middle East is one of the most volatile regions in the world, political and religious disputes can flare up in an instant on both sides of the Red Sea. The shoreline of Yemen and Saudi Arabia to the east are strictly off-limits to yachts. Because of the Islamic religion, non-Islamics are not welcomed as they are believed to be corrupt and spoiled.

To the west Eritrea, Sudan and Egypt welcome tourists but have a long history of civil war. Since the early 1960's Eritrea has fought to gain its independence from Ethiopia. After thirty years of war and famine, Eritrea finally declared its freedom in May of last year. Most of

238

the sailors we have met feel it's a little too soon to explore their country as the war has left the people there starving and in need of foreign aid.

Sudan is Africa's largest country and offers a convenient place of rest for northbound yachts. Port Sudan is halfway up the Red Sea and marks the beginning of the head winds, many yachts rest there before they begin to battle north. The north and south have had a long history of war and separation. In 1972 an agreement was reached between the divided country and south Sudan was finally given the independence they had wanted. As always not everyone was satisfied with the peace agreement and a small group in the south called the Sudanese People's Liberation continue to fight for equity. Although the coast is said to be safe, traveling inland should be avoided.

Egypt is a country that has one of the earliest recorded civilizations and five thousand years of documented history. The mystery of ancient Egypt has captivated tourists from all over the world for centuries and is visited each year by thousands of sightseers. Islamic fundamentalists have carried out terrorist attacks on tourists visiting Egypt and this has dramatically reduced the number of foreign visitors. The capital is Cairo and the largest city in Africa, Egypt has a population of sixty million with high unemployment and poverty. Cruising the coastline of Egypt up the Red Sea has gained in popularity due to the beautiful reefs, bays and climate. Venturing into the interior however, like Sudan should be avoided.

It is recommended for yachts sailing the Red Sea that they listen to the international news. If any disputes should occur between neighboring or divided countries, tourists are advised to steer well clear of the trouble until it has been resolved. The Gulf War in 1991 is a reminder that at anytime, and seemingly out of nowhere disruptions can occur and the best place to be is as far away as possible.

14° 59.5' N
42° 10.0' E
324v - Day 114

Still making unbelievable time, the wind is blowing from the southwest at twenty knots and we have been surfing the waves that sweep up behind us. Last night we hit thirteen knots as we slid down the face of one. If this keeps up we will make up the six days we are behind and arrive in Port Suez right on time. Zubair Island is on our starboard side, there looks to be no safe anchorage as the giant rock rises vertically out of the sea. We should expect a little turbulence as we pass it, the wind will blow around the island causing a disturbance.

We had radio contact with *Impulse* during breakfast, they will be anchoring tonight which means we'll probably catch up with them tomorrow. As long as the wind is in our favor we will be pressing on. Each day brings us another hundred miles or so nearer to Port Suez, we want to take advantage of every breath while it's still favorable.

Last night I woke up early, it was too hot to fall back to sleep so I decided to keep Lewis company on his watch. As I climbed out of the sweaty cabin into the warm night I was horrified to find Lewis casually watching a freighter that was only narrowly going to miss us. By the expression on Lewis' face when he saw me, he knew that we were far to close for comfort and had misjudged the distance it would pass. It made me a little nervous to think while Peter and I were asleep below, Lewis was playing chicken with a two hundred thousand ton piece of steel traveling at three times our speed. I did not need to say anything, Lewis knew he had made a mistake, if Peter had caught him however, he would not have gotten off so easily.

Unlike the Indian Ocean where we were all alone and could afford a lapse in concentration, the Red Sea will not be as merciful. Whoever is on watch needs to be alert and ready to push pride aside and ask for help should it be needed. Lewis' only fault is that he tries to take on too much himself and seems reluctant to ask for the help of others. He is the best sailor out of the three of us and because of this feels that he can manage on his own.

Lewis is a risk taker and what may seem reasonable to him would probably be completely unacceptable for anyone else. As a fireman Lewis is used to running into danger, he searches for it and then dives in headfirst. That is what he has been trained to do, that is normal to him. I however am a little more prudent and like to err on the side of caution. I asked Lewis as we held onto the helm and were rocked around by the swell from the giant propellers that I would feel more comfortable if he gave us a little bigger buffer in the future, nothing more was said on the subject.

17° 59.4' N
39° 27.5' E
328° - Day 115

Last night while I relieved myself over the railing I had the most magical experience of my life. I was alone on my watch, it had just gone midnight, the sky and sea were so black I could not tell where one ended and the other began. My harness was hooked onto a stay so I could lean over far enough to clear the deck. As I took pleasure in urinating into the Red Sea, *Aphrodite*'s bow dropped off each wave and sent a huge fluorescent spray far out to each side. The phosphorescence seemed brighter than usual against the ink black sea, there was even a glowing, twinkling trail to mark the sea I had polluted with my water. Each time the bow dropped, thousands more of the microscopic organisms glowed for attention adding to the fading trail of light behind us in the night.

As I watched the showering phosphorescence I saw lights shining under *Aphrodite*, but much deeper in the ocean. At first I thought it was the navigational lights somehow reflecting off the waves, but as the lights came closer and grew stronger I began to question what I was seeing and doubted my vision. I rubbed my eyes with my free hand to clear them, but when I looked down over the railing the lights under the boat were still there yet stronger and closer than before. It looked like divers were coming up from the ocean bed shining powerful torches toward the surface. The closer the lights got the more dazzling and magnificent they became.

One of them burst free from the surface in a brilliant explosion like a firework in the night sky. The glowing spray mushroomed out of the sea and fell back to the surface like tiny sparkling drops of rain. A second later the sea exploded as the dolphin dropped back into the water. Although I was unable to see the dolphins swimming around *Aphrodite*, the phosphorescence clung to the lower half of their body and left a magical trail of light underwater as they played around the boat. When the other dolphins reached the surface I was completely surrounded by lights weaving in and out of each other leaving magnificent patterns in the water around me. Streaking through the ocean the invisible dolphins looked like ghosts, I watched the lights in the water for ten magical minutes before they faded and disappeared deeper and deeper from sight.

Those ten minutes were the most entrancing I have ever had in my life, nothing I have seen before has moved me so much, I know that I will probably never experience anything quite like it again.

The day has been calm and relaxing, the feeling of last

night has stayed with me but I have not shared it. If I tried to verbalize it, I could never describe the experience or sensation of what it was truly like, it is one of those special moments I will keep to myself.

We are two hundred miles from Sudan and have left the main shipping lanes and are sailing closer to the western coast. *Impulse* is sailing with us, although they are out of sight they are just over the horizon and have been in contact with us for most of the day. We no longer have to contend with the giant freighters but will need to keep a closer eye on the charts and our position. The reef up the western side of the Red Sea has not been accurately documented and the charts have warnings on them indicating that there may be an error of up to two miles.

The three of us have spent the day outside under the shade of the mainsail. The cabin has been so humid that I slept outside after my watch last night. The wind is still blowing from the southwest, which we are all thankful for. Some wise guy has been entertaining us and all the other boats on the Red Sea by playing Whitney Houston and Brian Adams on the VHF emergency channel sixteen. Over supper we listened to *Run to You* by Bryan Adams and *I Will Always Love You* by Whitney Houston from the movie Bodyguard. Whoever it was has no respect for radio etiquette. In between tracks the "DJ" ignored the requests to, "Get the fuck off the emergency channel!" and quite happily carried on a conversation with himself in Arabic. With so much chatter it'll be impossible to hear the cries of someone in danger or requesting assistance.

20° 23.0' N
37° 58.0' E
336° - Day 117

I was awakened suddenly at 0200 this morning when my head smacked into the ceiling of the cabin. During the night the wind and swell had picked up into a storm and we were sailing right into it. The nose of *Aphrodite* was pitching up and down so severely I spent more time in the air than on my bunk. When we fell off the really big waves I was slammed up against the ceiling. My sheets, pillows and cushions are all completely drenched. Each time we took a nosedive the bow scooped up water and shot it down the length of deck toward the stern. My hatch, I have discovered, is not watertight.

Lewis and Peter were sitting in the cockpit with harnesses attached to the helm. After I moved all my drenched gear from the bow cabin and threw the cushions and sheets around the saloon to dry them out I put on my harness and staggered up to the cockpit to join the party.

"Thanks for waking me up boys!"

"Hell of a ride eh there big fella," Lewis said with a sardonic grin. He was wearing his bright yellow waterproofs for the first time and actually seemed to be enjoying himself.

"Come to join the fun?" Peter asked.

"Not by choice, as a tenant of these premises I have to make an official complaint, your roof's leaking!"

"Eh, what you on about?" Peter asked.

I pointed down to the mess of wet sheets, clothes and pillows in the cabin and told him to take a look for himself.

While Peter was inside I stole his seat under the dodger and glanced at the row of instruments above the hatch. They were busy at work, the LED displays flickered and changed constantly as they registered the wind speed, direction, our speed, our position, the currents and depth. The wind was peaking at forty-six knots and howling northwest across the ocean from Egypt, the waves were up to fifteen feet, short and steep. Our heading was true and we were on course howling to the north.

Once I had awakened and assessed our situation I realized we were in no danger and I could enjoy our first proper storm at sea. The black clouds were low and raced past close over our heads at a tremendous speed, the wind was warm and there was no rain in the sky making the experience almost pleasurable. The waves crashed into the bow as we met them at eight knots and sent spray into the air. Each time we ducked under the dodger to avoid a drenching. The sails were reefed right down to little pieces of cloth and *Aphrodite* was holding true.

It began just before I went to bed with Barry dropping down suddenly to 1002 mb, that was not a good sign, any sudden change in pressure is an indication that something dramatic is going to happen. The clouds rolled across the clear sky from the northwest over supper and brought the wind with them. We stayed up for the remainder of the night, when the sun broke through on the Saudi side the wind dropped a little but was still averaging over thirty knots.

The morning after! It's 0900, the sun is shining making everything seem more bearable. Now that there is enough light, Peter has the camcorder out and is documenting our first storm. Because of the conditions, it's too wet and rough to sit up on the deck so we are all sitting inside the cockpit enjoying the ride. We have been getting on much better as a team since we left Djibouti, the differences are still apparent but the weather is keeping us all occupied. The wind has been slowly swinging back around to the southwest now that the sun is up and has died down a little. The cabin area looks like we have been ransacked; cushions, pillows, sheets, towels, cloths and books are littered around the small space making it almost impossible to reach the bow cabin that is drying out. It's far too rough and windy to peg anything to the railing.

We have passed the halfway mark of the Red Sea and have sailed right past Port Sudan. To pull over now for a rest would be a waste of good wind and dangerous heading into the reefs. As George told me back in Cocos, "When in doubt, stay out!" We have only been at sea for five days and would much rather have a couple more days to see Cairo than Port Sudan. Once we're at the entrance of the Suez Canal we'll know that the worst of it is over and we can relax a little.

23° 31.5' N
36° 32.7' E
321° - Day 119

I have spent most of the afternoon trying to cover the bow hatch with bin bags in an attempt to keep my cabin dry. Stretching the plastic over the hatch in these conditions is like trying to stretch a condom over a watermelon. Trying to perform the simplest of tasks in these rough conditions is bruising and tiring. Every movement has to be premeditated and timed to perfection, if the movement of *Aphrodite* or the strength of a wave is misjudged, it's like being thrown across a room by a professional wrestler, except there are no soft mats to break your fall. I never realized just how many hard protruding objects there were on a boat, now I can safely say I have imprints of most of them somewhere on my body.

We made contact with *Impulse* earlier today, it seems

we are ahead of all the other yachts and leading the pack. We radio back our position and the weather conditions each day for the others following in our path. I told them not to be concerned if they come across some of our towels and a cushion or two along the way. The wind was strong again last night and Lewis brought the sails down first before he salvaged the towels, I don't know what he was thinking of! If he called for help I am sure we could have brought the sails down and salvaged the gear as well.

We are only thirty miles from the Egyptian coast, the wind has died down a little and is now blowing steadily from the northeast. We are motoring to try and make as much northerly progress as we can while the wind is light. We only have two hundred miles to the Gulf of the Suez and then another one hundred and eighty to the entrance of the Canal. There's lots of debris floating in the water, presumably washing down from the Suez. Planks of wood, metal drums and hundreds of plastic bottles. The river of trash we saw in the Indian Ocean sailing to the Seychelles probably originated from the Suez and washed down the Red Sea into the Gulf of Aden.

The whole world is hot. The mercury inside the cabin is pushing one hundred degrees, outside the cabin it's ninety-seven degrees and the water temperature is eighty-nine degrees. If my feet were not as hardened as they are, I would find it very difficult to walk around on the scorching deck. After four months with no shoes however, my soles are as tough as leather.

Our friend is back on channel 16. For half an hour now he's been antagonizing some poor bastard that we presume is from the Philippines. Every ten seconds or so he repeats his undying love for this man with, "Filipino monkey, I still love you, Filipino mooonkeeey!" He has yet to have a response from "Filipino monkey" but the lack of enthusiasm from his opponent has not dissuaded this man from continuing with his taunting. Trying to get "Filipino monkey" to bite, the man is now claiming his undying love for his mother and sister too!

25° 01.7' N
34° 31.5' E
331° - Day 120

It's a humbling feeling to watch the dark clouds roll in from the horizon in every direction, knowing that a storm is coming and that you can do nothing about it. At 1800 hours the sky became swollen with clouds that closed in around us. These storms only seem to come at night, they are so predictable you can almost set your watch by them. The last four nights have welcomed us the same way but last night was the one that made us all stay up.

The peaceful day ended at 2100 hours when the sky became saturated with black clouds and the first noise of thunder rumbled across the sky as the sun dropped into the horizon. The thunder was so deep, I felt the vibration in my stomach. As the night grew darker the lightning took over the blackness and filled the sky with light. Some spread across the base of the clouds like a network of veins that never reached the ground. Other bolts shot out of the clouds straight to earth with a terrifying crackle that followed seconds later and echoed across the night. The lightening was so consistent Peter pulled out the camcorder to record the never-ending bolts shooting from the dark stormy clouds.

"You're not touching anything metal are you Peter?" I asked as he panned the camera around the cockpit.

"Yep?"

"When your hair stands up on end, we'll know we've been hit then!"

Surrounded by so much electricity in the middle of the Red Sea we were the only metal around for miles. The tall aluminum mast reached up into the clouds like a lightning rod on the side of a tall building. I was certain that it would attract at least one bolt during the course of the night. Each time the sky lit up our pale faces reflected the eerie light as it shot across the heavens, our faces all turned to the mast each time a bolt stabbed at the ocean. The metal clip on my harness was attached to the helm, it was like I was strapped into an electric chair and I was just waiting for someone to flick the switch.

We made it through the night without being fried. Just before the loom of the sun broke the horizon a window appeared in the clouds and showed the stars above. I knew I was close to home because I saw something that I had not seen for over a year and a half, the unmistakable formation of the Big Dipper glowing in the sky.

I had Peter's camcorder out this afternoon and recorded our feeding ritual on the deck with close-ups of Lewis' sandwich and Peter picking his toe nails sitting next to him. I got the impression as Lewis and I joked around with the camera that Peter didn't want me playing with it, he didn't say anything so we continued documenting a day in the life of *Aphrodite*. I know that in a few years time Peter will watch the film and appreciate the close-ups of his toenails and the content of Lewis' lunch.

We have over two hours of tape that's been shot from Sydney to here. Lewis and I have asked Peter to send us a copy when he gets back to Australia. I know a lot of the everyday events will be forgotten in the years to come, the video will help us to remember what it was really like.

27° 37.4' N
34° 01.7' E
304° - Day 122

We have officially left the Red Sea and entered the Gulf of the Suez through the Straits of Gûbal. Although Port Suez is only one hundred and eighty miles away we have the current, twenty-seven knots of wind and six feet of swell against us. The engine is hammering at 1800 RPM but we are only barely managing one nautical mile an hour. At this rate it'll take us another week to reach the top of the gulf!

It's 1700 hours, the traffic is heavy now that we are in the narrower passage. We're only a mile southwest of the Morgan oil field and as the sunlight fades to the west, flames from the working rigs to the east mark the sky as they continuously burn off the excess oil that's pumped out from below the ocean bed. Tiny plumes of smoke rise into the night air from the twitching flames that light the ocean around them like street lamps down a dark alley. Helicopters are flying back and forth from oil rig to oil rig like bees pollinating flowers, cargo vessels are steadily steaming past us in the center of the gulf, it's been a long day but I have a feeling it'll be an even longer night.

Many of the rigs surrounding us are no longer in use and do not have lights to warn boats of their position. The huge platforms sit patiently in the ocean waiting for someone to pass too close and get snagged in the many cables and supports. We're hoping tonight will not bring a storm as we have no room to maneuver. The sky is still clear and the first stars are beginning to show themselves.

Thankfully the weather is a little cooler and I am actually wearing a T-shirt with my shorts, the days of parading around on deck in the nude or showering in the morning have past. I don't think the Islamic population

250

would appreciate naked men washing in full view as they sailed along their coastline. Unlike the friendly coastguard in Australia, who came around for a second peek, I don't think a display of our 'virility' would be quite as well received.

The plastic sheets I tied to the hatch are doing a really bad job of keeping the water out of my cabin, the ride is so rough as we are beating into the wind and slamming against the waves that I couldn't sleep there even if I wanted to. I have taken Don's old bunk which is little more than a cubby hole in the narrow passage that leads you from the saloon back to the captains quarters. The bunk is on the starboard side and opposite the engine compartment. The thin piece of plywood that separates me from the one hundred screaming horses is insulated on the inside but rattles back and forth with the swell. Each time the boat rocks to starboard the volume increases as the noise escapes. Peter has pinned up a sheet over the door to his cabin to keep his privacy, I am thankful for this as it helps to contain the stench that has now embedded itself in anything porous. Lewis is still occupying the saloon and switches beds depending on the weather.

28° 56.6' N
32° 49.5' E
295° - Day 123

Today marks the end of our fourth month since we left Sydney. I can hardly remember what my life was like before this journey, the life I know now is my reality and it's difficult to imagine living any other way. We all miss our families and loved ones beyond belief, the hardest part of this voyage is being away from the ones I love. Not knowing where or how they are is worse than anything

else I have endured so far. I have not spoken to Catherine
since the Seychelles, I write to her each day and have over
twenty pages, front and back to mail from the Suez. I need
to hear the sound of her voice, I want to tell her that I love
her.

I'm ready to begin the next chapter of my life, I've
had so much time to think about what I want, I'm all
wound up and ready to be let loose. I have so much that I
want to achieve, so much that I have to do that I'm getting
impatient. I know I will miss these days when it's all over
but right now I feel as though I have had enough. We are
all fidgety and ready to leave.

At 0800 I put the jib up and gave the engine a rest, we
have been sailing ever since. The wind was blowing at
twenty-seven knots right on our nose, motoring was just
burning diesel and barely managing to keep us stationary.
Although there is heavy traffic on the eastern side with
freighters steaming past us at twenty knots, and oil rigs
and platforms on the western side, I am actually enjoying
myself. The autopilot has been turned off and we are
sailing! Peter and I are taking turns to man the helm as we
tack back and forth across the gulf timing our path and
heading to miss the giant container ships. It's as though we
are crossing a busy highway with speeding cars passing us
on every side. Lewis is below and for some reason does
not want to participate in the games.

After a couple of practices Peter and I are running
well together, while one works the helm the other releases
the jib and trims the sails as we race back in the other
direction. We have the timing down to perfection and
speed toward the oil rigs making as much use out of the
wind as possible before going about. Each tack only gives
us about fifty yards headway. A group of men on one of
the oil rigs have gathered to watch us bounce back and
forth across the gulf, probably placing bets as to how far

we will get before we get flattened by a freighter or sail right into one of the rigs. We sail close enough to them that we can hear their muffled shouts over the wind and see their smiling black faces as they lean over the railing to look down at us.

Tacking back and forth like this reminds me of the afternoons I spent sailing as a kid with my dad in Christchurch harbor. I enjoyed the sailing, but savored the time alone I had with my father above everything else. The wind probably never even gusted over fifteen knots but in the tiny open wooden dinghy it felt like a raging storm. There were no freighters to contend with, only windsurfers and ferries. It was my job to pull the centerboard up when it started to drag on the sandbanks and to shift my weight when we went about. Expertly balancing the dinghy dad would look up at the sail to judge the wind direction and speed, then at me.

"Ready about son?" He'd shout.

"Yep!"

"Lee-oh!"

With a push of the tiller he'd swing us about and we'd both shuffle around the tiny boat to redistribute our weight before shooting off again.

I'm looking forward to seeing my family and friends. Although the journey is almost over, we still have another three to four weeks left to go. I get the feeling from Lewis and Peter that they feel the same way. Five months ago we couldn't wait for the journey to begin, some of us had waited a year, others a lifetime. Now we're almost as eager for the journey to end.

The last five days have been hard work, the constant night storms and head winds have drained our bodies of energy. We all need a rest and a sound night of sleep before we make the final ascent into Port Suez. There's a secluded bay a few hours away on the Egyptian coast. We will anchor there tonight, rest up and navigate the last fifty-five miles to Port Suez tomorrow.

We headed toward the sinking sun, sailing along the shimmering golden path reflected in the water that led us into the tiny bay of Marsa Thelemet. Surrounded by hills and desert, the golden sand is being blown by the thirty knot *Khamsin* wind. The only signs of life are a few dried out mud huts huddled along the shoreline that seem to be abandoned. The hills are sheltering us, the holding is sand and the water calm, never before have I looked forward to sleep more than now. We will leave tomorrow at 1200 after a nice lay-in and a large breakfast.

Port Suez - Day 125

We're glad we rested in Marsa Thelemet, as last night brought strong winds, storms and a mechanical problem. We stayed up all night and were thankful for the eight hours of undisturbed sleep we had the night before. Port Suez was filled with lights and dark shadows, the sky was covered with low black clouds and the wind was gusting to thirty-five knots. Most of the lights we saw in the night were from the many boats, barges, freighters, rigs and buildings around the bay. We decided because of the tight quarters we would motor up the East Side of the harbor away from the worst traffic and out of harm's way. At midnight the engine began to fail and strain as we motored into the wind and currents, by 0100 we had to cut the engine and sail. The propeller had jammed, it was too dark and rough to dive over and attempt to fix it, so we were forced to tack back and forth across the main channel.

Trying to judge the speed and direction of the many freighters and barges by just a few lights in the black sky was exhausting and testing. The lights from the buildings and homes around the bay camouflaged the navigational lights of the boats motoring around the harbor. Spotting them was almost impossible until the very last minute.

The line of lights at Port Suez twinkled in the night and hid the oncoming boats. We strained our eyes in the darkness looking at the thousands of lights around us, trying to determine which ones were moving and what direction they were heading in. The water was so black we couldn't see the bow waves until the last minute, because we didn't have an engine, maneuvering quickly was impossible. Not until the very last minute would a freighter show itself. What appeared at first to be just another light on land, would suddenly grow larger and black the lights out around it. On more than one occasion we were taken by surprise and had to run from the giant oncoming freighters. Lewis had the spotlight out and reflected the bright light off our white sails as a warning to the captains that they were about to run us over.

As the first sign of daylight marked the sky, the mouth to the Suez Canal showed itself. Dozens of freighters were anchored around the entrance, waiting for their turn to go through to the Mediterranean.

We called the Prince of the Red Sea on channel twelve to announce our arrival and to arrange a pilot to come and guide us in to the yacht club. He told us that he would be sending his son out to welcome us to Egypt. Heebi would be a few hours so we had time to clean the boat, fix the propeller and make ourselves a little more presentable after not showering properly for almost a week.

The water of Port Suez was black and dirty, far removed from the crystal clear Indian Ocean we had become used to. Debris was floating everywhere, white plastic bags drifted in the currents like jellyfish, planks of wood bobbed around by the light swell caused by the passing boats. Pools of diesel and petrol made colorful rainbows on the surface as the morning sunlight reflected off the oily puddles. It was decided that whoever was brave enough to submerge themselves in the filthy water to check the propeller would be rewarded with a hot shower immediately afterwards. With the promise of a warm freshwater shower, I volunteered for the task and with a brave face eased myself into the polluted water.

It was much colder than I thought it would be, the temperature had dropped from eighty-eight degrees down to a chilly seventy degrees. I was not tempted to dive down into the murkiness like I did in the Indian Ocean through fear of getting lost in the debris that floated around me.

I called up to Lewis and Peter to pass down the diving knife that we kept strapped to the helm. A potato sack had wrapped itself around the propeller and was wound so tight it took five minutes of cutting and tugging to finally free it. When I climbed back up on deck Peter had already started the shower and turned on the water heater.

Heebi was dropped off on *Aphrodite* by a pilot boat that almost crashed right into our side. He seemed like a friendly sort of guy and quickly took the helm and motored us into the marina.

His family has been working the canal since it was first opened in 1869. His grandfather was the great Prince of the Red Sea, the title has been past down through the generations. As Heebi shared his stories with us and the history of his family and the Suez Canal, he expertly steered Peter's precious *Aphrodite* with one hand, while appearing to try and pass the other boats and buoys in the harbor as close as possible. When he lit up a cigarette Heebi continued to steer with his foot. He wedged the wheel between his big toe while hunched over a match trying to shield the flame from the wind. As we passed through the entrance of the marina he pointed to starboard at a pilot boat that was perched atop a breakwater of rocks that jutted out into the harbor.

"The pilot, he forget the rocks was there!" Heebi said with a grin, shaking his head back and forth at the humor of it all.

It had seemed that one of the pilots, who was responsible for getting the freighters and other boats safely through the canal, had a little too much to drink the night before and had driven the motor boat right out of the water and parked it on top of the rocks before going home to bed. A group of men were gathered around the beached vessel, scratching their heads trying to figure out the best way to get it off.

Aphrodite's draft is five feet six inches, so when we left the main canal and the depth dropped off suddenly to six feet we all pointed to the depth gauge and told Heebi that it was getting too shallow. Heebi just gave us a cocky grin and told us not to worry. We watched the depth gauge drop down to five feet ten inches, nine inches, eight inches, seven inches, six inches! The three of us held on as Heebi continued to motor into the marina, he swung us around at four knots, dropped the throttle and killed the engine. *Aphrodite* gently settled against the pontoon and with a light kiss, the fenders touched the wooden railing with a squeak.

Heebi's father, Prince of the Red Sea number two, met us on the marina and welcomed us to Egypt. He embraced us like we were his children, which I thought was incredibly brave as the clothes we were wearing had not been washed since Djibouti, and as Lewis would say we were a little, "on the nose."

Wearing a white tailored suit, dark sunglasses, Italian shoes and heavy gold bracelets, The Prince of the Red Sea seemed to be doing pretty well for himself and looked like he was ready for a guest appearance on Miami Vice. He gave us all business cards and didn't seem to mind us taking pictures with him, in fact he seemed to rather enjoy the minor celebrity reputation he had built for himself. After the photo shoot he asked which one of us was Neville. As I made myself known Lewis made a crack about how funny it would be if there was a problem with my visa and I was banned from Egypt. The Prince of the Red Sea reached inside his breast pocket and handed me two letters. From the handwriting on the Airmail envelopes I knew immediately they were from Catherine, I was so happy that I embraced The Prince again who was by now probably bored with our company and needed some fresh air.

We tipped Heebi for his help and he offered to arrange a tour for us into Cairo, "Prince Tours" was another lucrative family business. The tour would include an air-conditioned minibus, free lunch and service to the Pyramids, Sphinx, the Cairo Museum, the bazaars, old Cairo and the River Nile. We accepted the deal and arranged to meet Heebi outside the marina first thing in the morning to begin the adventure into the largest city in Africa and one of the earliest civilizations in the world.

We motored away from the pontoon and tied up to a buoy on the West Side of the canal with the other yachts. No sooner had we secured the lines were we greeted by an old man in a dugout canoe with loaves of fresh bread. He hurled three up to us and waited patiently while we decided how to pay the man. We didn't have any Egyptian pounds so threw down a packet of cigarettes, the man seemed happy with the deal and paddled away.

The canal is just over one hundred miles long so most boats make the journey in two days. Northbound vessels begin the passage in the morning and anchor in Lake

Timsah by noon, one of the three lakes in the middle of the canal. After spending a night at anchor, southbound vessels leave Lake Timsah at noon for their journey to Suez. Most of the freighters that we saw at the entrance of the canal have already passed and will probably be in Little Bitter Lake or Great Bitter Lake by now.

The Suez Canal took ten years to dig, one and a half million Egyptian workers took part in the backbreaking project, over one hundred and twenty thousand workers lost their lives working in the canal. On November 17, 1869 the canal was opened, joining the Mediterranean Sea with the Red Sea for the first time and halving the distance for ships taking cargo from Europe to the Far East. The canal has been closed twice, once in 1956 for a year and for a second time from 1967 to 1975 following the Arab-Israeli war. The canal reopened in 1975 once cleared of wreckage and mines, and was enlarged in 1976 to 1980 for the growing number of tankers, giant cargo vessels and the ever-increasing number of ships using the canal.

Eight per cent of the world trade is transported through the canal annually along with five per cent of the oil exports. Over eighteen thousand ships pass through the canal each year. Huge vessels up to sixteen thousand feet long, two hundred feet wide and with seventy feet draughts pass through the canal with a net one hundred and forty eight million tons of cargo a year. It's hard to imagine so many packets of cigarettes in one place.

We're all still pretty tired after the last week of storms and head winds, Lewis and I scouted around Port Suez but were too exhausted to really absorb any of it. We headed back to the yacht club early to relax and make phone calls to our families. I left a message with Catherine's answering machine pleading her to call me at the club as it has been weeks since we last spoke to each other. I gave her the number and told her that we would only be here for two days, after that I would not get a chance to call her until we reach Italy.

We took care of most of the chores in the late afternoon. We all know we are going to have an exciting day tomorrow and wanted to get an early night. We replenished our fuel tanks with fresh diesel, our water tanks and even managed to clean up some of the boat before collapsing into our bunks and falling into a coma-like state of sleep.

Port Suez - Day 126

What a day! We were dropped back at the yacht club well after dark, I am too excited to sleep so have made myself a cup of tea and am sitting on the bench under the starry Egyptian sky. Lewis and Peter have gone to bed, I know Lewis is fast asleep as I can hear his deep steady snoring from here. Peter went below half an hour ago after smoking his last cigarette of the day, I know he's still awake because he's having a coughing fit right now. I'm tired and exhausted but won't be able to sleep for a while, I have too much to think about after what I saw today.

Cameel and Muhammad picked the three of us up at 0800 in an old white Toyota minibus. We had a lot to fit in, so Muhammad wasted no time explaining the day's agenda and suggested we begin the tour. We clambered in the old van and with a grind of gears and a cloud of diesel smoke Cameel, our driver for the day, found first gear and we were on our way.

The road was rutted and riddled with potholes, but the Arabic music that was blasting from the radio did a grand job of drowning out the creaks and groans of the protesting suspension, Cameel's beaded seat cover squeaked and rustled as it massaged his back with each bump. The air fresheners and beads hanging from the rear view mirror swayed in time to the Arabic music that Peter had asked to be turned down on more than one occasion. Lewis and I were having a great time and sang along to the music, screaming and chanting in rhythm to the radio, excited by the trip we were taking into Cairo. Muhammad thought this was very amusing and on one occasion joined in with the harmony, the only difference was that he actually knew the words to the song.

Peter was quiet, concentrating on capturing the experience on the camcorder that he had brought with him. With the window down he recorded the one-hour journey into Cairo. Aside from the blockade with armed soldiers, mounted machine guns and piles of sandbags, the straight road that cut west through the desert was nothing but featureless and barren wasteland. As we got closer to the city's perimeter, billboards appeared along the side of the road and the traffic got heavier and more congested.

Our first stop with "Prince Tours" was the monument erected for Anwar Sadat, the Egyptian President who was shot and killed on October 6th, 1981. I heard Peter narrating as he panned the monument claiming he was recording "Anwar Sadat's house." We moved on, driving deeper into the heart of Cairo, the home for sixty million people. Regardless of the speed Cameel drove he kept the old van in third gear the entire time. The diesel engine screamed for mercy when we reached high speeds and shuddered and shook when we pulled away from junctions. The traffic got worse, no one was paying attention to the signs on the road and it didn't really matter what lane you were in, the right of way seemed to be determined by who had the larger vehicle and how much they valued their body work. Peter made a crack about how he could make a fortune with the insurance companies fixing the dented and scratched cars that surrounded us.

Somehow Cameel managed to weave his way through the lanes to the Cairo Museum without getting us into an accident. When we piled out of the van my head was beginning to hurt and I had a strange sensation of feeling claustrophobic, something that I have never experience before. I was missing fresh air and the quiet, wide-open landscape of the ocean.

We had just two hours to explore the Museum, I could have spent two weeks there. The three of us split in the atrium and went our own way. When I was twelve I drew a picture of the golden mask of King Tutankhamun, even at that age I was fascinated by the detail and colors, and spent a week reproducing the design on a giant sheet of paper with colored pencils. I saw the mask for the first time today, I felt like I did twelve years ago, I marveled at the timeless beauty and penetrating stare of the young king. Even though the tiny room was heavily guarded and full with tourists pushing and shoving around the glass case for a closer look, I was lost for a few seconds. Staring into the eyes of the young king, I tried to envision the great civilization that once prospered and ruled upper Africa in a magical time, so different to the world that I now live in. I imagined the sculptors and artists that handcrafted the gold and precious stones over three thousand years ago, wondering if such magnificent craftsmanship could ever be reproduced today with the same tools and painstaking attention to detail.

No flashes were allowed so I set Lewis' camera on a slow shutter speed and cleared a space in front of the display. Standing with the camera braced against my chest I checked the f-stop and hoped that no one would walk in front of me or push me during the critical fifteenth of a second the shutter would be open and recording the golden mask onto film.

I left the museum in a profound state of mind, wondering if we could ever again hope to create such timeless designs that will be admired in another three thousand years. I felt sad just for a second because the answer I gave myself was no, we couldn't.

After lunch Cameel weaved his way across town to the highlight of our day's tour, the great Pyramids of Giza. I felt better with some food in my stomach and had a little buzz going from the "Seesha" I had smoked after the meal, (black honey and tobacco you traditionally smoke in Egypt from a bong). We were rested, well fed and ready to witness one of the great Seven Wonders of the World.

All the pictures I have ever seen of the Pyramids were taken in such a way that they appeared to be located in a remote part of the Sahara desert. The reality of how close they actually are to Cairo suddenly dawned on me when I caught a glimpse of Khufu's (Cheops) pyramid through the buildings. Cameel swung the tired Toyota around the corner (still in third gear) and there they were, the remains of a great civilization now shadowed by a city that is over-populated, polluted and poverty-stricken.

A mystery still surrounds the pyramids, how they were built, who built them and their location. Scientific evidence shows that the size, placement and position of each pyramid is so precise that even with today's technology it would be practically impossible to replicate the structures. Khufu's pyramid, the largest of the three was constructed for the king who ruled Egypt during 2551 - 2528 BC. It took thirty years to construct, over two million blocks, each weighing two and a half tons. Its base is equivalent to seven city blocks, it is thirty times larger than the Empire State Building and can be seen from the surface of the moon.

The pyramid faces true north, the collective length of each side equals 36,524 inches, move the decimal point back one and it is also amazingly the exact length of a solar year. There is only a 0.1% error in the lengths of each side. The height of the pyramid is 5,449 inches, the average height of land above seawater, something that today we are only able to calculate with satellite technology. The three pyramids are aligned with the stars on Orions belt. Some say that aliens constructed the pyramids as a sort of radio beacon into space, most people attribute the designs to a great civilization and many many years of back breaking work.

Eager to get a closer glimpse I jumped out of the van and started hiking up the hill toward the Great Sphinx that appeared to be under construction. I hadn't managed to get more than fifty yards up the embankment when I was ordered to come down. It seems tourists are only allowed to visit the pyramids with the assistance of a guide and preferably a camel or horse. I took a quick picture and returned to the others waiting for me by the van. Lewis was smiling and shaking his head, wagging his finger and tutting at me. "Ease up there big fella." He said.

As we mounted up in preparation for our ascent to the base of Khufu's pyramid, an old man greeted us and pressed alabaster beads into our palms for good luck on the journey. We assumed that it was part of the tour, thanked him and stuffed the tiny beads into our pockets, eager to begin the adventure back into time. A few seconds later he started to shout and scream, demanding that we pay him for the gifts that he had so generously given us. After a moments confusion we realized that this entrepreneur was not part of the tour and was only in it to make a buck, it was obvious by his tone and shaking fist that he had no interest in our good fortune. He argued that because we had accepted the beads we had to pay for them. I pulled the piece of blue rock out of my pocket and studied it between thumb and forefinger, it was not particularly impressive so I returned the bead back to the old man as did Peter. Lewis being as generous as he is, paid the man a very charitable fee for a rather nondescript stone.

With a "giddy-up" and a prod in the bottom from the guides the two horses and camel began the march up the hill. The sun was high in the clear sky and was hot, I had forgotten my baseball cap so bought a "ghutra" (a large diagonally-folded cotton square) and an "igaal" (a double-coiled cord circlet) from one of the young kids in the car park. I felt like Lawrence of Arabia with my new headgear as my horse plodded through the desert sands.

The expedition to Khufu's pyramid through the Sahara lasted a little over five minutes. The guides kept a tight grip on the reins and skillfully led us up the north side to the entrance. When Peter dismounted he was greeted by an Arab who offered to take his picture in front of the great pyramid. Lewis and I warned him to be careful as we were certain that there would be a bill at the end of the photo shoot and suggested that he politely decline the offer. The man assured Peter that he would not charge him for the picture and even offered a spare "bisht" for Peter to wear, complete with belt and dagger. Again Peter told the man that he would not pay him, the man agreed and helped dress Peter in a flowing, floor-length gown, Peter actually seemed to be enjoying himself at this point. As Peter coached the man on how to use his camera the Arab suggested that Peter climb on top of his camel for the finished effect.

The picture was taken and I have to admit Peter looked pretty good dressed up as an Arab and sitting on a camel in front of Khufu's pyramid, but sure enough when Peter got off the camel the man demanded to be paid.

"What!" Peter shouted, his words echoing across the sacred burial site, "You told me I would not have to pay!"

"I told you that I would not charge you for the picture or my robe," the man said with a crafty grin, "I did not say that I would not charge you for sitting on my camel!"

Peter of course became angry and told the man to "rack-off" as he undressed, throwing the garments onto the ground. They argued for a good five minutes, Peter never did pay him.

Not wanting to have the experience ruined by an argument over a couple of Egyptian pounds, (about sixty cents), I wandered off to explore Giza. Over the years the soft limestone blocks used in the construction of the pyramids have been seriously eroded by the elements, leaving jagged steps that reach up into the blue sky. Colossal slabs of highly polished white limestone, a material much harder and durable than marble, once coated the pyramids and protected them from erosion. These one hundred inch thick, twenty ton slabs were stripped away long ago to help in the construction of Cairo leaving the softer blocks exposed. Khafre pyramid, the second largest, constructed for the son of Khufu, is the only one that still bears a layer of white limestone at the very top.

The Great Sphinx, the guardian spirit of the burial site, has been resurrected on more than one occasion when it was consumed by sandstorms. The pharaoh's head, that is believed to be Khafre's, and the lion's body beneath is in constant need of repair. As limestone is a porous material and needs to breathe, the cement that is used to replace the eroding statue never really sticks. The paws of the lion's body have been completely replaced with cement. Scaffolding has been erected on one side of the sphinx while restoration work continues.

When I returned from my explorations, two middle

aged English couples had joined our group, I could tell they were from my native homeland before they even introduced themselves - the black socks worn under sandals gave them away immediately, (something my father also insisted on wearing when we went on holidays).

We were led into the entrance of Khufu's pyramid by an Egyptian boy who disappeared into the dark passage before the English couples had even managed to make their way up the first set of steps, it was going to be a long climb. The ascending passage was so cramped and steep (about a 45 degree angle) I had to literally get on all fours in order to squeeze through. Peter was behind me, huffing and wheezing with each step and Lewis was talking to one of the couples in the front who seemed to be concentrating their energy on the climb. We climbed up the dimly lit passageway that led us into the heart of the pyramid and into the King's Chamber three hundred and thirteen feet below the apex.

Unfortunately the tomb was looted long before archaeologists ever had the opportunity to record the find. The sarcophagus, made from blocks of red granite was the only remaining item, Khufu's body and all his earthy possessions that Egyptians believed they would take with them into the afterlife were gone. Some people travel for miles to meditate in the inner chambers, I found the sacred burial site a little disappointing, the hieroglyphics were badly worn and covered in graffiti so I only spent a few minutes walking around the empty stone room.

When we emerged out of the dark cool pyramid back into the heat of the day, the sun was beating down onto the desert with such fury it made us all squint and my eyes ache in their sockets. As we staggered out of the passageway one by one, each shielding our eyes from the light, I tried to imagine what it felt like to be one of the thousands of slaves sent inside the pyramid to construct the network of chambers and passageways. It's hard to imagine being forced to spend your entire life preparing for the death of another.

Our guide was patiently waiting for us outside with the horses and camel. It was Peter's turn to ride the kneeling beast so we all mounted up and began our descent back to the car park. Halfway down the embankment Peter and I exchanged transport as I had not had my turn on the camel. With groans of protest the beast was forced, yet again, to kneel on the stony ground. When I climbed on his back he protested by groaning and wailing at me. His long slender jaw moved side to side in a chewing action as if rolling another giant spit wad. I felt certain that it had my name on it, he was going to let me know of his discomfort by blowing a solid lump of phlegm into my face that would sting and explode on impact like a paint ball pellet. As if sensing the camel's intentions my guide shouted at it in Arabic and tugged on a rope that was attached to a silver ring that was piercing the delicate skin of the camel's nostril. The camel screamed at the young boy in protest, and straightened his rear legs almost throwing me off. Clutching the bamboo knob at the front of the saddle, I waited for the camel to stand fully upright and bring me back onto an even keel. With sad eyes the camel turned and looked at me and with a tired gait followed the young boy who led the animal by tugging on the rope. I felt sorry for the beast and with affection and a twang of guilt as he carried me down the sandy path, stroked the coarse hair on the base of his neck in a vain attempt to comfort the animal.

The ride was pretty unpleasant as with each step another layer of skin from the inside of my thigh was scraped off by the coarse blankets draped over the saddle. By the time we reached the car park I was actually looking forward to the comfort of the vinyl seats in the Toyota van.

Cameel and Muhammad were waiting for us and ready to whisk us off to the next experience on the tour, the Egyptian bazaars. We thanked our guide and each tipped him a few Egyptian pounds for his help before saying goodbye to the pyramids of Giza and the tired camel.

Within minutes we were back in the crowded city streets of Cairo and battling with the other motorists. After his rest, it seemed that Cameel was tackling the traffic with renewed vigor and aggression, it didn't take us long to reach the markets.

Each time we climbed out of the van we had a little less energy, it was late in the afternoon and we had had a long day. We were not used to so much moving around and were beginning to think about our *Aphrodite*, quietly waiting at her anchor, rocking back and forth with the swell, it was a soothing thought. *Aphrodite* was like a mother to us, she looked after us, protected and sheltered us, and at nighttime she would rock us to sleep, whispering quiet noises into our ears, I was missing her.

The bazaars looked as glamorous and magnificent as I am sure the tomb of King Tutankhamun did when Richard Carter first shone a light into the King's burial chamber. Everywhere we looked gold dazzled the eye, ebony statues gleamed and shone like dark African skin, papyrus hung from the walls covered with brilliant paintings of great pharaohs, alabaster, precious stones and crystals covered every shelf, each of them casting colorful rainbows across the room. This was not like the stalls I found in the Seychelles or Djibouti, this was the Bloomingdale's of bazaars where gold Visas and American Express were gladly accepted. I felt like a beggar in my worn out corduroy shirt and salty shorts as I walked down each aisle admiring all the wonderful, expensive sculptures.

I have souvenirs from each country I have visited over

the last year and a half, I was looking for something that I could afford and would also remind me of this day in years to come. I only had about seventy Egyptian pounds in my wallet (about twenty dollars) and another thirty dollars back on the boat to get me to Italy and pay for my share of the pilot fees. I owed Lewis two hundred and five dollars, I felt uncomfortable with him lending me so much money and did not want to borrow another penny from him, although he would have given me another two hundred dollars if I needed it.

When I saw the sculpture I knew it was what I wanted and probably well within my price range (with a bit of haggling). It was behind the counter so I asked one of the salesman who was hovering around me if I could take a look at it. The fish was carved from a solid block of blue alabaster but as I studied it closer it appeared to have tiny flakes of gold embedded down its five-inch body. It was weighty and well carved. Although the detail lacked the precision of some of the finer sculptures with the "Please do not touch" signs hanging from them, it was nice piece and had a good feeling about it. The detail showed scales and fins along both sides of its slender body, its expression was one of happiness and contentment.

"That is eighty Egyptian pounds sir." The man said behind the counter.

"Sir?" That was not a good sign. I had a bad feeling that this store was far too civilized for some good old-fashioned haggling, but I was going to give it a shot anyway! I told the man that I liked it and pulled out forty pounds from my wallet.

"This is all I have." I told the man as I made my move.

He looked at me and smiled sympathetically, "I am sorry sir I cannot let this piece go for any less than seventy pounds."

I had enough money but did not want to spend it all on a stone fish.

"Alabaster is the lucky stone of Egypt sir," the man said taking the fish from my hand and holding it up to have a closer look, "the fish is also a lucky symbol for Egyptians as they come from the Nile that is the life source of our great country."

This guy was good, it was going to take some real theatrics to knock him down to a reasonable price. I asked him to wait while I spoke to my friend to get the seventy pounds that he was asking.

Lewis was on the other side of the shop rummaging around a bucket of stones and semi-precious gems. I asked Lewis to give me fifteen pounds but to act as though it was all the money he had left. Waving his arms back and forth and showing me the contents of his wallet, Lewis handed me the fifteen pounds and shrugged while he showed me the inside of his wallet as if to say "this is all I have!" I pleaded with Lewis to lend me some more but he insisted (and rather well I might add) that he had given me his last piastres. He even turned the pockets of his jeans inside out as if to prove that I had taken everything.

When I turned to walk back to the counter the show we had put on had not gone unnoticed by the salesman, I was concerned however, that the pocket turning was a little too dramatic and may have given the game away. I added the fifteen pounds to the forty pounds I had already left on the counter and looked at the man and gave him a helpless sort of shrug. He was hesitating so I rummaged around in my pocket and emptied out the last of my change, about sixty piastres. The man walked away and spoke to an older man sat on a stool by the entrance. The older man looked over at me and studied the fish in the salesman's palm, with a nod he sent him away.

"Would you like me to wrap it for you sir?"

"That's not necessary, but thank you very much."

When we clambered back into the van I gave Lewis his fifteen Egyptian pounds back and thanked him for his help. Cameel started up the Toyota and swung it around to head back east to Port Suez.

On more than one occasion the three of us fell asleep on the long journey back, Cameel and Muhammad chatted quietly in the front and much to our relief had the radio turned off.

When we got back to the yacht club it was well after dark and Port Suez was quiet and still. The lights from all the freighters anchored in the bay reflected off the calm water that lapped up gently against the moored yachts. We had all made calls to our families last night and were expecting some messages when we returned from our day in the city. Before we rowed out to *Aphrodite* we asked the man in the tiny booth watching an old black and white television set if we had had any calls, he looked up at the notice board and just shook his head and returned to the Arabic television show.

Eager to speak to our families we stayed up for another fifteen minutes and left messages. I used the last few minutes on my phone card and called Catherine's beeper number. She had changed her personal greeting, it said, "You have reached Catherine Roddie, please leave a message after the beep and I will get back to you. If this is Neville the phone number you gave me for Port Suez was incorrect, please leave the correct number and I will call you again." I got a new number from the yacht club and left another message for her. Peter and Lewis did the same thing before we rowed over to the boat.

Peter stayed up with me for half an hour to smoke a couple of much-needed cigarettes and talk about our last leg across the Mediterranean. Peter is missing his family and wanted to know when we would reach Fiumicino. I told him that unless we were held up through the canal we should arrive right on time, the 24th November. I know how he feels, I was hoping that Catherine would call tomorrow as it would be the last chance I would have to speak to her for a while.

Peter has eventually stubbed out his last cigarette of the day and gone to bed, leaving me alone with my lucky fish. Turning it in my hand the speckles of gold reflect the moonlight and twinkle like the stars in the clear night. Although I have not spoken to Catherine I am content with the thought that she had tried to call me.

I have gathered my blankets and pillows and will sleep on the deck tonight, I wish Catherine was here by my side, I miss feeling her body against mine, I miss her smile and I long to hear her laugh.

8

Suez Canal to Fiumicino

(1,201 nautical miles)

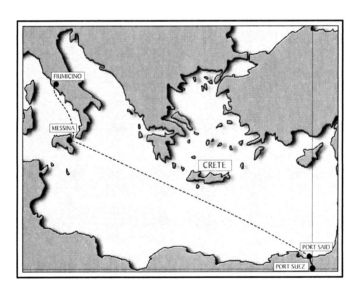

8

Suez Canal to Fiumicino

Port Suez - Day 128

Our pilot joined us this morning at the ungodly hour of 0730, ready to hold our hand and help us navigate the sixty or so miles of canal to Lake Timsah. We will anchor there this afternoon in the far northwest corner by Ismalia and wait until tomorrow morning when hopefully, not as early, our new pilot will join us and guide us through the second half of the canal to Port Said.

We had arranged for the pilot to meet us today between 0900-1000 so when we heard him banging on the side of the boat an hour and a half early asking, "Permission do com a bord," we staggered out of our bunks and greeted him with ruffled hair and sleep creases on our cheeks. We had not expected such an early start to the day and judging by our appearance we did not need to tell our pilot that we were not quite ready. He waited patiently for us while we got dressed, brewed some coffee and tidied up the cabin, by 0800 the caffeine had kicked in and we were ready to begin our first leg of the journey toward the Mediterranean sea. We were all still pretty tired, so we let Said (pronounced "say-id") chauffeur us through the canal while we munched on our wheat biscuits and sipped our coffee. Although we kept a close eye on him, Said was doing a pretty good job so we lounged around in the shade, ate breakfast and enjoyed the scenery.

On both sides the golden sand of the Sahara desert

dropped into the canal, there were no buildings to mark the shoreline, just sand that disappeared into the hazy horizon that was not too far away. Heat waves rose from the hot desert and made the air shimmer and move as though it were water. The sun was low in the sky but the day was already hot, thankfully there was a light wind to help cool the air.

The canal is in constant need of dredging as the frequent sandstorms that sweep across the desert are constantly trying to fill it in. There are no locks in the Suez Canal as there is not a great difference in water level between the Red Sea and The Mediterranean. We kept in the shallow lane on the port side, trying to leave just enough room for the freighters to pass us. It's kind of a nice feeling thinking that for the first time on the trip we may have actually been in their way. As we left so early we were leading the convoy of freighters north to Lake Timsah, with the current under our bum and Said leaning on the throttle we were steaming along at nine knots.

Said seemed eager to transit the canal in record time and on a number of occasions Peter had to tell him to ease up on the throttle and to save some of our fuel for the Mediterranean. He responded immediately with a smile, knocked the throttle back with the palm of his hand and at the same time nodding at us as though seeking approval. A few minutes later however, hoping that we would not notice, our speed would very slowly increase again. Although Peter has gotten better and is slowly beginning to press his authority as the captain of *Aphrodite*, he still has a long way to go. Peter has the right to steer his boat through the canal but seems to be more comfortable letting somebody else take the responsibility, as usual he's not too sure what to do.

He had a little too much to drink again last night and after his fourth beer, in his friendly stage, he started to congratulate me on my navigational skills.

"You've done a top job Nev," he said, "a top job!"

I humbly accepted his praise but insisted that it was a team effort and that we were all equally responsible for the success of our journey to date. Peter's glassy eyes failed to notice the looks of sarcasm Lewis and I exchanged. We have both spoken about the continuation of Peter's circumnavigation with his family back to Australia and agree that it would take a miracle for Peter to make the journey without the help of a crew. Unless he just became reliant on us and decided not to exercise his leadership skills and to sit back and enjoy the trip I have serious doubts that he could make it on his own. The fact that he made me captain back in the Seychelles is an indication that he does not feel comfortable dealing with pressure or decisions, something that I find hard to believe for a man who has his own business. Even after four months with Peter I still feel as though I don't really know him that well. Lewis on the other hand is like a brother to me now, I know we will keep in touch in the years ahead and hopefully one day sail again together.

By 1030 we had left the canal and entered the first of the three lakes, Little Bitter Lake. The temperature dropped as we motored out of the canal and across the flat water, the fresh breeze blowing over the lakes surface was cooler and more welcoming than the hot breeze of the desert. Although the sky was cloudless and the bright sun was steadily climbing overhead, the water temperature was a chilly sixty-eight degrees. With Said leaning on the throttle we cleared Little Bitter Lake in a few minutes and entered Great Bitter Lake where it got even colder.

I had not anticipated sailing in cold conditions and only ever really focused on sailing in the Indian Ocean and around Africa. The Mediterranean was an afterthought (I guess a part of me never really thought we would make it this far). It's the final leg of our journey before we reached our last port of call, but with a slight chill in the breeze I am beginning to wonder where I put all my socks and t-shirts. Rome is on the same latitude as New York so the further north we sail the colder it's going to get. Lewis and Peter are both prepared as they intend staying in Italy for some time, I will have to layer all my clothing in an attempt to keep myself warm. The warmest garment I have is a surfing shirt I bought in Bondi Beach before I left Sydney. Somehow I don't think that it's going to be enough when we reach the Mediterranean. After traveling around Australia and spending a year and a half in tropical conditions I've forgotten what it's like to feel cold.

I've taken advantage of the peaceful day by reading up on the Mediterranean. All the books say the same thing, the winter months are the worst with violent storms and dangerous conditions, I knew somewhere along the trip we would pay the price for such a late passage, I have a feeling that the Mediterranean is going to ask us to pay up.

By 1500 we had reached Lake Timsah and were anchored by a brand new tugboat also waiting to transit the canal. We dropped Said off on the jetty and gave him his fee (twenty Egyptian pounds) along with one packet of Marlboro to smoke on the journey home, two pencils for his children to use at school and two coconuts from Cocos Keeling. Said was very grateful for his bag of goodies and left to catch a train back to Port Suez.

Lake Timsah was alive with paddleboats, couples laughed and splashed each other as they paddled around the dirty lake. The Arabic music playing on the shore wafted over to us in waves carried by the soft wind. The tiny beaches around the harbor were packed with locals dancing and enjoying themselves. Ismalia was in full holiday cheer, everyone was having a great time.

Although legally we were not allowed to go ashore as

we had not cleared customs, immigrations or spoken to the harbor master, the temptation for Lewis and I was too great. Even the state of the water and Peter's protests and appeals to my sense of responsibility did not prevent us from joining the party. We had no idea how our unannounced visit would be received so we climbed up onto the beach and sat down away from the others. As we were the only white people on the beach, and seemed to magically appear from nowhere, it didn't take us long to arouse suspicion. Within minutes a crowd gathered around us like we were a beached mammal and everyone wanted a look. The parents and grandparents of the children who were sitting down around us were not so intrigued by our presence and continued chatting amongst themselves. Everybody started firing questions at us all at once, most of them were male college students who were studying law in Cairo. We were asked where we came from, where we were born, did we support the government of our countries, what religion were we, what countries had we traveled to, where were we going, what professions were we in.

We stayed on the beach for over an hour talking to the students but by 1700 we were no longer intriguing, every conceivable question had been asked and with their curiosity satisfied we were left alone again as the crowd rejoined their families. We swam back to Peter who was actually quite happy, he was just finishing his fifth beer and boasted that he had had some great conversations with some of the people on the paddleboats. We joined him in a few beers and relaxed on the still lake listening to the music still playing on the beach and wondering what our families were doing.

Ismalia - Day 129

The VHF radio crackled into life around 0800 and woke us all up, so much for a lay in. At first we were not sure who the caller was trying to reach but when, "Sailing boat next to tugboat in Lake Timsah, sailing boat next to tugboat in Lake Timsah," failed to answer the caller for the fifth time, it finally dawned on us that we were the ones being summoned. Lewis stuck his head out of the cabin and sure enough two men were standing on the deck of the tugboat waving over to us. They were inviting us aboard and claimed they had some cargo they wanted to give us. It all sounded very suspicious and as we were not allowed to come into contact with any other boats in the harbor we were a tad skeptical at first.

On channel four the skipper told us they were taking the tug to Port Sudan and wanted to get rid of all the alcohol they had on board. At the mention of beer Peter was quick to forget about the authorities and asked Lewis and I to raise the anchor.

We moored alongside the tugboat and asked permission to come aboard. The stout little boat was brand new and had never been used. The winches, chains, ropes and decks were all spotless. The skipper, Van Nieuwenhuijzen introduced himself and his crew of three men who looked as rough and worn out as we did. They worked for the World Ship Delivery Company and spent eight months out of the year delivering boats for clients all over the world. The pay was good and as we were led into the cabin that resembled a luxury yacht more than a working tug, Van Nieuwenhuijzen told us that they were making two hundred and fifty dollars a day each with all expenses paid for. I told Peter as we filed into the brightly lit decorated kitchen complete with electric stove, microwave, toaster and coffee maker that Lewis and I should be compensated for our time and effort for helping him get *Aphrodite* to Italy. Lewis and the other men chuckled at my remark but Peter did not take the joke well at all and got quite upset.

Looking around the galley it made us feel like we had been roughing it for the past four months. Everything was in pristine condition. The counter tops had never been cut on, the floor had never been dented by tin cans, there was no soot above the stove and the head worked with a simple flush rather than half a dozen manual pumps that we were used to.

Van showed us the pile of alcohol they wanted to donate to us, there were four cases of beer, forty loose bottles of Heiniken, three bottles of whisky and two cases of water and soda thrown in for good measure. As they were destined for Port Sudan they needed to unload all their alcohol before arriving. As we staggered up to the deck with garbage bags full of beer bottles and began piling up the cases, the skipper told us that if they got caught with so much alcohol in Sudan they would run the risk of getting thrown into jail. He told us that it was much worse in Saudi Arabia, if you got caught with alcohol there they would hang you from the nearest tree!

I felt like a smuggler as we quickly passed the cases one by one over the railing, stashing them and the cans of beer in Peter's head. Our pilot was due to arrive at any moment and we didn't want to get caught red handed. We were almost finished loading the goods when a pilot boat pulled up alongside and three Arabic men were watching us from the deck. Voortman, the first mate, was quick to react and darted off inside the cabin, returning a few seconds later with chilled chocolate flavored milk in tiny cardboard cartons. Slurping down the milk through the tiny straws, the Arabs patiently waited for while we stashed the last of the beer in the head.

We hadn't fooled anyone, Muhammad our pilot for

the day, and the other two men knew only too well what we were up to but couldn't be bothered to do anything about it. It wasn't worth their time to tell the port authorities as it would mean paperwork and a delayed trip for us and no "backseesh" for Muhammad, besides they got some proper chocolate flavored milk for free, something that I was craving more than beer or soda. I long for a heaping bowl of crispy cornflakes drowning in chilled fresh cow's milk with ripe banana slices on top, instead I have a billy mug with three soggy wheat biscuit semi drenched in water and UHT milk sprinkled with dried dates, not quite the same thing really.

By 0900 we had left Lake Timsah and begun our six-hour journey to Port Said. Muhammad was far more relaxed than Heebi and seemed happy to let Peter man the helm while he sat back and enjoyed the ride. The day has been clear and sunny but the brisk breeze blowing from the northeast has kept the mercury in the cabin under eighty degrees. As Lewis and I swilled back bottles of mineral water and soda, reminders of the Arab-Israeli war of 1967 passed us at three knots on the western bank. The hull of a giant tanker that was sunk by torpedo in Great Bitter Lake leaned heavily to one side just out of the water's reach. It had been towed to the bank and dumped, left to rot, a reminder to those who use the canal of the unsettled relationship between Egypt and its neighboring countries. The fatal shot that ended its seafaring life is still apparent on the starboard side. Half of the hull was blasted away leaving a twisted and mangled wound, making it look as though a giant sea monster ripped a bite out of the ship. A few hundred yards up the bank the bare concrete structure of a hospital overlooked the canal. The black windows watched us as we slowly passed, the walls and balconies were dotted with bullet holes and scarred with larger holes from mortar shells that filled the air and echoed across the desert twenty-seven years ago.

The army was present on both sides of the canal right up to Port Said. Our first glimpse of the mighty Suez force was a lone soldier riding a camel north on the eastern bank. Later we saw the Suez army building a bridge as we passed. They had just started the construction across the five hundred foot stretch and would have it complete within thirty minutes. The dark green flatbed army trucks each carried a section, the floating pontoons were slid off the back of the truck into the water then unfolded laterally to accommodate the vehicles that would drive across. Lewis shouted "Welcome to Egypt" as we passed by the bank, the men waved and smiled at us with rifles slung over their shoulders.

By 1445 we sighted Port Said, although we still had over an hour before we would drop off Muhammad and enter the Mediterranean I scrambled around in the cabin to get the charts out for the Mediterranean and check the waypoints that were already programmed into the autopilot. Lewis double checked the coordinates with me and went over the charts that we were going to use to see us through to the Messina Straights between Sicily and the mainland. The familiar feeling of the unknown as we drew closer to Port Said once again twisted in my stomach and filled me with anxiety. This is the last leg, something that we were all looking forward to. We missed our families and wanted a quick and safe passage to Fiumicino.

32° 01.7' N
31° 31.7' E
297° - Day 130

It looks as though we may have our wish. Last night we were back on our evening watches for the first time in almost a week, the clear sky and open sea invited us with a soft fifteen-knot breeze from the east that pushed us gently towards Italy. We cleared Port Said as night fell around us, following the leading lights that guided us at thirty-seven degrees into the Mediterranean and away from Africa. We sailed through the dozens of freighters anchored around the mouth of the harbor patiently awaiting their turn to transit the canal, and with our sails raised to the top of the mast began the last leg of our adventure together.

The sun has been in the sky for only two hours, the wind blowing from the Atlantic Ocean is brisk and even the water looks chilly. I took a "deck shower" after my mug of coffee had warmed me up and given me the confidence to bathe. The bucket of green Mediterranean sea that I pulled over the railing was cold and covered my entire body with goose pimples when I dumped it over my head. The heavy exhaling and jumping jacks I did in an attempt to get the circulation back into my body woke Peter who thought I was mad when he saw what I was doing. Lewis also heard the commotion and raced up on deck thinking that we were in some kind of danger and was pissed off when he found out that he had got out of bed after only four hours of sleep just to see me exercising in the buff.

We made potato salad for lunch as Peter needs more room in his toilet for all the beer we picked up in Lake Timsah. The sack of spuds we bought in the Seychelles is still over a quarter full but the remaining potatoes have grown tiny willies and are attempting to mate with each other. The white roots are getting all tangled up so we spent half an hour before lunch "fixing" all the spuds and returning them to the bag emasculated. The onions were shedding their skins but generally behaving themselves so no surgery needed to be performed.

Even though the waves had picked up a little and the

breeze peaking at twenty knots, I decided to bake a pizza for supper. Lewis helped me prepare the ingredients and by 1800 we were chewing down the last of our pineapple slices and ham rations, we are so close to Italy we feel that we can raid the cupboards and eat whatever we desire. The ride is getting rough and the pizza Lewis had eaten, has made an appearance. It's 2100 and we have just reefed the main sail right down. The wind is steady at twenty-three knots and has swung around to the northwest forcing us to tack back and forth. I have a feeling we are in for a long night.

32° 47.4' N
29° 32.7' E
259° - Day 131

The books were right! We have been beating into wind gusting to forty-five knots for almost twenty-four hours now. The genoa finally went on us last night just after midnight, the tearing sound as the strip of red material was ripped from the sail was so loud we all heard it over the wind. Immediately *Aphrodite* was thrown off balance, the next wave grabbed us and turned us just enough for the wind to catch the other side of the mainsail. The boom whipped around with a snap and within seconds the port railing was submerged underwater as the auto pilot fought to steer us the other way. Peter reacted quickly and pushed the button for manual override, I grabbed the helm and swung us around away from the wind.

With the wind behind us it was all so different, the ride was smoother and the howling and squealing stopped, all of a sudden things didn't seem so bad. There was no temptation to sail back to Port Said. We all wanted to reach Italy and were not about to run away from our first storm at sea. We were going to face it head on, look it in

the eye and tell it to "rack off!" I wanted some good yarns
to tell everyone when I got home and besides I was a
Hockley, the sea has been in my blood for generations, I
was born to do this stuff, or so they told me!

Lewis and I pulled down the tattered genoa and threw
it into the saloon. We dug the cutter out from under my
bunk and dragged the sail up on deck. We fed the slides
into the track and gave Peter the signal to bring us around
when he was ready.

There were a few seconds when *Aphrodite* was
broadside to the waves and most vulnerable. Peter had to
time it perfectly by judging the wind speed and the twenty-
five foot waves chasing us from behind. We waited for the
right moment for a lull in the wind, when it finally came
Peter swung us around, *Aphrodite* responded beautifully
and within seconds was facing the next wave that we had
just managed to beat. Lewis and I raised the cutter that
helped to steady the bow.

The weather has been rotten all day, it's now in the
late afternoon and the sun has still not shown itself. Dark
clouds have been rolling across the sky, the sea is mad and
the wind is pissed off. The waves have opened up and are
peaking at thirty feet now. The tops of them are beginning
to get blown off by the wind, sending trails of white foam
across the surface of the sea. The clouds are full with rain
and ready to dump tons of water onto us at any moment.

We are sailing close to the wind and heeling right over,
everything is pulled in tight and we are crashing through the
waves heading toward Crete. The swell is so rough that
even with forty-five knots of winds we are only averaging
four knots over ground. We are all wearing wet weather
gear and harnesses are attached. I have just managed to grab
a quick nap and now Lewis is doing the same, we want to
make sure that we're all relatively rested and ready for the

night. We could all use at least twelve hours of sleep but for now have to take whatever we can get.

33° 26.0' N
27° 47.4' E
290° - Day 133

Today I feel like an old salt, standing at the helm trying to shield myself from the stinging rain, as another wall of cold Mediterranean Sea towers forty feet above me. I brace myself as five tons of seawater crashes down over the deck, swamping the cockpit, and threatening to carry me away. My harness is attached to the helm, without it I would be swept into the darkness, with little hope of being rescued. Turning to look at the mountain of ocean roll south towards the African coast, it's hard to believe we're only nine hundred nautical miles from Fiumicino. It seems at times that we may never make it.

It's gotten worse, the wind is hitting sixty knots regularly and the waves are towering over us at forty feet. The clouds have opened up their doors and have been bombarding us for three hours with giant drops of rain that sweep across the water at sixty knots, it's impossible to look into the wind as each drop stings the skin like an angry bee. There's so much water in the air it's hard to breathe.

This is how I imagined it to be, and this is what I had wished for one hundred and thirty-three days ago, when I first stood upon the calm deck of the *Aphrodite* in Sydney harbor.

Seeking an adventure, I wanted an experience that would stay with me in the years ahead. Sitting in an office building one year from now, it is important for me to have a place I can go to help put my life into perspective. I have learned many things over the past two years and have realized that life has more to it than I had ever dreamed possible.

Never before had I breathed air so fresh that it would make my entire body tingle with pleasure, watched the sun rise each morning, drunk rain straight from the heavens or just soaked in the world around me and relished in the simplicity of life. Every experience I have had on this journey has made an impression on my life. The people I have met, the places I have visited, simple things that I once took for granted, I have now come to cherish. What saddens me is that I know the journey is almost over and my fear is that I may get swept up in the current of living again and forget what I have learned.

I have never felt more alive than I do right now and yet I have never felt so uncertain. Maybe the two are partners. If everything in life was predictable, would you really be living or just playing a role? I am nearing the end of one chapter of my life and God willing, will be starting another in a few months.

We are all close to total exhaustion. The cold wind and relentless waves are gradually pounding the energy from our already tired bodies.

Although *Aphrodite* is doing her best to protect us, she is beginning to show signs of weakening. Lewis noticed a crack in the boom just behind the bracket that attaches the kicking strap to the foot of the mast. The jibe we had two days ago is almost certainly responsible for the damage. Even with the mainsail reefed all the way down the strain on the boom is so enormous it could crack all the way through at any moment. To make matters worse the cutter flapped out and tore to shreds like tissue paper in just seconds by the raging wind. The violent shuddering of the destroyed sail caused the sheet to break under the strain releasing it into the wind like a giant kite.

We finally managed to gain control of the shredded cutter and stuffed it into the sail bag throwing it into my cabin with the torn genoa. We're going through sails as quickly as toilet paper. The only sails we have left now are a storm jib roughly the size of my sleeping bag, the inner cutter and the giant spinnaker that can only be flown in gentle conditions. Something tells me that we will not be using the lightweight sail again.

The conditions are too severe to sail anymore, with so much strain on the rigging we have made the decision to barepole. We'll bring the mainsail down and run with the waves under engine power. Peter fired up the Yanmah and headed directly into the wind meeting the waves head on, he kept our heading true while Lewis and I tackled the last sail we had up.

With *Aphrodite* pitching up and down so violently it was like trying to unsaddle a bucking bronco that was already let loose and pissed off with the world. With the hull slamming against the water as we fell off each wave into the dark canyons below, it seemed like it would only be a matter of seconds before the shock would split the fiberglass hull in two like a walnut shell. We heard a faint cry being carried away by the wind and turned to see Peter yelling at the top of his voice warning us to get down, we both looked up. A wall of water was bearing down on us and seemed to touch the top of the mast as we sunk down to greet it. We strained our necks and looked up at the wave in awe. The wind blew the top off the crest like it was blowing the froth off a pint of Guiness, showering us with foam and water. Peter pushed down on the throttle to meet this one at five knots, the engine started to splutter and stall, then died. Even above the roar of the wind and the rumbling of the wave about to sweep over us it all seemed to go deadly quiet without the diesel engine thumping reassuringly in the hull.

Lewis and I didn't have time to get back to the cockpit, we couldn't risk unclipping our harnesses to make a dash for it so we wrapped our arms around the mast and on our knees hugged the aluminum pole, waiting in silence for the wave to hit us.

We met the wave head on, the bow sprit sunk itself deep into the wall of ocean and for a moment it looked as though we were going to just punch a hole right through it. Within a second the power of the wave took control and lifted our bow toward the sky, we all held on as we climbed up the mountainous wave. Below we heard the clutter of plates and pans shoot across the galley as cupboard doors flew open by the impact, more dents on Peter's newly installed hardwood floor, (his wife is going to be pissed when she sees the state of it). We reached the peak and hovered for a second on the very ridge, the highest point of the sea around us.

The dark sets of waves stormed across the ocean leaving trails of foam and bubbles in their wake, it was nature's battlefield, and we were caught right in the middle. The wind blew with such a fury it threw seawater into the air to meet the rain. Streaks of white foam scarred the surface of each wave as the crests were flung into the air. It was difficult to distinguish sea from the darkening evening sky. The black rolling clouds raced by close over our heads mirroring the waves below. Everything, the wind, rain, sea and clouds were racing southeast, we were the only ones trying to battle northwest, we could not fight Mother Nature any more, if we kept trying she would tear us into tiny pieces.

The wave released us from its grip leaving us to the mercy of the next one. It passed underneath our belly causing *Aphrodite* to nose dive into the crater it left behind. Lewis and I staggered back to the cockpit like two drunken old men, hunchbacked and unsteady on our feet as we dove into the dark valley below. Even with our wet weather gear we both still got a drenching. The cold seawater and driving rain had worked its way up our

292

sleeves, down our neck holes and soaked us to the skin.

We made it to the cockpit and clipped on our harnesses. The three of us were together again and almost in a state of shock, staring at each other through wide unbelieving eyes.

"Well gentlemen, I don't know about you but I think we should get the fuck out of here." I shouted over the wind.

"Sounds like a cunning plan there big fella." Lewis agreed.

"I think there's a problem with the engine." Peter finished.

I took the helm while Peter and Lewis went below to check on the engine. A few seconds later Peter poked his head out of the cabin.

"There's water in the fuel, I'm going to have to clean out the filter!"

I nodded, wondering how water had found its way into the fuel tanks. My mind started to run wild, was there a leak in the hull? Were we taking on water? I asked Lewis to check the automatic bilge pump and look under the floorboards, thankfully the hull was dry and the bilge pump was working.

Peter cleaned out the filter and started the engine, it ran a little rough but gave us just enough power to make a U-turn. We swung ourselves around pointing the bow back to Port Said, hoping that the storm would not take us that far. Everything seemed to calm down when we were running with it, although the wind was still screaming at sixty knots it seemed softer than before and the waves were not swamping the deck. All of a sudden the conditions didn't seem so bad until the next big wave swept up behind us and gave us a push. I wrestled with the wheel to keep our nose pointing true, if we broadsided the wave we would get knocked down, ten knots, eleven knots, twelve, thirteen! We surfed the wave for forty feet before it let us go and continued southeast without us. By running with the storm we had solved one problem but created another. It was already getting dark and within an hour the world would be black. With no stars or moon to light the ocean it would be harder to tell when the big waves were coming, we had to slow ourselves down.

We never dreamed that the old tires we salvaged in Darwin would need to be unfastened from the deck, we could never have imagined being in conditions so severe. Although *Aphrodite* is a sturdy old girl and with her sails down can stand a lot of beating, we're at serious risk of capsizing if the conditions get any worse, and if the storm lasts for another twenty-four hours we'll be on the Egyptian coast.

We're all wet, cold, tired and hungry. Peter is complaining of chest pains and has just gone below to lay down for a few minutes. I don't know if it is the strain of the conditions or the thousands of cigarettes he's smoked over the past nineteen weeks. Either way I hope it's not serious as we're days away from medical help should anything go wrong.

Clinging onto the wheel for support *Aphrodite* is suddenly hit broadside by another wall of ocean. I know the bad ones come in sets so I shout down to Lewis and Peter to hold on. The starboard side becomes fully submerged under water as we list violently over. We are carried sixty feet before the wave releases its deathly grip and continues south without us. Strange thoughts run through your mind when you feel as though they could be your last. Surprisingly I am not afraid of the conditions, but more annoyed that I have not got a warm pair of pants or a dry sweater to wear.

Another wave powered by sixty knots of wind is ready for us. They seem to be lining up to take turns.

Aphrodite sinks down into the depths of the ocean before the giant swell lifts us up into the black sky and carries us with it, closer to Africa. The world around us is dark and unforgiving. It is 1800 hours and already the skies are black. The cold wind has been blowing hard from the west, shaking everything in its path.

"14.9!" I bellow down into the cabin, struggling to be heard over the raging ocean and angry winds. Lewis, who is busy preparing himself another snack, pops his head up from the relative comfort and warmth of the cabin to take a glance at the glowing LED instruments. With a mouthful of crackers and vegimite he shouts, "Good on yer! Looks like you've set the record again, big fella!" As if I have had control over any of it!

It all seems so surreal. Bob Marley is playing on a CD, Lewis is making himself lunch and Peter is taking a nap. What else can we do? Life goes on out here regardless of the severe conditions. You can't shout out, "Hey, pull over I want off!" We're all in this together by choice and ironically, I can think of no other place I would rather be.

I have forgotten who's shift it is, although for now it doesn't really matter. Lewis and I are taking turns behind the wheel.

With the engine barely running and night rapidly approaching we can't risk being carried by a rogue wave. We know it's out there and if the storm continues through the night, which it looks like it will, it'll only be a matter of time before it will reach us. With only an hour left of daylight we have decided to unlash the tires from the deck and prepare the sea anchor. If the conditions don't let up in the next few hours we'll toss the weights over the back of *Aphrodite* in a last resort to slow us down and steady our movement.

The ropes holding the two tires to the cabin roof were so wet and the knots so tight we had to cut them free. Peter emerged from the cabin coughing, he's claiming to feel better so he lit up a cigarette before helping us prepare the anchor.

The waves are averaging thirty-five feet, every tenth one towers over us at forty to forty-five. The wind is still howling through the rigging forcing us south. I have just taken our position and have some good news and bad news.

The good news is that I have taken over one hundred miles off this leg. We are still destined for Fiumicino through the Messina Straights but I have gone over Peter's coordinates that he had plotted a month ago and discovered a rather big error.

His calculations had shown that the final leg from Port Said to Fiumicino was one thousand two hundred and ten miles when in fact it's only one thousand one hundred miles, a savings of one hundred and ten miles! What Lewis would call "a bargain." His coordinates also show that if we continued on our original course we would have collided with the south coast of Italy rather than the more conventional method of sailing around. If this damn storm pisses off, we may actually arrive in Fiumicino right on time!

I almost forgot. The bad news is that we are closer to land than I had originally thought, if we continue at our present speed we'll be washed up on the African coast in the early hours of the morning! We have no choice, the sea anchor has to go over.

We gathered two hundred feet of heavy line and secured the tires to the end. Lewis tied the knots, we didn't want a repeat of the knot I had used back in Australia that was almost responsible for the loss of our skipper. It was backbreaking and tiring work, although the waves were not breaking over the deck, the spray from the raging sea, the heavy sheets of rain and the movement of *Aphrodite* threw us all over the deck. Peter was manning the helm, he had to keep our nose pointing downwind. Somehow he had managed to light a cigarette and the ash blew into our faces from the red tip that glowed angrily from the wind. We secured the line to the deck and waited for the next wave to pass under us, when we were at the very bottom of the trough we were going to push the tires overboard.

We dropped down between the two waves and kicked the tires over the edge. Traveling at six knots the two hundred feet of line soon unraveled itself from the deck into the disturbed sea, with a loud crack the line went taught almost wrenching the cleat from the wooden deck. Instantly *Aphrodite*'s movement became slow and laborious, like a convict dragging a heavy ball and chain she struggled like a leashed dog trying to escape the weight that she was dragging behind her.

Our speed has dropped to under three knots, we have kept Peter's Rambo knife out should anything go wrong and we have to cut the line in a hurry, we've done everything we can possibly do, now we can only wait and hope.

After all the effort we're starving, cold and tired. Peter has put the kettle on for coffee, the gimbal stove has never worked so hard and is swinging back and forth trying to keep the kettle over the flame. Lewis and I have made more crackers. Unfortunately we have exhausted all our supplies of vegimite and have been rummaging through the cupboards trying to find something to spread on the thin pieces of cardboard. Lewis ended up sprinkling flakes of tuna on his while I made a double decker sandwich with onions, tomato paste and mustard. It tasted quite disgusting and for the first time ever I actually feel a little seasick.

My nap is long overdue, it's been fifty-six hours since

I slept for more than twenty minutes. I collapsed in my bunk still wearing all my clothes, I only had enough energy to take off my waterproof trousers and jacket, I left everything else on including my harness. It didn't really matter, everything was wet anyway so I curled up in a wet soggy ball and fell into a coma.

"Hey big fella, you up?"

I couldn't fucking believe it. I told Lewis to get lost and let me sleep for at least an hour.

"It's six in the morning Neville," he whispered, "I thought you might like some breakfast, I found another jar of vegimite buried under the pasta!"

I didn't believe him, no way I had slept for seven hours and I was certain there was no more vegimite! When I climbed out of my warm damp bunk and went to put on my waterproofs Lewis told me that I wouldn't need them.

I staggered up on deck picking lumps of sleepy dust out of my eyes the size of sugar cubes and couldn't believe what I saw. The sea was as flat as a pane of glass and the sky was a cloudless light blue with a warm glow to the east. Peter was grinning triumphantly at me behind a cloud of cigarette smoke, we had survived the storm and Lewis had found more rations of vegimite to see us to Fiumicino!

41° 14.0' N
12° 30.4' E
340° - Day 143

My eyes burned this morning as I looked east over the flat water towards the coastline and the loom of the rising sun. They burned not from the sun's glare, the morning mist covered the horizon and dulled the first light, but they burned from the tears that formed in my eyes. My vision softened as I sipped my coffee and smiled at the thoughts of a journey that has come to an end.

I have just finished my last shift aboard *Aphrodite*. It's 0600 and the dull sun is trying its best to warm the world. It's forty-five degrees and I am cold. Lewis and Peter are still curled up in their sleeping bags fast asleep, probably dreaming of the arrival that is already here.

It's November 25th, 1994 and we have arrived one day behind schedule. Although we're still ten miles from Fiumicino, for me the journey is over. Ten miles after sailing eleven thousand, two hundred and fifty-six means that we have landed and just need to wait for the seat belt sign to go off. I'm not in a hurry for this to end, as I know I will miss these days when they are gone, but a part of me is ready to swim ashore and begin the next journey of my life.

The storm lasted for four days and blew itself out while I was sleeping. When it passed it left us with no wind for the final seven hundred miles. We motor-sailed all the way to Messina where we stopped off for fuel and after a night of rest, anchored in the busy little harbor, we continued up the west coast of Italy.

As usual I am letting Peter sleep in so I can enjoy my last morning on *Aphrodite* quietly alone. The water is calm and a light breeze has just picked up from the northwest, I have raised the sails for the last time on this journey and the gentle breeze is just strong enough to push us forwards at two knots. As the sun dried out the horizon and cleared the mist, the mouth of the Fiumicino River that runs inland to Rome has shown itself, we've made it!

Fiumicino airport - Day 151

The journey has come to an end and this is the last entry I will make in my logbook. I'm waiting for my flight to be announced and am ready to begin searching for my next dream. Although I haven't plotted any waypoints and have no charts to see me back to New York, I know that I will find my way there and am looking forward to beginning the next passage in my life.

The next passage

Lewis called me up from Rome two weeks after I had flown out of Fiumicino. The entire Hockley household was wrenched from a deep sleep at five in the morning by the phone that would not stop ringing. My dad yelled to get me up, "That Australian sailor is on the bloody phone, tell him not to call so early in the future!"

I smiled as I walked downstairs in my warm pajamas to take the call. Even with the trip long over Lewis was still waking me up for my shift. It was as though he had the right to call me anytime he pleased, for him this was normal. Like the one hundred and forty-three times before, he greeted me in the same familiar way.

"You up there big fella?" He asked.

"I am now you bastard. What do you want?" I said with a smile on my face.

"Just called to wish you a happy Christmas."

"Thanks, oh by the way I've sent you a present, two hundred and five dollars!"

"That's very generous of you." He said, "When are you flying to the States?"

"Today actually, my flight leaves this afternoon."

I flew to America the day after Christmas and arrived in Orlando, Florida with a six-month holiday visa and a lifetimes worth of goals and dreams. After so many years I was jubilant to have finally made it back to the country I had spent the last six years of my life dreaming about, I got as far as the immigration desk before I was stopped. The two officers escorted me away from the line of tourists and led me into their office for questioning - they wanted to ask me about my length of stay and the countries I had visited over the last year. Unlike Pat back in Darwin these boys were not as care free and would not have had any problems sending me back on the next plane to England if they thought I had the slightest intention of illegally working in their country or overstaying my visa. I assured them that I was not going to be seeking employment and that I was merely visiting old college buddies. I showed the officers my return ticket dated for June 28th 1995 as proof that I would not overstay my visa. I didn't mention my ban from Australia but as I put my return ticket away I promised myself that I would never use it and would someday have it framed on my office wall as a symbol of my perseverance and the realization of a dream.

After half an hour of questioning I was finally allowed into the country of my dreams. Catherine who had waited for me all this time was worried that I had missed my flight or was sent back to England because of the bad reputation I had acquired for overstaying my visa. When I saw her she smiled and ran to meet me. We held each other in the airport as tightly as we did nineteen months earlier before I flew to Australia, she whispered in my ear that she would never let go of me again.

I lived in Florida for five months, Catherine spent most of her time traveling with Hawaiian Tropic, it was my turn to sit by the phone and wait for her to call for a change. I spent my time in Daytona Beach working on my portfolio, developing designs and ideas that would help me find a sponsor in New York. As much as I liked my coconut carving and my other sculptures they were not quite portfolio material so I set about creating more relevant designs. I was offered sponsorship by two companies in Florida but declined them both, knowing that

New York was where I had to be.

One month before my six-month holiday visa was due to expire I applied for a six-month extension, it arrived three weeks later, the very same day Catherine and I were going to drive up the coast to New York in the Budget rent-a-truck we had loaded with all our worldly possessions. My six-month extension was not renewable and was due to expire on December 27th, 1995. I only had five hundred dollars and a few months to find a design firm that would sponsor me.

Summer in New York City that year was as hot and humid as the windless days in the doldrums. After a month of walking around the city in ninety-five degree heat with close to one hundred per cent humidity, wearing a suit, tie and carrying around a twenty-pound portfolio, I was not any closer to finding myself a sponsor. It took all my effort to remain positive. One of the things that helped me not give up, even when everything was looking so hopeless was thinking of *Aphrodite* and the days I had spent at sea.

After three months of interviews, phone calls and chasing dead end leads I began to resign myself to the fact that most companies were not hiring full-time staff in the summer, let alone someone who had spent the last two years traveling and had no recent experience and no work visa. The thought of flying back to England though was one that I was not prepared to entertain. Unlike Australia I could not overstay my visa and jeopardize my future in America so I was determined and desperate to find a sponsor in the little time I had left. I knew I had the option to travel back to Florida but I only wanted to move forwards, I didn't want to consider going back.

Twelve weeks before I would have had to fly back to England, a thought that filled me with despair, things began to look up. I interviewed with a new company that needed a designer to help build their identity and work on the multi-media projects they were developing. They sponsored me and on November 2nd, 1995 I got my work visa.

Catherine and I found an apartment in Long Beach, New York that overlooked the ocean, we moved in on Christmas Eve. Within a few weeks I had my return ticket above my desk and had decorated my office with pictures from Australia, Africa and the Indian Ocean. Catherine and I got married in New York on Park Avenue on August 15th, 1996.

Even to this day Lewis still calls me up. Last week the phone started to ring at three in the morning, I knew who it was before I had even answered the call. Lewis spent two months in Italy before traveling back to Sydney. He still works for the fire brigade and has stayed in touch with Petra, the fiery redhead he met in Cocos, they have been seeing each other ever since.

I have not spoken to Peter Lawton since Fiumicino. He did somehow manage to find his way back to Australia, Lewis said that he had some assistance for part of the journey home. I called his repair shop in Canberra where he was back knocking out the dents of damaged vehicles, his wife answered the phone and we talked for a few minutes. Peter was out in the shop but she said he would call me back, I never did hear from him.

Life goes on, although we have all returned to the mainstream of living and the experiences are now just a memory, my life has been changed by them. I find myself thinking about the windy days and the rolling sea, the never ending sky and the lonely calms, and I know that I will one day live in my dream time again.

The pages of my logbook were handmade with the bark of the Dephne bush paper tree found in the Himalayan region of Nepal.

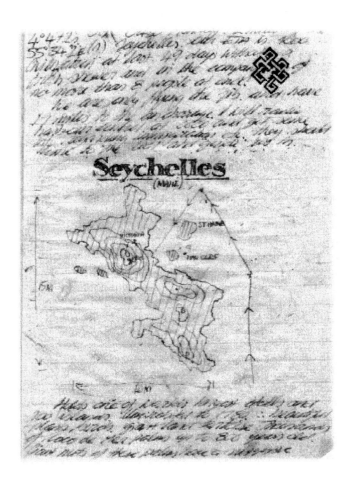

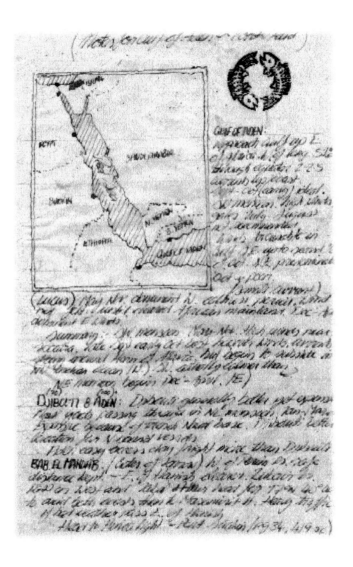

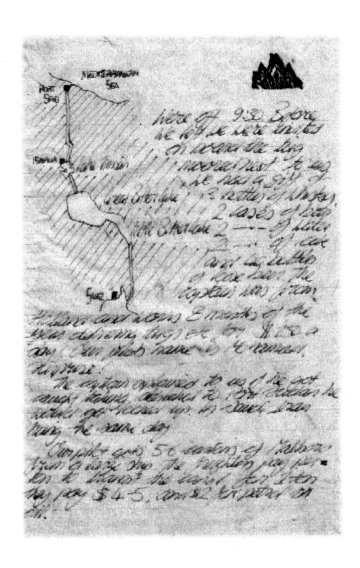

Glossary

The terms outlined in this glossary serve to provide you with an understanding of the nautical language I have used throughout this book. This glossary by no means constitutes all sailing terms, there are far too many to list, and quite frankly no one really knows what most of them mean anyway.

Bare Pole
It's much more exciting than it sounds. When the wind starts to blow really hard, so hard that you cheeks begin to flap uncontrollably, it is wise to remove all sails, hence leaving the mast bare.

Barometer
Or as I like to call it, "Barry", an instrument used to measure atmospheric pressure. If "Barry's" pressure drops a lot, hang on, because strong winds are coming.

Bilge
The lowest part of the interior of the boat, where water, coconut shavings, cigarette butts and the onion you dropped while making pizza a month ago, but couldn't find, collect.

Boom
It's the sound that's made when invariably everyone smacks their head on it at some point during a sailing trip. Its other function is to secure the bottom of the main sail.

Bow
The pointy end of the boat.

Buoys
A flotation devise that is used to mark channels and hazards while serving as a socializing point for seagulls.

Canvas
A slang word used to describe a sail when sailors have forgotten its real name.

Cleat
A fitting that lines (ropes) are secured to.

Cutter Sail
A sail flown from the bow of the boat behind the genoa.

Dodger
Aptly named as one "dodges" under this canvas shelter in the cockpit when large waves break over the boat.

Draft
The only real way to drink a beer. (I believe the nautical term refers to the depth of the boat under the waterline).

Duck
I use this name for an inflatable boat (I don't know why!)

Fender
Protective cushions hung from the side of a boat.

Furl
To reduce the size of a sail in stronger winds by wrapping it around itself.

Galley
The kitchen area on a boat where the one-minute noodles are prepared.

Genoa
A large sail that is flown on the front of the boat.

GPS
Global Positioning System. A system of satellites that allows sailors, who have no idea what they're doing, a method of finding their way home.

Head
The part of your body you hit the most while using this facility.

Heading
The direction you are sailing, rarely the direction you want to go, as the wind has an uncanny knack in blowing you the wrong way.

Heave to
This is equivalent to pulling over to the side of the road in a car when you need a break. The sails are arranged in such a manner as to slow or stop the forward motion of the boat when in strong winds and limited sea room.

Helm
The wheel or tiller of a boat that turns the rudder.

Jib
Smaller than the genoa, this sail is also flown from the front of the boat.

Ketch
A sailboat with two masts.

Lazerette
A small aft space below deck used for storing spare parts, stowaways and illegal contraband.

Leech
The long diagonal edge of the sail that faces aft.

Leeward
The direction you turn when relieving yourself on deck.

Lifelines
Lines running around the deck of the boat to prevent unsteady sailors from falling overboard.

Line
On a boat most ropes are called lines, what genius thought of that one!

List
Wind pushes against the sails causing the boat to lean, the more the boat leans the longer the list of reasons you can think of why you don't like sailing in stormy conditions.

Main Sail
This is the large sail that is suspended from the mast, the bottom edge being attached to the thing you hit your head on.

Pole
A pole is used to hold sails up to catch more wind.

Port
The left side of the boat when facing forward.

Reef
To partially lower a sail, so in strong winds you can fool yourself in thinking you're actually in control.

Running
Sailing with the wind behind you, one of my favorite tacks.

Sheet
Not to be confused with a blanket or quilt. A sheet is a line (rope) attached to a sail, another fine nautical term that makes no sense!

Sloop
A sailboat with a single mast.

Spinnaker
A very large and usually brightly colored lightweight sail that is used in gentle wind when running.

Spreader
Supports extending from both side of the mast to help create stay tension.

Starboard
The right side of a boat when facing forward.

Stays
Cables used to secure the mast to the boat.

Stern
The flat end of the boat.

Tack
To change a boats direction by heading into the wind.

Trim
To adjust the tension of the sails by pulling on sheets.

Waypoint
A position created by a latitude and longitude.

Winch
A mechanical device used to pull on lines to help trim sails
(now we're getting technical).

Windward
A direction you definitely do not want to face when
relieving yourself on deck!